# WESTERN INNER WORKINGS

*Sangreal Sodality Series*

Western Inner Workings, Volume 1

The Sangreal Sacrament, Volume 2

Concepts of Qabalah, Volume 3

Sangreal Ceremonies and Rituals, Volume 4

# WESTERN INNER WORKINGS

## Sangreal Sodality Series
## Volume 1

## William G. Gray

SAMUEL WEISER, INC.
York Beach, Maine

Published in 1983
by Samuel Weiser, Inc.
Box 612
York Beach, Maine 03910

ISBN 0-87728-560-8

Library of Congress Catalog Card Number: 82–62846

Typesetting by Positive Type
Printed in the United States
by Maple-Vail

Publication of this series was made possible by the Sangreal
Foundation, Inc.

# Contents

Introduction ..................................... ix
1 Behind Our Beliefs ..............................1
2 The Cult of Kingship ...........................17
3 Sacrificial Circles ..............................33
4 Greatness of the Grail ..........................49
5 Individual Identity .............................63
6 The Art of Abra-Melim ..........................77
7 Abra-Melim Again ..............................93
8 The Mysteries of Melchizadek ...................109
9 The Simplicity of Brother Lawrence ..............123
10 Paganistic Principles ..........................139
11 Cosmic Cycles ................................157
12 Cycles Continued .............................173
13 Still Cycles ..................................191
14 Sacred Ceremonialism .........................207
15 Mediation and Meaning ........................223
Valedictory ...................................239

# About the author

Wm. G. Gray was born in Middlesex, United Kingdom, at 2:10 p.m. on the 25th of March, 1913. Astrologically this gave him: Sun in Aries, Moon in Scorpio, and Leo rising.

On his father's side, Bill Gray comes from a long line of churchmen with his grandfather being an Anglican rector and his heritage extending back to Archbishop Walter de Gray of York. His mother was Scottish-American and in mid-life became a prominent astrologer. This was young Bill's first introduction to the occult and through his mother was able to meet many members of the Golden Dawn and other esoteric groups.

He joined the British Army as a communications technician and served several years in Egypt where he came into contact with additional material relevant to the *Inner Tradition.*

Shortly after his return home, England became involved in World War II and Bill's military outfit was immediately transferred to France where he was in action until evacuated during the Dunkirk disaster. It was at this time that he swore to devote the remainder of his life to the Western Spiritual Way of Life. After the holocaust, his health broke and he was invalided from the British forces.

For a short period, Wm. G. Gray was a member of the Society of the Inner Light. This organization was founded by Dion

Fortune, the author of many books on the Western Tradition which had been of great help to him in his early occult studies. Bill Gray's own especial mentor was a Rosicrucian associate of "Papus," Dr. Gerami Encausse. To this advanced initiate, Bill Gray attributes his own psycho-spiritual development.

Wm. G. Gray did not commence writing until the late 1960's when he wrote an essay on Qabalah purely for the benefit of a few close associates. They were so enthusiastic about the article that he was encouraged to expand it into what is now one of the classics of Qabalistic literature, *Ladder of Lights*. When Israel Regardie was asked to read the manuscript, he was full of praise in acclaiming it both unique and original. Since that time Wm. G. Gray has written eight more books about the Qabalah and the Western Tradition before undertaking the present Sangreal Sodality series.

Wm. G. Gray is married to an ex-service woman who, like his mother, is a professional astrologer. He established himself as a Chiropodist in the West Country of England and there has devoted his free time to the study and advancement of the Western Inner Tradition.

• • • • • • • • • •

SANGREAL SODALITY chapters are being organized throughout the western world. If you would like information on organizing your own group, please write:

Wm. G. Gray
c/o Samuel Weiser, Inc.
P.O. Box 612
York Beach, Maine 03910

# Introduction

This book condenses what might be called a unique experiment in spiritual sociology. It presents a centerline approach to our hereditary or so-called "secret" spiritual tradition as Western people who have evolved our own special culture from the entire field of consciousness available to humans following particular paths of progress during the course of our existence on this earth.

All cultural developments are dependent on two main abilities: an ability of *literacy*, which enables humans to think in terms of descriptive ideology, and *numeracy*, which enables us to think in terms of relative valuations. By combining these two abilities correctly, we are able to process our consciousness in ways which have the end effect of making us not only the people we are but, more importantly, the sort of people we want to become.

Behind all the apparently variant and conflicting spiritual systems which humans of Western origins have adopted in their search for individual and collective identity, lies a single and genetically inheritable strain of inner awareness which might indeed be termed "occult," or hidden, because so few people are objectively conscious of it. It is that precise awareness which this work is intended to awaken in those who hold it latently, or to sharpen and focus it for those in whom it may be stirring already.

First, in this book, we shall deal with the purely literate side of our inner tradition, then later on we hope to tackle the numerate concepts which take us closer to the spiritual structures of our natures.

This literary legacy of our Western Inner Way is vast and constantly enlarging though it has become increasingly repetitive in recent times. Much of our modern esoteric literature is little more than a persistent rehashing of previous publications. Granted, there is a need to present valid old themes in terms of our times, but there also exists an *ad nauseam* point at which otherwise intelligent interest in any topic is reached and plain boredom with over-exposure prevents real progress and possibly valuable new discoveries being made. We seem to be hovering dangerously near that mark in this *fin de siecle* period. There are magic circles and vicious circles, but when the two become coincidental, no good is boded for anyone caught within them. So in order to provide a liberating stream of thought leading out of stagnating pools of pedantry, this series of Sangreal studies which deal with specifically vital points of our Western Way is herewith offered.

These writings do not claim to reveal startling occult secrets concealed for centuries by mysterious "Masters" or other superior superpeople calmly controlling the destiny of this world from their mountainous hide-outs or from hidden planets lurking in distant corners of Cosmos. What they afford is an opportunity for self-selective training along the central spiritual lines which hold our esoteric cultural heritage together as a whole. This, in turn, affects the lives and future of us all as a distinct species of life on this planet.

For many years, the publishing market of the English and European literary world have been flooded with a variety of books dealing with Oriental occultism. This has proved of great interest and attracted a considerable number of devotees, disciples, and what might be termed sub-culturalists, all seeking spiritual satisfaction which they evidently could not obtain from existing "orthodox" religions and established mystical systems. There are two main reasons for this. One is that such resources proved inadequate to supply the urgent spiritual needs arising in the souls of those who were incarnating in the West. The other is that such souls appeared unaware of, or unwilling to develop the wealth of potential already present within themselves as a genetic spiritual inheritance of the Western world. So they took what seemed to be the easiest way out of their difficulties and grabbed at anything exotic and available that looked like a ready-made remedy for their inner deficiencies.

This can be compared to people living in areas of enormous wealth in terms of natural resources while developing none of them, and surviving by dependency upon other countries which have processed and marketed their natural resources. As any economist knows, this inevitably leads to social stagnation and ultimate degeneration of national character. The spiritual equivalents of this are worse still. From both a material and spiritual viewpoint, the healthy state of any community is best preserved by organizing and developing its inherent resources until these become as self-sufficient as possible, and surplus-exchangeable also. The ideal condition for a complete human community would be total self-sufficiency, a state more difficult to materialize than perpetual motion.

In our times it is not unheard of to enounter communes of usually young people who claim with justifiable pride that they are virtually self-supporting. On investigation, however, this generally means that they grow their own farm produce, carry out property maintenance, and possibly make their own clothing. Commendable enough, but nothing more than any rural population might have done better a few centuries back. It is all too frequently found that our modern back-to-the-landers are embracing foreign philosophies and Oriental outlooks on life which are at considerable variance with indigenous spiritual systems. Not that this is wrong per se, but only that it encourages undue dependence on imported ideology and neglects the cultivation of our inborn genetic consciousness.

It might be better for all of us if more esoterically inclined people realized deeply enough that we do indeed have a specifically Western Inner Way quite apart from any established religions or sectarian organizations. Those are but branches stemming from that Tree of Life which grows out of the inner ground whence our spiritual roots commence their climb towards Ultimate Light.

Surely it is time that some souls already incarnate recognize the significance of a spiritual factor *bound up with their own blood* which was once called the *Sang Real* or Blood Royal. This is our inner inheritance which of itself offers what used to be termed *salvation* for whoever belongs with it and follows the Quest for immortal identity which it encourages in the hearts that bear it consciously.

The present collection of writings has been assembled and co-ordinated principally for the purpose of alerting souls of that class into action. Each chapter may be considered as a separate thread of one single theme connecting our inner lives together like an unbreakable blood-link between family members of a common faith. If this work fulfils but a fraction of that function, it will have served an unique purpose.

You, in particular, whose eyes and mind are at this moment engaged with these words, should know instinctively whether or not this applies to you as a living soul. Perhaps you don't know exactly why, in terms of technical explanations or complicated verbal statements, but this is where you must rely on your heart rather than your head. The Sangreal is something you either belong with by birth and blood inheritance, or you do not, but might yet claim it if you would. There is nothing to prevent your attaining it in due course if you truly intend to. So if you are uncertain where you stand at the moment, it will do you no harm to read on and probe possibilities, will it?

Although the material contained in these chapters is not exactly a "course" in the usual sense of the word, it should be treated as if it were in order to obtain the best value from it, otherwise it will amount to little more than information which could be obtained elsewhere by spending the necessary time, trouble, thought, and resources needed to accumulate and assemble it. Even information cannot be collected without expenditure of all those essentials, plus considerably more time than it takes an average reader to follow it second hand. So you cannot very well lose on that score, can you?

Hence the intention is to place this book before you so that it can be handled as a work program, with carefully calculated questions at the end of each chapter. This together with the various exercises and practices suggested in the text, will make an entire training course as fully detailed and valid as any you might expect to find in so-called "Occult" or "Mystery" Schools of our present times. The main difference between anything you might be taught by such "esoteric associations" and what you hold in your hands now is this: Whereas an organization would impose disciplines on you and provide personal encouragements or criticisms regarding your efforts, in this case you will need to be capable of doing that for yourself, guided by whatever "inner contacts" you may make in the course of your studies and practices. In other words, you will be entirely responsible for your own progress.

There really *is* an "Organization" behind this work you are invited to participate in, but it is a purely spiritual one in essence. If you would prefer to find it in some kind of physical form at a later date, then *you,* together with others of similar inclination, will have to provide it with the means of such manifestation through yourselves. That is exactly the opposite of what has usually happened in previous times. Hitherto, various concerns have extended correspondence or other types of training courses for attracting fresh membership, then selecting suitable graduates for initiation into the society itself. Here, you are being provided with training materials which, if you are capable of handling them correctly, will enable you to construct a Society, or consolidation among its successful students resulting in what can only be termed a "Sangreal Sodality" of Western esotericism.

Boiled down to basics, this amounts to an attempt at forming a conscious linkage on material levels of life between all who sincerely feel or believe that their spiritual past, present, and future is bound up with the Western, rather than an Eastern Inner Tradition. That is to say, those who "have it in their blood," and really belong by simply being the souls they are, regardless of what section or cult may be claiming their attention during their present incarnations. Whether they call themselves Rosicrucians, Druids, Pagans, Qabalists, or anything else of a distinctive Western nature, such are but branches as it were, of something much greater than and inclusive of all sectarianism. This is our Western Soul, or Ethos, in which we participate perforce of our birth within it. Therefore its nature is both normal and natural to our very existence.

That is the standpoint on which the Sangreal Sodality depends: a kind of superloyalty above all sectional interests to the Life-Principle which produced us as a distinct species of people on this planet, having a particular function to fulfil in the spiritual structure of humanity as a whole; to develop and cultivate consciousness of the fundamental life purpose so that we shall become better able to serve the evolutionary ends of life itself as Deity, or however otherwise anyone sees such an ultimate to universal existence.

Now you who are reading this may not be interested in any such end-aim, in which case be assured there will be plenty in the way of esoteric information and subject matter to keep your mind occupied for the sake of intellectual pursuit alone. Assuming, however, that you may be inclined to take the theme seriously enough to follow it through to the end of your endeavours, here is what you are advised to do.

First of all, assess your life style and obligations, and then make the best arrangements you can for devoting the minimum required time and attention to these spiritual studies. You will need about five minutes in the morning, a few seconds at lunch-break, and some twenty minutes or so in the evenings, quite aside from your ordinary reading time. Remember always, it is best to do a minimum of work *regularly* each day, rather than a lot one day and nothing for many days afterwards. By all means, keep one day a week solely for recreational purposes, and a clear month for your normal vacation per annum. Your daily program should be built around the following fixed points:

1. *A morning meditation* consisting of five or so minutes of concentration upon a topic chosen from the current lesson or chapter studied the previous evening.

2. *Mid-day Invocation,* or a very brief but intense spiritual signal sent from the depths of your soul toward whatever Inner Power you believe or hope may be trying to help guide your individual life along its best Path.

3. *Evening exercises,* which amount either to the ones recommended in each Chapter/Lesson, or straight forward meditation on the chosen topic. In any case, a short write-up of results should be made as a sort of report in what used to be called a "Magical Diary." An ordinary desk diary would do if it had enough space, but the conventional thing to use is a loose-leaf file where each sheet can be added in proper sequence and ruled according to the amounts written every day.

4. *Sleep subject.* This is the selected subject which is "slept on" so that the deeper awareness contacted subconsciously during the night can deal with it effectively and produce interesting reactions when connected to normal waking consciousness during the morning meditation. It is usual to pick these subjects from the lesson in hand.

These events will form the skeleton of a spiritual framework on which to build the "inner stronghold" needed to contain the increasing consciousness of anyone who involves himself in this kind of self-development. Since they need somewhat more detailed description, this is what they actually entail:

1. Having read the material of the Chapter/Lesson in hand, choose ten or more distinct items from it that especially interest you and make a list of them. They do not have to be the same as the set questions at all. In fact, it is best if they are not, but rather derive from some points that you have thought of for yourself in connection with the lesson. You can select them in any order you like, but only *one* is to become the "Subject for the Day." You may write it on a piece of paper and put it under your pillow if you think that might help. Having duly "slept on it," bring it to mind as soon after rising as you conveniently can, and work with it in this way:

Put yourself carefully in the Western meditational position. This means no more than sitting comfortably on the firm seat of a chair which has an upright back or none at all. A dining chair or kitchen stool will be fine. Face a West Quarter. The spine is to be kept erect, feet flat on the floor beside each other, thighs about right angles to the legs below the knee. The hands rest lightly on the thighs, usually palms down and fingers extended. The head may be bent slightly forward, eyes closed with inner gaze aimed at the bridge of the nose. Breathing should be slow and regular. Peace and quiet in a dim light away from noise is best but ear plugs and an eyemask may be used if needed. Some find it helpful to wear headphones with suitable musical or sonic background, but everyone has to find what is best for themselves. Deep lounging chairs or couches with soft cushions will most definitely *not* be right for Western meditation, nor will lying in bed and dreaming offer a satisfactory substitute.

When you feel entirely settled, fix your whole concentration on the chosen topic and try to hold it in mind for at least five minutes. You may certainly do this dressed in pyjamas and dressing gown, or any other pre-breakfast style you fancy, but you must be correctly postured and mentally prepared for this brief exercise. Use a "pinger" to mark the time if you want to, but at the end of it make a brief note concerning the quality and depth of the meditation. This can be done easily by estimating results according to these three standards:

G (Good): Steady and constant awareness of the topic, coupled with a feeling of inner expansion concerning it, possibly with a new sense of its relevance or an increasing appreciation of its significance;

A (Average): Awareness of a drift from the subject, and a continual need to keep re-focussing the mind with some effort, but on the whole satisfied with the value of effort expended;

P (Poor): Total drift from the matter to other lines of thought, difficulty in focussing the mind with any clarity, and awareness of disinterest or inability to control the workings of your consciousness. Dissatisfaction with yourself.

It must be remembered that this applies to a normal mindstate. If you are temporarily affected by physical sickness or extremes of mental stress, do not attempt the exercise but for the sake of diary continuity simply write S by the date.

Do not try to think out any results of your early meditation. That will come later. Make everything as concentrated as you can for those few moments, then let it sink into your subconsciousness. Date the diary entry, note the time and quality evaluation, make a mental acknowledgement to your "Inner Contacts" however seems best to you, then get on with your mundane life.

2. Some time in the middle of the day around noon, send out your "spiritual signal" to whatever inner influence you hope may be helping your human efforts at living as a worthwhile soul. This takes longer to describe than to do. It consists of deliberately clearing your mind momentarily from material affairs, and sending out a sharply defined thought aimed at your "Inner Instructors" who are responsible for guiding you along your Life Path. You may use a mentally worded formula if you like, providing it is short, succinct, and emphatic. There must be no vagueness or dissimulation about it. A "forceful fling" is the basic idea. Do not attempt to elaborate the exercise with extended prayers or anything else. The methodology itself is important here. What is vital is that you manage to clear your mind for those few seconds needed to perform the practice, and that you do it so that it fits in with your normal routines and activities. Preferably, it should be done amid pressures of work and people. This will take ingenuity but many ways might suggest themselves. For instance, you might blow your nose slowly, wipe glasses, look as if you were consulting papers, or even tie a shoelace. With a little practice it can all be done in ten or fifteen seconds, but it is quite a valuable part of your training.

3. In the evening you will need enough time for your exercises and written work. This consists of a short write-up on the subject of the day for your diary. Think it over for a few minutes, then try to condense your thoughts into as few words as possible with the most meaning in them concerning your subject. Do not use vague, imprecise terms, do not ramble or employ extravagant phraseology. Remember the old time guidance given to trainee journalists: "Take a whole chapter and compress it into a few paragraphs. Take those and reduce them to a single sentence. Then take that and boil it down to a single word. If you can succeed with this, then you are made because all you have to do is make whole sentences from a few words, and long articles or stories from a sentence or so."

It is the principle of the thinking processes which is

important here because this last exercise involves the compression of consciousness back into basic energy, and that is an essential element of many occult procedures. How you accomplish this is entirely a matter for you to decide since everyone varies somewhat in method. You must do it in whichever way is easiest in your case. It is far better to put down only two or three words with feeling and meaning in them than pages and pages of pompous and futile meanderings of pseudo-mysticism. You should make a rule to keep your diary entries strictly within ten lines on each topic. Any extended writings should be done elsewhere.

4. Last of all, select your subject for the next day's consideration. You ought to drift off to sleep while contemplating it if you can manage this. It helps a lot.

When you think carefully about these four different ways of dealing with consciousness, you might realize that they form the four main points of a complete cycle. Starting in the morning, we have an intake of inspiration from the previous period of sleep-state inner awareness. This is reacted with by a steadily fixed focus of concentration. At noon, there is a sudden and almost explosive release of intentional conscious energy aimed in the direction of an inspiring Deity. In the evening, normal thinking consciousness is used with care and deliberation in a constructive scheme of inner ideological activity. Lastly, during the night, a fresh intake of inspiration is sought from higher than human levels of life. By such systematic usage of consciousness covering the human scale from one end to the other, the foundations of future enlightenment are most surely and steadily laid.

So by working with consciousness in this way, you will be training yourself in the systematic use of its basic elements for the specific purpose of co-operating with the "Inner Intelligences" responsible for maintaining and manipulating the finer forces behind our objective cosmic universe. *And that is exactly what all "occultism," "mysticism," "magic," or practical religion should be about.* Just as an artist starts by mixing and applying the three primary colors in definable forms, a musician begins with scales and simple harmonics, and a writer by learning the alphabet and then how to combine it in conformity with thought, so must students of spiritual processes commence with the practice of elemental consciousness as applied to their particular field, thus:

1. By *inspiration,* or reception of "inner intelligence" from higher than human sources. This is best accomplished during sleep when the objective mind and brain are at rest and do not interfere with or distort close contacts.

2. By *concentration,* or intentionally focussing consciousness with maximum force and attention. This is best done after awakening when the mind and brain should be clear after a night's sleep.

3. By *aspiration,* or deliberately aiming as high as possible for inner help with life. This is best done when pressures from living in this world build up the greatest need of guidance from beyond it.

4. By *construction,* or careful use of thinking consciousness so as to produce meaningful patterns of awareness in connection with chosen subjects. This is best done at the end of a day when an already activated mind has time and opportunity to arrange this task properly.

Surely by now you can see the reasons why such a course of systematic consciousness is being recommended? It is about the most prudent and practical method for modern people to start working with the main material of what was once called a "Magical Art." That is to say, intentionally directing consciousness itself. By beginning to build up a revolutionary life style centered around the pivotal points of spiritual cognition in this regular and rhythmic way, humans can convert themselves into living dynamos which will supply the vital currents needed so urgently for energizing and activating the inner affairs of our Western world. That is the "Great Work" which this book is dedicated to promoting with every possible word.

So far as the test questions at the end of each Chapter/Lesson are concerned, they should not be attempted before the contents of that Chapter have been thoroughly assimilated. Leave them alone for at least two weeks after reading the Chapter. It will be no use to suppose, "Oh, I know that one, I'll do it now." At a later date you might come up with an entirely different answer. It is actually a good plan to read your answers a few months after you made them and see then if you still agree with what you wrote at first. You might surprise yourself. By far the best arrangement to make with your work is to take it steadily Chapter by Chapter allowing yourself an absolute minimum of two weeks each, as if every one were sent to you separately after such an interval, and you had to complete the required work before receiving another.

Remember that anyone can buy a book of this nature and read it from cover to cover in quite a short time. That does nothing except provide a person with superficial interest and information. Reading a textbook on music never made anyone a trained musician. The one and only way this book can be of real value to you is by practising the exercises in it and *experiencing* its contents in your life. This naturally demands both time and effort which will vary considerably between one individual and another but cannot possibly be less than the reasonable minimum that is necessary.

A hidden value of the Chapter/Lesson outside of the printed diagrams or words you can absorb through your eyes and think about in your mind, is the inner instruction and guidance you will receive from spiritual sources of Intelligence which will make contact with you because of what you are reading and doing. In other words, your active studies and practices will create energy patterns of consciousness which are distinctive in a way which is sure to attract the attention of discarnate entities who are especially concerned with the spiritual advancement of souls within our Western Inner Way. All traditions have their own such guides and guardians as you will discover later if you have not suspected this by now. You can only be taught *part* of the Way on paper, but if you use that properly the rest should be revealed to you from "inside" by those able to teach without either words or visual signals. This is how these lessons should work and why they would be useless to a superficial reader. So please treat them for what they are, a means of contact between yourself and higher than human orders of life in a common cause to which we all owe allegiance.

If you are seriously determined to follow the Western line of Light, you would be well advised to confine yourself quite firmly and conscientiously within the framework of our tradition alone for at least the duration of preliminary training. That is to say, confine your consciousness to Western styles of mystical and esoteric work and thought until they become integral to your own nature. This does not mean there is anything wrong with other traditions. It only means that you cannot hope to gain much from Western esotericism unless you concentrate on it exclusively until it flowers in your own soul. For instance, you would not expect to become a great musician or anything so specialized while you were diverting your time and energy to many conflicting subjects in different fields. To gain proficiency in any area, you need to devote all possible energy and attention to that special subject while you study it. The same applies to our Western Inner Way. You are simply being asked to tackle the spiritual problems of your life with Western techniques in particular. That is all.

This means that you should suspend any active contacts you have with incompatible systems or schools of thought. For instance, you cannot very well claim to be a serious follower of the Western Way while you are attached to Zen, Vedic, or other Oriental and possibly conflicting methods of metaphysical conduct. Be one thing or the other but don't try to be both at once because it won't work. Eastern and Western spiritual systems are complementary to each other, but they go in opposite directons toward the same ultimate end in spiritual life. Nobody can run in two directions at once, so when you are absolutely and finally certain which way you want to go, close down any contacts with inharmonious associations you might be consciously keeping open.

For example, you should use Western esoteric symbolism alone for coordinating your consciousness. Look around your rooms and remove all obvious symbology from other systems except those common to all like pentagrams, hexagrams and so forth. African and Voodoo masks would be environmentally wrong, and so would Shinto or Tibetan images, Hindu deities, or Chinese ideograms. There is no need to dispose finally of valuable artwork, however. Just put such things out of your sight until you are capable of translating them into Western terms of thinking. Replace them with equivalent Western symbols. For example, you could replace a statue of Kwan Yin with a stylized Madonna figure, or use a deck of Tarot cards in place of the I Ching.

While we are on the topic of decor, here is something you can do of special occult importance. Set up a focal point in your home wherever you mean to carry out your meditations and exercises. The basic idea is to construct a symbolic nucleus connected with the Western Inner Way which will enable you to align your consciousness quickly and neatly into a workable pattern every time you use it. This is much like setting up a map reference point so that you could easily know exactly where you were in relation to the territory around you. It also provides a fixed localizer whereby your presence may be more powerfully sensed by the Inner Intelligences responsible for guiding and guarding our spiritual tradition on their levels of life. Of course, it is not the actual physical symbols which attract their attention so much as the images and thinking about them created in your own consciousness.

There is no need to go to any great expense or trouble in choosing and setting up a focal symbol for the Western Inner Way in your home. The simpler and easier to think of the better. It does not even have to be in view so long as you know where and what it is. You could perfectly well keep it in a closed box or behind a picture on the wall providing you can call it clearly to consciousness wherever you happen to be. What really matters is that whichever symbol you choose should have something uniquely connected with yourself built into it somehow—anything linking it with you and no one else.

For instance, you could trace a plain Cosmic Circle Cross on a card and write your signature anywhere around it. You might draw the Tree of Life and put a small photograph of your face on one or all of its Spheres. If you are a convinced Christian, you might have a Cross with your picture at the center, or a Crucifix with your photo, your name, or both at the bottom. You could take any particular symbol of the Western Way, such as a Celtic Cross, or a "Grail" type of illustration, then attach yourself to it by name, token, or perhaps a small lock of your hair. Any such thing designed to connect you and Western esotericism together will do.

The reason why there is no insistence on a standard design is because it is quite important that you should exercise your own inventiveness and ingenuity to establish your special sense of individual contact with the deep spiritual stream of our tradition. This may take some time and effort to think out and accomplish but that is all part of your training. When you have settled on a design which seems natural and comfortable for you, set the symbol somewhere safe where it is accessible to you or can be visible at will, and then *leave it there.* Do not move it from its location any more than necessary. Remember you can carry its image around in your mind wherever you like, and also it does not always have to be the same. You might need to alter it later as your experience and development directs.

The function of this personal symbol is much the same as a passport or identity card on material levels. It establishes your bona fides on inner lines of life among those who are concerned with the advancement of the Western Soul. It is also a sort of fulcrum on which you focus your attention when "gathering up your thoughts" for any particular purpose. First, fix your mind on your "spiritual security symbol," and then push it around in search of whatever you are aiming for. Thus your special symbol becomes a mento-spiritual device for automatic starting in any particular direction you intend, and additionally provides a useful return point if you need one in a hurry.

Do bear in mind that these studies and practices of themselves will not make you rich, famous, or bring you any material gains to gratify your greeds or ambitions. Your own reactions with them may indeed arouse abilities in yourself which might obtain such things in this incarnation, if that is the best you genuinely demand. However, the specific aim of this work is to make you aware of the Holy Heritage within you which you are entitled to claim as a mortal who is within the Western Inner Tradition. Whether you will ever go on further, and become an active initiated member of its Mysteries, fulfilling your obligations for passing such a contact along to others, is entirely for you to learn and earn by yourself.

The old days when Sacred Kings were ceremonially sacrificed on behalf of their people are over. More is demanded of modern people and in a higher way. Those who might have been chosen to die in olden times are now expected to offer a fair proportion of their lives and resources in the service of our spiritual tradition. No more, no less. Nothing that is not offered gladly with complete free will and joy at acceptance would be welcome. Sacrifices offered grudgingly, resentfully, or with reservations are utterly worthless in the Holy Mysteries. So are so-called sacrifices in the hopes of gaining corresponding rewards. These are nothing but bribes, and no genuine agency of the Mysteries from Divinity downwards could possibly be influenced by them in the slightest way. Nothing of a spiritual nature *can* be bought or sold, because the act in itself would automatically invalidate that very nature by its transaction.

There is no denying that you have a hard and difficult Path ahead of you if you determine to follow the Western Way in all its implications. Ours has never been an easy or undemanding tradition offering undeserved rewards for inadequate efforts. On the contrary, it has always been a tough, troublesome, and challenging one, calling for considerable strength of character, determination, and unremitting self-discipline. Nothing less is expected of those who dedicate themselves unreservedly to it. So do not make any rash or unthinking commitments which you are not absolutely confident you could at least make a good attempt at fulfilling in fact. You could regret this if you did.

If you happen to be a youngish or inexperienced person, there is one important thing you should learn at an early stage of your esoteric training. That is the need for, and commonsense rules of, spiritual security. This means keeping your own counsel, as the saying goes, on matters of your inner interests. Possibly more rubbish has been written about "occult secrecy" than most subjects, but there was and still is a very good and sound reason behind it all. Perhaps you had better consider a few points carefully before proclaiming your personal concern with esotericism too loudly before all and sundry.

First of all, your deepest spiritual levels of life are normally beyond the reach of inimical influences directed from external sources. If, however, you yourself intentionally expose these to risk, you could sustain a lot of damage to your inner sensorium and who would be to blame? The same is true of your physical body. If you lost more than a third of your skin surface, its internal system would perish through shock and infection and you would die. Without the bone of your skull to protect your delicate brain, how long could your body stay alive? Have you ever thought your soul needs an equivalent protection? In a world like this one, it most certainly does.

Think for a few moments how deeply your feelings (or soul senses) can be hurt by unthinking activities of other humans. They might not mean to hurt you but they have, simply because your soul "happened to be in the way" as they crossed your life path. That is not unlike your foot being heavily trodden on in some crowded place. Your pain and injury are no less because there would then be both bodily and mental suffering to contend with. So there can be spiritual damage to incur if you deliberately expose or extrude your spiritual system to any adverse streams of consciousness. By no means are all Westerners sympathetic to, or even interested in the secret side of their Tradition. Many can be hostile to it for various reasons, and they are likely to react unfavorably with your extensions in their direction. If commonsense does not teach you this then sad experience certainly will in the end, but by then it may be too late.

Another consideration is this. Centuries of experience have shown that careful confining of conscious energy within specific cyclic limits does build up a reservoir of power inside such areas. Given the right inner dimensions and sufficient content of consciousness, an efficient potential can be maintained. Once that container is breached, all its contents flow out wastefully and even destructively. Consciousness is not unlike a broad stream which can be dammed by a containing wall so designed that a volume of pressure may be concentrated to a single flow point which will drive a dynamo or perform useful work which the stream could not do otherwise. Break the dam and the water supply is spread over too wide an area for accomplishing much more than wetting it. Apply these natural laws to spiritual levels and you should see what is meant.

You can see an application of these principles in the old custom of always keeping any "special wish" a strict secret or "all the magic will leak out of it." That is a very good description of what happens. The "magic" of anything *does* "leak out" when it becomes commonplace and devalued. Any child learns that in the process of growing up. So if you value the magic within your own tradition, you will keep it where it rightly belongs—inside your soul to be shared only with those in whom you can place implicit love and trust or those bound to you by bonds of brotherhood and belief. We have been clearly told, "Do not give dogs what is holy, nor feed your pearls to pigs. They will only trample on them, then turn and tear you to pieces." None of us can say we have not been warned.

If you ever mean to become a "Grail" then you must first learn how to contain the "Holy Blood" energy within you by building up in yourself the symbolic "Cup" which will act as a reservoir so that its precious contents are available only to rightful partakers. You will learn, too, that what is *sacred* should be kept *secret* in the sense that it is never profaned or "exposed outside the Temple." Otherwise its inner power will be lost to you indefinitely.

Therefore you should start as you mean to continue, by keeping your occult studies confidential, and never talking about them except as may be necessary with those few people you know beyond doubt that you can trust. Do not leave lessons, papers, or anything connected with your studies lying around casually for anyone to read out of curiosity or from critical motives. Ideally, keep all written work in locked files or brief case. At least put it in a private drawer out of the way of prying eyes. You may think there is nothing in the work which might not be read by anybody—*and you would be right*. That is not the point at all. What matters most is your own behavior in regard to the material itself. If you treat it with contempt or casualness, how can you expect to get anything worthwhile out of it except mere information? Yet that information is a symbol of the real inner wisdom you hope to gain. So is your behavior a symbol, and when symbols are rightly interpreted and acted on they provide the answer to problems. *Verb sap!*

On the surface it may seem ridiculous to take security measures concerning matters that anyone could buy or obtain from a library. Nevertheless, act as if it were something confided to you by a relative or friend who was relying on your discretion and honor to deal properly with such a trust. What this correct attitude will do, in fact, is help form a good habit of mind and soul which encourages reliance from inner sources of intelligence. Ask yourself this question: Would you discuss or reveal details of your private affairs to anyone you knew would broadcast them in an unfavorable light to an unfriendly audience? If the answer is "No," then why should you expect non-incarnates to be so stupid? Become the sort of soul whom they can trust, and once they become completely convinced of this, you will begin to receive indications of their interest in you soon afterwards—if you know how to recognize this.

There are no shortcuts on the Inner Path. There may be the quickest and most direct methods but every inch has to be travelled and *experienced* by pilgrims questing for the Grail they hold within themselves all the time. The Path only leads them to awareness of that truth. Yet none attain such consciousness without pursuing their Paths to that point. Whether this is learned early or late in embodiment, it amounts to the same thing. Evolution has to be earned by effort on every level of life. What you earn you keep, but anything you are given may just as easily be taken away again. "Easy come, easy go" applies to mystical matters as well as material ones.

So the main purpose of this work ahead of you is to encourage you (and others, of course) to play a full and essential part not only in belonging with our Inner Tradition, but more importantly *working* with it so as to improve and preserve it at present in order to project it reliably and acceptably into the future. Do not depend on others to accomplish that task. Even though you probably believe there are many more capable souls than yours dedicating themselves to such striving, nevertheless you should work as if the entire future of our Western Inner Way depended on *you alone*.

A long time ago, Gautama Buddha said to his oriental disciples, "Though you know you may have as many incarnations as there are grains of sand on that shore, you should live each one as if it were the only life you would ever have." More than sensible advice. Today, occidentals might well consider the same principle applies to their lives within the Western Way. Imagine yourself as the only living representative of Western esoteric culture trying to collect your consciousness of it in such a way that you could pass on its essence *en bloc,* as it were, to another generation, in the hopes that they might eventually recover the whole intact by a process of reconstitution. How would you suggest tackling this job if it came to you? Tape recordings, time capsules, micro chips, and similar technology are ruled out. It has to be something out of your own consciousness which may be formulated and imparted like a spiritual seed that will in time reproduce an original fruit. There is a theory that the Tarot cards were conceived for that purpose. Can you think of something better?

No tradition should be something dead from the past hanging around our necks like a millstone in the present. It should be thought of as something spiritually vital in those of us alive today which must be handed over to our descendents in a condition of conscious animation so that they may continue living in a way which will be worth our returning to this world and recognizing. Thus, we should really be passing along an inner inheritance we hope to claim ourselves when we become re-embodied on this Earth. Looked at in that light of self-interest, a tradition begins to take on new meaning. Plenty of people feel this instinctively, but have neither called the idea into their consciousness nor found words to express it within their minds. You should not only be in a position to do both, but also ought to be able to contribute your particular share to our collective spiritual future. The vital question is—will you? Nobody but yourself can decide that.

No tradition is better than the people who embody it, whether they are themselves embodied or not. A tradition *is* the soul of all its people, good, bad, or indifferent, being only greater in magnitude than any one of them. If you know yourself to belong within the Western Way of Light, then listen for the call coming from your own Blood and hearken for the "Song of the Sangreal" with your inner ears. Ahead of you lies the Work of the West. Opus Occidentis, in Latin, and therefore OPOC for short as a codeword. *Do it.* If, on the other hand, you are uncertain where you belong, then the words ahead are sure to help you find some useful and appreciated place among humans who will be glad you are with them. There will be something for everyone who seeks enlargement of soul for any reason whatever, and no effect of such a kind is ever wasted in a world needing it so much. May your soul in particular be blessed past the end of time.

# · 1 ·

# *Behind Our Beliefs*

It is very difficult to trace the theme of our Western Inner Tradition through its literature. So much of it lies quite beyond the scope of words and has to be communicated mostly by symbolic or other means that are seldom understood by modern people. Yet literacy may extend esoterically into what may seem like a new language, but is actually a very old one that is genetically remembered. Much of it resembles the language you "spoke" yourself when you were a very small baby and knew no other tongue than "thought-talk."

The preceding paragraph, for example, is written in language comprehensible to quite ordinary people of this age who have what we would regard as a very average education. Millions of us communicate in such terms these days. Two or more centuries ago, relatively few had received an education enabling them to read or understand the literature of their times, let alone ours. The further we go back in history, the less widespread literacy was. Our Inner and secret spiritual Tradition not only depended mainly on oral transmission for its survival, but it continued along a number of considerably varied lines. In other words, there was no absolutely hard and fast doctrinal formula to follow as in the case of conventional religion or philosophy. Those had set rules to observe, and if you ignored them, you would probably be expelled from membership. With the Inner Tradition, there were but a few basic and fairly simple positions to hold, and beyond those you got what you could from where you might.

Now you probably think this was rather a systemless sort of system and a very poor means of keeping any Tradition going. Maybe you suppose it might have been better if some organization had been established which could have reduced everything to rules, regulations and fixed formularies which could be administered for the benefit of an arcane membership. If you have been thinking along any such lines, you would be wrong. Perhaps not entirely so, because there have been a few bodies of belief which considered themselves appointed by God or lesser authorities to preserve specific parts of our Tradition for posterity, though how far they succeeded is entirely a matter of speculation and opinion.

Thus there is no physical and human "Hierarchy" *as such,* behind our Inner Tradition for very good reasons. If you want to know those reasons, you have only to look at *any* hierarchical human organization on Earth and you should see them right away. The brutally blunt facts of the matter are that humans as a whole are *not* sufficiently developed as a spiritual species to be trusted with the actual administration of Life Laws on high energy levels of existence. The very fact we are human beings means we have far too much of a fallibility factor to permit our use as agencies for Cosmic Intelligence to operate beyond a very limited point, and that is *that.*

There *is* an "organized Hierarchy" (if we should recognize it as such) which influences our secret tradition from inner levels of life, but it is an entirely spiritual system of operation which works through conscious collusion with embodied agents and other human facilities available among us. Most importantly, there are absolutely *no* elements of coercion, compulsion, or the slightest persuasive pressure applied to any soul for the purpose of obtaining its cooperation in furthering our Western Inner Way. The essence of our Tradition is individual *freedom* to make or mar destiny in relation to Divinity. The immediate aim of Inner Intelligences connected with the Tradition is to awaken a sense of such responsibility within all souls belonging by rights thereto.

This means, to put things in old fashioned terms, that your own "salvation" or "damnation" is in your hands alone, and you will *become as you will be,* whatever that amounts to. Maybe you have heard the famous dictum: *Do as thou wilt,* and speculated on its meaning. Many mistaken minds assume it means "Do what you like." That is a misconception. The whole secret of the phrase lies in the meaning of *thou.* It does *not* mean the ordinary personality people think of as "you," the John or Jane Doe part, that belongs with your incarnate body and should die some time after it does. *Thou* specifically means the Real You of your Immortal Identity which relates directly with Divinity and is the True Self you were meant to become at the end of your earthly existence when you have *earned* emancipation from embodiment. Perhaps Jesus put it plainest in the Garden of Gethsemene when he cried, "Not *my* will, but Thine be done." So the dictum *"Do as thou wilt"* means exactly, "May the Will of God in me be done." *Never* on any account say, think of, or use that old invocation without realizing its full implication.

Back to beginnings again. In earlier times some of our secret Tradition may have been comprehensible in terms of language among a relatively small minority of "initiated" individuals, but what about the bulk of human beings who could neither read, write, nor follow complicated ideology? How did they carry things along? Yet not only did they carry the essential elements of our Tradition from one generation to another, but they did so without endless arguments, fuss, elaborate procedures, or other artificial aids to mental stimulation. In fact, they bore the fundamentals of the Tradition within themselves with a minimum of mentalization, yet a maximum of "feeling-appreciation." In modern terms they were Orphics rather than Hermetics.

We have to remember that in former times the mass of Western population was very roughly divided into urban and rural communities, the former close-packed, merchantile-industrial and highly competitive in character, while the latter were family grouped agriculturists, slow to change, and generally conservative in nature. The town-dweller tended to think in terms of artifacts, and the country-folk thought more in terms of nature. That is to say they did most of their thinking and conceptualization according to what they depended on for their livelihoods and subsistence. It was only to be expected they would translate our Inner Tradition into such frames of reference. Let us try to see what this means, because it has a great deal of bearing on the inheritance we have received from our forefathers.

The consciousness of country people was attuned to the cycles of solar seasonal life. Their's was the oldest awareness of the Cosmic Cross pattern divided into hunting and cropping periods. Their God and Gods were all around them in the skies, fields, seas, trees, herbs, and the very stones themselves. Natural noises from those sources were "voices" from an invisible world wherein apart from Gods, dwelt strange races of non-human beings, some friendly, some hostile, and others indifferent to their human neighbors. Occasionally these odd little "spirit-people" appeared in the shape of animals, but sometimes they might be seen by specially gifted human eyes as creatures of not quite human semblance, with a peculiar culture of their own. It was not considered very wise to seek close relations with such beings because of their unreliability, but tales were told of humans who gained some uncertain advantages from contacts with the "Fairy-folk."

The substance behind all this shadow is considerable. By the exigencies of their lives, rural individuals were frequently in the habit of spending long periods of solitary or single-companioned contact with the elements of life and bare necessities thereof. They were therefore more or less forced into wordless communion with what they encountered in the course of their work, and in the end came to comprehend a strange language common to Nature itself which "spoke" of its own mysterious behavior. Some of the "words" had physical sounds, like the crying of wind and calls of creatures telling about weather changes or the presence of eatables and enemies. Most of the "language," however, was only "audible" to those accustomed to listening for Silence. None of it was in words common to human civilized consciousness, moreover it was too difficult to translate into such limited terms. Enough to know it was there, and somehow it knew you were there, too.

Most of our secret Tradition was not "passed along" in wonderful Temples by robed Hierophants to habited Initiates or anything like that at all. It filtered through the humble souls of ordinary peasants dealing directly with the "Silent Speakers" in everyday condition of existence. They did not have to *understand* what they received. They simply had to "hold it in them" and leave it alone till it "came up" in its own good time. This they knew all about. Had they not planted endless seeds in the earth and waited patiently until fruits arrived in their turn? Now they realized something was being planted in *them* which might not flower for many generations, but eventually would come to light and produce both flowers and fruit of a very special kind. None of them could have told how they knew this, or explained anything in human words yet know it they did, to a degree which gave them a sense of purpose in life which many moderns lack. Had they been forced to say what they were living on earth for, they might have replied something to the effect of, "To keep it going like."

Maybe none could have defined just *what* had to be kept going, but all knew without words what was meant. *Life* had to be kept going, and that was exactly what peasant work was concerned with. Life and lives of humans, animals, plants, and minerals in continual cycles of change and exchange amongst each other for some purpose nobody could explain, but they all felt was behind them somewhere. The rural worker felt *needed* by this strange Power and believed he or she was "part of its push." He was not only involved with Life, but what he did helped it along its way. Animals bred because he herded and selected them. Crops came up because he planted them. Trees gave good fruit because he pruned and manured them. Wine was available because young people danced on the grapes old people had cultivated. Everywhere was evidence of what men and women could do with the assistance of friendly spirits who "spoke" and encouraged them as they worked on and improved what Nature had provided.

Of course there were the "bad spirits," too. They sent the blight on crops, barrenness on beasts, killing frosts out of season, withheld rain when needed, and did all sorts of anti-human acts.

Sometimes ill-intentioned humans would invoke them to injure other folk whom they held grievances against. Such malice became known as "witchcraft," the work of the wicked, and it was feared and punished as such in various ways among different communities. All sorts of protective devices were tried against influences of ill-will directed against honest agriculturists. Sometimes these seemed to work and quite often they didn't. Struggling between Good and Bad, the peasantry of Western Europe survived somehow with the support of the Life-Spirit they silently shared together.

It was inevitable that they should discover the "specialness" of certain places from sheer experience. Particular localities and especially features therein such as springs, rocks, caves, and hilltops had their own peculiar "atmosphere" which might be good, bad, or just "otherworldly." Chinese peasants had learned this in early times, and developed sensations experienced at definite points into a kind of science called "feng-shui" or knowing the rightness or wrongness of places. Western workers were no less sensitive in their natures but were content to take things for granted as they found them and react accordingly. Thus they would avoid "bad" places as much as they could, cultivate the "good" ones, and maybe save the "odd" ones for special meeting points with their dimly remembered "Old Gods."

What all this amounted to was that the average countryman and woman *feelingly* shared the Great Life around them expressed through the energies of Nature. By straightforward absorption from the consciousness of Cosmic Life they received the Inner Tradition, not in any verbalized and intellectual form, but as an instinctual and vital appreciation of experienced energy patterns which condensed in their consciousness and genetics as a spiritual stream derived from their deepest roots in reality. As the poet said, their instructive sermons came from stones, and they read from "books in the running brooks."

Townsfolk could accomplish very little of this. Their lives were superficial and disturbed in comparison, so their contacts with Nature were virtually cut off by interference from each other and the problems of urban life. They were restless and impatient as a rule, unable to settle down and reach inner worlds by silent contemplative contact. They may have been more intellectually active than their country cousins, but they missed the "spiritual solidities" which rustics were prepared to take for granted without elaborate examinations and soul searchings.

By populating the countryside with creations of his non-volitional consciousness from Gods down to fairies and other oddities, the rustic of old times was seeking a symbolic means of relating himself with an inherent Intelligence which he sensed lay behind his daily world of experience. He was careful to divide his "Spirit world" into concepts superior to himself—the Gods, and his spiritual inferiors—the fairies. This indicated his evaluation of himself on the scale of inner existence.

However, by personifying and relating with the invisible powers and energies of life encountered on Earth by humans trying to support themselves and their families, our Inner Tradition of the West became cultivated and propagated from one generation to another. No matter how superior and sophisticated we may suppose ourselves in the midst of our modern technology, *our roots are rural,* and if we seek them we shall have to trace them to the soil from which they sprang. This means digging down deeply enough in ourselves to find the sources of our basic beliefs in life and recognizing them for what they are—early attempts to relate with our own origins and find pointers to our future Cosmic conditions.

It is encouraging to note a growing concern in our times with this vital task. Think of the number of apparently "new" movements inquiring into our significance as an Earth-species linked in the past with Life elsewhere in our Universe. To name a few of them: Tellurianism (Earth as a living organism), Ufology (contact with other Solar Systems), Sacred Sites (attempts to rediscover old contact-points on earth with Cosmic Powers focused on this planet), Ley-lines (ancient directional relationships between Earth-points of special significance), Hill markings of possibly religious or social meaning in past times, Stone-Circle interpretations. All these coupled with a host of other connected topics like interests in herbalism, country crafts, folk-singing, naturism, holistic healing and so forth, are gaining importance in modern consciousness. This all arises from a single root-stem in our souls: *recognition of the urgent need to re-establish our oldest spiritual tradition in terms of our times.*

What we are trying to do with any or all of the above mentioned activities is come to a conscious and rational relationship with the spiritual realities of our inner universe particularly applying to Western people of this world, but seen through sets of "scientific symbolism" which modern minds have been conditioned to accept. After all, it is only a question of old wine in new bottles. On the whole, modern people tend to be suspicious of priests, yet tolerant of psychiatrists who deny that the psyche they are dissecting is alive. There is no doubt we are a crazy mixed-up civilization, and those seeking survival through it seem to realize there is only one sensible thing to do: *reach for our roots and hold on to them.*

We are trying to place in your hand keys which will unlock the spiritual secrets of yourself as an evolving soul upon the Western Inner Way and towards an ultimate end of *Perfect Peace Profound.* These "Keys" are mainly symbols and contacts of consciousness which connect directly with the depths of our secret Tradition. But, *nobody except yourself* can fit them to your own locks and turn them. Who else but *you* has the right to liberate yourself into a state of enlightenment? It is totally foreign and alien to our Inner Tradition that any soul should be deliberately invaded by another with intentions of compelling conformity and enforced agreement in spheres of spiritual activity. All must be free to accept or reject *as they will.* Groups with common customs and aims do have the right to insist that those applying for inclusion among them should conform with established practice, but the burden is strictly on individual souls whether or not to seek close association with any corporate body of belief within the Western Way.

Now you may realize just why it is so important that there should *not* be any Earth-organized authority laying down rigid rules about what our Tradition should or should not be. Our real Inner Tradition is something *born out of us* because of individual spiritual experience over many centuries and millennia of life shared with higher states of being than ours which are concerned with our evolution *because of our own efforts* towards an ideal condition of existence beyond embodiment altogether. Thus our Tradition is composed of contributions from every single soul that has ever tried to live within it, augmented by their contacts with spiritual counterparts engaged in furthering the same life-stream. Insofar as all these units of experience point towards a unified End and Origin, we share the same consciousness constructing them. That is what our Inner Tradition amounts to.

Going back to the elementary rootings of our Tradition, we shall find it began similarly to most traditions. It developed out of early encounters with the elements in attempts to survive on this planet by food production through hunting, herding, planting, and fishing, the common factor being fertility. The simple facts of life boiled down to birth, breeding, death, and believing. Out of those fundamentals, our conscious relationships with Cosmos sprang up and began to make patterns which later turned into distinct traditions depending on how much they were interpreted.

This is very much as if a class of children were all given exactly the same three primary colors plus black and white, then told to depict the same abstract theme with them. There would be a certain amount of blanks, a number of "copycattings" and some strikingly interesting original designs. That is what early mankind did when confronted with a similar problem in terms of life-fundamentals on Earth. All our religions and most of our philosophic beliefs to this day are based on concepts concerned with birth, breeding, and death, or the triplicity theory of life overshadowed by the mysterious fourth factor connecting death back to birth again. Our Western Tradition did no more than paint its particular picture of Cosmos with the same primaries as everyone else, but it did so in accordance with its own unique spiritual experience.

*Birth* was seen as an event which brought a fellow human into this world, and since he must come from *somewhere,* there had to be another world invisibly connected with this one. Who that individual was, why he had come, and what he was supposed to do here, depended on:

*Breeding.* Even early humans were aware of selected reproductive strains among herd animals and themselves alike. They knew about prime males fighting each other to the death for herd rulership which granted the winner conjugal rights over the finest females. They had practiced this themselves and found it produced a line of fierce fighters and adaptable mothers. They were also discovering that seeds selected from the best specimens of plants were likely to produce the finest quality crops. Breeding was a life-factor which humans were learning to deal with to their advantage.

*Death* meant little more than migration from the vicinity while you left your body behind for your friends to dispose of as they thought fit. If you were respected and would be welcome back, they treated your corpse as well as they could, but if you were an unpopular type they got rid of the remains in some disgraceful way like leaving them to be eaten by wild animals or buried in a bog—anything to point your spirit in other directions and discourage you from coming back for another incarnation among them.

*Belief.* Most people felt there was a Father-God somewhere in the Sky and a Mother-God in the Earth. This was because they sometimes heard Him growling away up there when He was getting a mood on Him. Then His shadow would lie heavily above the land as He enveloped Earth in His embrace and muttered. Suddenly His terrifying phallus of Fire would stab into Earth and He would roar His triumph over Her with fierce passion. Sometimes Her rumbling responses could be heard quite clearly afterwards, dying into sighs of satisfaction. Again and again the action would repeat, and dense streams of Divine seed would descend all over Earth to fertilize Her willing and waiting womb. Eventually His passion would subside, and He would climb off Earth back into His clouds again, smiling from the Sun, while Earth lay soaked and gently steaming. Her plentiful progeny would arrive later, and Man would eat some of them, as Earth would eat Man's body up when he had finished with it.

All later and complicated forms of religion are extensions of this rather lovely and simplistic version of Father-Mother-God in creative climax. Even today we instinctively revere the saying: "God is Love," and that is precisely what it means. The word used for "Love" is AHBH in Hebrew, pronounced sometimes "Ah—Vah." It means literally "to breathe after," and is figurative of the increased rapid breathing accompanying sexual excitement. So here we have an early ideology of God being the Male-Female complementary energies of creation eternally seeking fulfilment in each other. It is a particularly interesting thing that the Western Christian association of God with the name Jesus means exactly that from a double Greek derivaton: Ge (the Earth-Mother) and Zeus (the Sky-Father). So there is a connection with our oldest roots in the word-symbol for our "Salvation."

In ancient times, there were two main systems of territorial survival among mankind. One was by nomadic herding, and the other by crop farming. We can think of them like cattlemen and homesteaders of the last century. The story is told in the legend of Cain and Abel. Cain was the agriculturist, while Abel was the herd-keeper. Presumably Abel's sheep and goats invaded Cain's crops and destroyed them, thus inciting Cain to kill Abel and so become the world's first recorded murderer. God was said to have preferred Abel's sacrifice instead of Cain's, perhaps because it was a meat-offering, Sacred King style. However the tale maybe interpreted, it illustrated the root causes for war among mankind: ideological differences, jealousies, and territorial disputes. We do not seem to have improved much there, have we?

Before herding and farming really got going on Earth, however, the real human Hero figure was the Hunter, the swift, strong male killer who kept his tribe fed because of his skills. Without Hunters, the tribe would perish and die. They all knew that. Moreover, Hunters often lost their own lives or were badly lamed in pursuit of quarry. Everyone honored them and valued their services. Not only did they hunt animals for their people to eat, but they sometimes had to hunt other humans who showed hostility to the tribe and threatened their livelihood in some way. The Hunter then became the Warrior, and in either role he was liable to be killed on behalf of his people for whose sake he risked his life.

Life came from the Gods and went back to Them in the end. You could call souls into this world only one way, but you could send them out of it by quite a lot of different methods all culminating in death. Birth came by white seed, but death usually came with red blood, as if it were caused by violence suffered in service for the people. It almost seemed as if the Gods demanded a certain number of lives that way, and if such was indeed their Will, who was Man to question it? Would it not be a wise and splendid idea to offer the Gods a life or so as a free gift in hopes of obtaining favors?

So the cult of sacrifice sprang up along many different if related lines. The original notion was probably straightforward commerce with the Gods. If favors were sought, then the gift had to be appropriate in value, say fruit and flowers for minor favors, birds and small game for bigger ones, lesser herd animals for larger ones yet, and really valuable beasts for important requests. It was inevitable that the top currency in the scale of God–Man exchanges should be a human life. Even there, a set of values applied. Old men were of small worth, since they were due to die soon anyway, and their usefulness was over. Women were not considered suitable as a rule, except sometimes if they were young and attractive. Children were acceptable in a pinch, especially firstborns, but the highest possible human price was placed on the finest and fittest males, tried, tested, and in prime condition. Sacrifice one of them occasionally, and the Gods must surely appreciate the honor paid to Them and reward the generous givers lavishly.

Sacrificial customs cannot have been going very long before it dawned on all concerned that the best and noblest, and consequently most valuable sacrifice would be a voluntary Victim, one who gave his own life freely and gladly. What more could any God ask of Man? It might be thought there would be some difficulty in getting nominations for this office but on the contrary, young men were prepared to fight each other for the privilege. It was an honor to be prized above everything else.

Think of the inducements. At least a year of luxury living at the expense of the tribe, choice of the best girls, every kind of delectability their society had to offer, in return for what? A life they had to risk all the time in hunting or fighting anyway. Moreover, their death would be relatively painless and at least swift, in the presence of an admiring and applauding crowd of friends and families. Not only would these people cheer them on till the end, but they would reward them after death by making them into memories of the highest importance to the tribe. They would be made "honorary Kings" and remembered as such forever. That was surely worth dying for.

If anyone suppposes no young man would do this today, let them figure what would happen if a "luxury year" were guaranteed in return for a quick death by stabbing at the hands of an expert surgeon at the end, with world-wide TV coverage. The TV offer alone would bring more queues of young men than could easily be imagined. Fanatical devotees to "causes" would gladly sell their lives if enough money or support were forthcoming. There has never been a lack of volunteers to die by martyrdom.

However this cultus of the Sacred King began amongst the tribes which later became the population of the Western world, it grew to a very high point of spiritual importance among them, and is a main foundation of our secret Tradition to these times. We still lay coins or tokens under the foundations of important buildings in memory of the human bodies we once sacrificed during earlier days. It is very important that the whole significance and function of the Sacred King system be understood, because otherwise nothing of our Inner Way will make much sense or reason.

Christianity cannot possibly be comprehended without a full knowledge of the Sacred King concept, which never seems to be explained properly by any official exponent of Christian Churches. It is a theme which none seem anxious to face, and any suggestions of it get hastily swept under covering carpets of conspicious wooliness. One wonders why. By "cultured" standards it may not be a nice or pleasing proposition, but why should it be? On the contrary it is a blunt and uncompromisnig confrontation with the most basic facts of our own natures. Birth, Breeding, Blood, and Belief. You cannot escape these however much you try to wriggle away from them. They are the Four Fates which encircle your life while you have a human body in this world. They also lie behind your entrances and exits therefrom, so you might as well have a closer look at them. Before we go any deeper, however, it might be a good idea to condition your consciousness in a number of simple ways. Here are some of them:

1. Go into the countryside by yourself as far away from humanity as you can. Choose a nice day. Settle down somewhere and really *experience* your surroundings. Look at every leaf and see if you can find two *exactly* alike. Crumble earth through your fingers. Do deep breathing exercises. Lie flat on the ground with your eyes closed. Listen intently for natural sounds and try to ignore any that might reach you from civilized sources. Can you feel any kind of Divinity or Life-Spirit in contact with you? Take a lot of thoughts home with you to work on.

2. Whether or not you are a Christian, go alone into a small rural church if you can. Look around. The altar is the sign of an unoccupied tomb. On or near it should be the representation of a Cross, possibly with a crucified figure on it. There are millions of Christians in this world. Why should they revere this particular symbol of Divinity? What, if anything, does it mean to you? Would you die for whatever you believe in? If you had to die anyway, wouldn't you prefer it was for a good purpose rather than uselessly and needlessly? Can you feel any sense of "Divine Presence" in the place? If you think It is there, do you suppose It knows you are there, too? Go home and do some more thinking.

3. Look at your finger tips very carefully, using a magnifying glass if you can. Those patterns are unique to yourself, as you should know. So if you are marked out from every other human by nerve patterns in your skin, can you believe there might be equivalent patterns in your soul establishing your identity as an individual, patterns in your genetics, your blood, connecting you with ancestral origins leading back to the far past which we have been considering? Something is still teaching you today from those remote sources. Had you realized this? You inherited a great deal from your parentage apart from your body. Have you ever wondered how far back it goes and what you might do with it if you felt so inclined? Give a lot of serious thought to these queries.

## Questions

1. Interpret the phrase: "Do what thou wilt."
2. How did our Western Inner Tradition divide between urban and rural communities?
3. To which do you feel most drawn?
4. Do you have any particular "Sacred spots," and if so describe them with your associations.
5. Give examples of "back to nature" movements in our times.
6. What are the "Three B's" of our Inner Tradition and how would you define them?
7. Define early concepts of sacrifice as bargaining with the "Gods."
8. Explain the Sacred-King concept.
9. Choose the ten most important sentences in this Lesson.
10. Assuming you have done the last three exercises suggested, which did you find the most significant and why? If you have not done them, why not, and which would you start with?

# · 2 ·

# *The Cult of Kingship*

Our average ancestors in far off times were not sincerely religious people as we might interpret the term today. They saw their "Gods" as we might see our modern concept of state, as remote powers controlling our lives behind the scenes, yet capable of interfering with us in restricting, irritating, or sometimes beneficial ways. In our times, the state may enforce legislation which limits individual liberties in quite a number of ways, but it can also implement and has a great deal to do with our welfare and improved living conditions. That is largely how early earthlings considered their Gods: like our state, difficult to deal with unless you knew the right manner of approach.

Why bother with the Gods at all? Why not leave them alone to get on with their affairs in Heaven, while we tried to cope with ours on Earth? What made Man want to deal with Deity in the first place? That is indeed a leading question to which there cannot be a conclusive answer as yet, because we are still seeking it. There can be two very strong likelihoods.

The first reason is because the Gods, as humans believed then, had incalculable influence over all factors affecting humanity for good or ill. For example, the Gods controlled the weather on which supplies of foodstuffs and sea-passages depended, to say nothing of floods and droughts which brought disasters everywhere.

Displeasure of the Gods sent diseases and plagues to man and beast alike. Their approval led to benefits like plentiful harvests and prosperity from trading. Brought down to basics, it paid to appeal for patronage from the Gods. That was the only insurance practiced in those times.

Humans found the second reason a lot harder to understand. It was instinctual and inherent in themselves. Something drove them toward Deities not from fear or for seeking favors, but because they sensed a degree of affinity between themselves and the invisible Immortals. In a remote way they realized they were distantly related to those Gods and wanted to improve that relationship. This trait in specific members of the human race shows some evidence of genetic lines leading back to the "Old Blood" which originated from outside this Earth altogether. Humans in those days could not have known this with their objective consciousness, but then they relied a lot more on intuition (teaching from "Inside") than we do now—often to our loss.

Voluntary offering of human life to the Gods (or God) as a sacrificial act of supreme value, became the basis of our Tradition, and *it remains so now in terms of our times.* Originally, the greater and more important an individual was, the higher value his sacrifice had. This meant that the ultimate sacrifice any tribe or nation of people could make would be their King or Ruler. An ordinary, no-account person would be rather an insult to any national-sized Deity. It had to be at least someone very special and selected with the utmost care, preferably one thought to have "the Blood" in him. Only the very best was good enough for the Highest Gods who must not be approached or invoked for trivial causes. (Besides, no tribe could possibly afford to keep killing its leaders for minor reasons.) So the Supreme Sacrifice of Royal Blood was reserved for desperate occasions, or took place at periodic intervals, possibly several years apart at first. Lesser sacrifices were far more frequent, of course.

Originally these sacrificial customs were common to all human cultures, but as these diverged from each other, they became increasingly specialized, every separate culture evolving its own special systems. For instance, in many places a sort of envy had arisen among young nobles who considered they, too, were worthy of a "Divine death," and did not see why they should not be entitled to such an honor. This led to electing "surrogate Kings," and if the numbers of eligible males allowed, the "Supreme Rite" might take place as often as twice a year, at Summer and Winter.

By early megalithic times in the West, the practice of human sacrifice had reached a very sophisticated stage of development. Elsewhere the custom was declining and eventually would almost die out. This seemed to be for political rather than religious reasons, because human life was always held cheaply. Dynastic and dictatorial societies were arising wherein the controlling elements had no intention of sacrificing themselves to any God while they held the riches of rulership in their own hands and commanded armies strong enough to keep the population in its place. Sacrificial practice was beginning to debase anyway, because unwilling and protesting victims were being offered more to please the crowds than the Gods they were supposed to appease.

This was probably what led to the substitution of animal for human sacrifice. Animals could not protest, and they were being killed for meat and hides anyway. A convention arose that the garlanded beast had to bow its head submissively before being butchered alive at the altar, and whoever held it soon learned the knack of inducing such a gesture. Animal sacrifices always had to be garlanded as a token to represent both a crown and symbol of sacrificial purpose.

Where purely voluntary immolation was kept up strictly, its methodology had become very impressive. Victims were selected only from an elite of the right age group (usually between 20 and 30) which had been brought up especially for the purpose. Preferably they would all be "of the Blood" or be related in some ways to lines with Sacred Kings in their families. Selection varied from drawing lots to being picked out by a blind person. This gave the Gods some choice in the matter because an element of chance was introduced.

Death was mostly by stabbing to the heart with a flint knife or sometimes a spear, usually at the hands of an Elder who was an expert at the job. The victim was generally held in place by his close friends or companions against an upright or horizontal stone specially set for that purpose. Later he was bound in position with cords, which is one reason why the Cord became a sacred symbol in the Tradition. It should remind people of the dedication they owe to Divinity. As a rule, the death was swift and relatively merciful, better than what a young man would normally face in battle. Among some tribes, however, it was considered more heroic to die slowly and painfully to show what suffering could be borne without flinching or uttering cries of pain. The moment of death was normally sunrise when the first Solar rays reached the willing Victim's breast.

After death the Victim's body was processed for distribution among those on whose behalf he had died. Because his blood was the visible sign of his death and was evidence of his Kingship, as much of it as possible was saved to share among a privileged priesthood and elect of the people present. Occasionally the vessel in which this was distributed was made from the skull of a previous Sacred King or some equally honored personage. The head was often buried or set in a niche at a sacred spot where it would act as a protective talisman, while hands, feet, and entrails were burned. The meat got cooked by women whose special duty this was, and shared out sparingly to members of the populace. They gave their late leader the most honorable burial of all—in their own stomachs. Long after this practice ceased, it still remained a high honor for dead leaders' bodies to be cooked in the funeral pyre of a cremation fire, while their praises and eulogies were solemnly sung.

This was far from being the end of the story. Death by itself was not the object of the exercise at all. Much more was expected. The liberated spirit of the Victim had a duty to do by his people. He had to go to the Gods on Their own ground, so to speak, and intercede on behalf of his kinsfolk and people. His task was to tell the Gods exactly what was happening among his folk on Earth, what their needs were, speak of their hopes, fears, wishes and intentions, then beg the Gods for kindness, consideration, and all the benefits They could bestow on earthlings. In short, he was an Ambassador and Mediator from his tribe to the Kingdom of Heaven.

Maybe this was all he was expected to do at first, but subsequently a further direction was given him which was very far reaching. He was asked to remain with the Gods to learn what he could about them and all they were prepared to teach him for the improvement of his people. Then he was supposed to return among those people on Earth by ordinary incarnation, and grow up to teach the Truths he had learned in Heaven for his kindred to hear on Earth. In that way they hoped to enlarge their understanding of life on other levels, and learn how best to live on this one.

This is the function of Sacred Kings in all times. First, he must lead a self-sacrificing life, and second, he must teach or disseminate in each incarnation whatever has been learned during discarnation which may be of benefit to fellow-mortals. That was how it was done in old times. Note very carefully that Sacred Kings were supposed to die only on behalf of their own people, especially those to whom they were related even in distant ways. It was important that there should be a linkage of Love among them all, binding them together in the bonds of Brotherhood and family feeling. They had to belong with each other "because of Blood." The vital factor of Blood was the Sign and Symbol of relationship with Deity through the Royal Line of Sacred Sacrificial Kings.

At first, such relationship could be claimed by those who "had the Blood in them" by reason of actually drinking some, or participating in the "Holy Feast" at the conclusion of the ceremony. As numbers of would-be participants grew out of all proportion to the supply of cooked meat, someone thought of mixing a little blood with a lot of what passed for wine at the period and offering that around. Others would dilute the blood considerably with water and scatter this in drops over the heads of the crowds, assuring them that a single contact with one drop was sufficient to bestow the precious blessing, if it were asked for with fervent faith.

It was one thing to send a Sacred King to Divinity, but quite another matter to get him back again. There surely had to be some technique of managing this. By now, there was an organized and hierarchial priesthood who was inventing, organizing, and arranging these ceremonial events. In the end some one came up with the sought for solution. If Death could be operated as a sacred affair dedicated in service to the High Gods, then so could Birth. Circumstances only had to be suitably ordered. Eventually, matters were broadly worked out along these lines.

Just as selected youths were brought up for the specific purpose of being chosen as Sacred Kings, young girls might be specifically taught and trained so that a few among them might become the mothers of returning Sacred Kings seeking re-entry to tribal circles. At first they were fertilized by picked priests who were known to be "Blood-bearers," but sooner or later the crude principles of artificial insemination were discovered, so that it seemed the girl had had a child by miraculous means and she could truthfully say: "No man hath touched me," because the "magic touch" was administered by a senior woman. The usual method was inserting the small end of a hollow horn with a fresh collection of male seed in it, and blowing down the wide end to expel the seed into the girl.

Some thought the seed should be collected from a number of donors, each with some special gift. One man would be learned, another rich, another a keen hunter, another a warrior. The idea was that the resulting infant would be possessed of all their best qualities. Their knowledge of biology may have been very slight in those days, but there can be no doubt of their good intentions. Thus was born the idea of God-Fathers, for it was supposed a boy could have several fathers but only one mother. Hence also why the "Blood" was supposed to descend directly through the female line. All girls accepted for such service had to prove familial connection with some Divine King ancestry.

Suppose the result of such ritualized impregnation was a female? The organizers of the enterprise were not unduly worried. Either the child was brought up similarly to her mother, or she might just be exposed at birth to die naturally. Perhaps someone might take pity on her helplessness and bring her up as his or her own child. Or maybe not. It had to be as the God decreed. If she were permitted to grow up in a sacred Sisterhood, she must pass her life in perpetual virginity unless selected for the office of Divine Mother. No man must defile what was dedicated to the service of the Gods. Death by disgraceful means was the punishment for such desecration.

Many were the variations and local customs on this central theme surrounding the Sacred King story. Does a lot of it sound very familiar? It should, because it is the basis behind Christianity which has become the majority religion of the West in theory, however it is interpreted or misinterpreted among its many sects, branches, and their divergencies. There were just as many differences among followers of the Sacred King system, except that none of them had definite names for their religion as such. To them it was only a matter of people doing the same thing in different ways according to how they felt like relating themselves with their Gods.

As religions in the Orient and Middle East became more sophisticated and established set doctrines, teachings, philosophies, and formulae, they grew away from the Sacred King practices while retaining some of the principles. They had begun to realize that original purposes were being achieved. Humans were developing higher standards of intelligence and culture. As they evolved, so did their God-concepts. More and more individuals were coming back into incarnation and making valuable contributions to civilization apart from the Sacred King sacrifices being offered. It was evident that the "Blood" was breeding through normal channels and becoming far more widespread, though it was being kept within Royal and noble circles insofar as this was possible.

With the coming of formal Temple worship and substitution of animal sacrifices for human, Sacred King practices did not so much die out as reach a higher level of interpretation. Sacrificial cooked flesh was still served out and eaten, but now it was mainly mutton or beef, both of which were costly, though poor people could purchase doves instead. Some progressive Temples were offering flowers and vegetables together with incense in place of the savoury smell of roasting flesh which was said to attract the Gods' interest in what was going on. The priesthood had discovered there were big profits to be made by selling sacrificial animals and offerings to large congregations of worshippers. Additionally, it ensured their own food supplies indefinitely free of cost, since they bought cheaply or accepted voluntary donations, then resold these at inflated prices to the public.

The Sacred King system left positive traces of itself over the faces of most religions. Temple virgins still existed, though sometimes these turned into Temple prostitutes, selling their services for the benefit of whichever establishment they worked for. Ruling monarchs kept the claims of Royal Blood for themselves and their nobles. They realized well enough that the true Blood Royal carried the obligation of a ruler to die for the benefit of his people, but they figured they were entitled to pay for someone else to deputize for them, or else donate a largish sum to some Temple in return for squaring the Gods to accept an expensive substitute. By Roman times, the public office of Rex Sacrificulus became established. This "Sacrifice King" was appointed to offer sacrifice in place of the legal Ruler. He ranked higher than other priests, and his wife also became a priestess who officiated at functions held in honor of Goddesses. Roman Vestal Virgins were sworn to chastity altogether for their period of service, usually thirty years, and their duty was to tend a sacred ever-burning flame. Note their full office was for the maximum lifetime of a Sacred King.

Despite the drift away from human sacrifices for religious reasons, the Tradition itself remained deeply rooted especially among rustics and country folk who always resent marked changes from long-practiced customs no matter how much for the better. Those in the West were the last to abandon their sacrificial practices in public, and privately among very select circles, they probably continued voluntary Sacred King rites much longer than many might suppose. Its memory is not entirely forgotten even into our times.

Now let us look back a bit and see what all this means to us as modern people and how it affects our Tradition in contemporary consciousness.

In the first place, if you are of Western origins the ancient patterns are already in your genetics like the rest of us, and there is nothing to be done other than acknowledge the fact and live around it. There is a modern tendency to ignore ancestry of any kind, either physical or spiritual, to overlook or deny any such thing as hereditary and previous existence, and generally to live as if humans were entirely a product of their environment and education. This is just as short-sighted and foolish as taking the opposite viewpoint that because ones' ancestors were such and such, one should automatically be entitled to positions of privilege and power over the lives of other humans. A fine balance has to be found between both extremes.

Regardless of what your ancestors have passed down to you in the way of property or real estate, they left you an invisible legacy which you carry round with you in genetic traits. Much of this is of your own making in former incarnations. Because you were that kind of an individual, you are born into the type of family whose genetic patterns match your spiritual status. This does not mean you are a helpless being whose fate is fixed from the beginning because of your birth. You are capable of changing and converting it very considerably by your intentions and behavior in this incarnation. What is important is that you recognize the fact that your far past and remote future are connected by what you are doing and believing *now*.

People realized this well enough in old times. That was mainly why important families were so concerned with "lines of descent" and "tables of geneology" with all those "begots" to them. It was not entirely to prove their connections with "Blood Royal," but this had the useful function of setting up "people points" along which to look back for directions toward Divine origins. Just as in early days stones would be set up for sightlines at visual distances apart, across deserts or unfamiliar country so that travellers might always find their way home eventually, so human ancestors might serve as trail-markers leading over immeasurable distances right back to blessed beginnings. It did not matter if they could not all be traced. Several generations would do to take sights along—enough to point anyone in the general direction which should be followed.

It wasn't that observers were being encouraged to be continually retrospective or backward looking. Once they could appreciate their "come from," they were supposed to turn around and line themselves up as their "back-points" indicated, then aim themselves at the future in a continuous progression to that line in straight or curved directions according to their inclinations.

So that is the practical use of ancestor knowledge so far as it goes—getting your bearings along the time-axis and general impulse-origins of your Cosmic life. That should at least enable you to make a rough estimate of your present position as an entity, which can be quite useful if you are trying to gain a sense of purpose in life and possibilities for future existence.

There is "Blood Royal" somewhere in you and it is being reawakened. You can lay claim to it in yourself by dedicating your soul to what it stands for, your sincere self-sacrifice to the God Within, who is your own True Self.

An interesting custom for spreading the "Blood" was that of *droit de seigneur* or "right of the Lord," which was the customary claim by most Western nobles to the virginity of any suitable female vassel on his estate. Normally, this would be one about to marry a favored serf, so the child would at least have a home of some kind. For this reason the custom got known as *prima noce* or first night. The underlying reason had nothing to do with offering sex-delight to lucky lordlings. It was not considered as a pleasure, but a duty and obligation incumbent on nobility to "pass some of the Blood" along lower lines than theirs, thus improving the stock among the peasantry and spreading the Royal Blood further still. As might be expected, it was usually considered a great honor to foster a child with noble connections in the family. Additionally, it might be expected there would be monetary or other material favors attached.

By now it should be clear why Christianity soon obtained footholds in Western civilization. It was the "Old Religion" brought up to date and simplified to an easily workable formulae. In the Near East, this was quickly recognized and promulgated. You have to see the overall picture in terms of their times and then estimate for yourself any similarities with our own days.

The older megalithic and pastoral religions had been largely superseded by much more complicated systems of philosophy and stylized formularies, many of them very lovely and artistic in conception. There were plenty of cults, creeds, and ethical codes to follow. By this time, "the Gods" were becoming more a matter of social conventions than religious convictions. Though magnificent and well staffed Temples were raised in their honor, they were regarded as symbols of state rather than spiritual realities. In Jerusalem, the palatial Temple had become what we would now call a thriving tourist enterprise. It had become more of a shrine to Jewish national culture than a purely spiritual center of worship.

A great proportion of the population were plebians and bond-slaves living close to the poverty line without a lot of hope in life or very great encouragement to live it. According to the priests, the next world seemed to be run by the rich, too. Social insecurity and unrest was reaching a high pressure point, and Judea in particular, was an occupied country held by the extremely efficient Roman Army and civil administration. Coinciding with the underground current of rebellion fostered by the "Resistance movement" of Zealots, named after Simon Zelotes, came the mission and teaching of Jesus. Rumors of a fabled "Messiah" or Liberator Figure akin to our King Arthur, had been going round for some years.

The word "Messiah" meant an anointed one in the sense that old Sacred Kings were usually anointed with special oil before their sacrifice. It marked them out by scent as a Willing Victim, and as such acclaimed them as worthy of the highest honor among their people. The Messiah that Jews were hoping for at the time would be a military leader who would take all their sins on his shoulders, free them from Roman oppression, and set Israel up as an independent power in this world. He would probably die in battle during the struggle, thus sacrificing his life for their sake.

The eventual execution of Jesus by the civil authorities after accusations of blasphemy from the Jewish Temple which realized he was not likely to free the Jews from Roman rule, might not have caused any great consequences among the populace except for one thing. The circumstances of his birth, teaching, death, and subsequent communication with his disciples afterward could be interpreted according to the ancient pattern of Sacred King practice, regardless of what Temple priests thought. Some people had strong suspicions that those same priests were discrediting Jesus purely to keep power in their own hands, and now that they had persuaded the Romans to kill him like a criminal, they supposed their sinecures were safe. How long would they be safe for, if Jesus really had been a Sacred King and went up to tell the Gods how badly his people were being treated? There were rumors about that already, and just look at the facts of his life.

To begin with, his mother had been a Temple Virgin who might possibly have been pregnant from a sanctified source before being placed in the care of a respectable Elder. The child's name was Jesus (Savior in Hebrew), and stories were told about his remarkable childhood. His lineage could be traced back to David and he was of undoubtedly Royal Blood. Multitudes had heard his teaching and had been told of his miracles which seemed applicable to Jew and Gentile alike. His partisanship was certainly on behalf of the oppressed and underprivileged, though he had preached spiritual liberation rather than revolutionary tactics. It was true his death was due to condemnation by hated authorities, though he went to it willingly under the title of "King," even though that was meant semi-mockingly by the Roman proconsul Pilate, who had it written over Jesus' thorn crowned head on the cross to annoy the Jews he disliked. So it could be said that Jesus died while described as a King by officials of Government.

It was also true he had been nailed to the cross, instead of being bound with cords, and it was a Roman javelin thrust which made certain of his death, releasing both blood and serum thereby, so really the Gentiles had more claim to his "Kingship" than the Jews. Officially, his own people had disowned and rejected him, which traditionally meant that anyone was free to accept his sacrifice. On his way to be crucified, many people in the streets had done just that, shouting out, "His blood be upon us and our children." There must have been many Gentiles that day in cosmopolitan Jerusalem who knew quite well what they were shouting about. In such a crowded city then, there were surely a few Celts and Gauls, possibly in the Roman Army, who had some idea of what they were witnessing.

Apart from reports of his body being missing from its temporary tomb, and stories of his appearance after death to communicate with his personal circle, a final clincher confirmed his

Sacred Kingship to the satisfaction of many who still believed in the Old Faith. At the end of the Passover Supper he had shared with his intimates, he picked up an ordinary round of flat bread, and telling them "THIS IS MY BODY," he passed it among them to break and eat. Then he followed this with a plain Kiddush cup of sweet wine and told them: "THIS IS MY BLOOD." He evidently went on to say this was a new form of the old Mystery Faith and he was willing to shed that blood for them and many others in order to lighten their human burdens of wrongdoing and wickedness. Words like that could only have been spoken by a Sacred King of the highest order. Lastly, he asked them to remember him by repeating the ritual.

The idea of "God-eating" is an old one, and so is the substitution of animal or vegetable flesh for the body of a God. Egyptian Temples had been using round bread-cakes with a cross on them for quite a while. This act of a Willing Sacrifice offering his own blood and body in advance of his death was indeed a new and surprising practice which had nothing whatever to do with normal Passover proceedings. It must mean that Jesus and his followers belonged to the Old Religion, and whoever wanted to signify their beliefs therein had only to symbolize this in future by a similar rite in order to claim kinship with Kingship. It was also remembered that a woman disciple had duly anointed Jesus' head and feet with precious perfume, and he had acknowledged the act graciously despite complaints from some members of his circle about the expense involved.

The beautiful simplicity of everything fired imaginations, particularly in the Western world where solemn sacrifice of dedicated Victims was still practiced periodically, though far less frequently than formerly. This new custom of what might be called a "Reformed" version of Man's oldest Faith meant combining the offices of Kingship and Priesthood in one and the same person: to offer oneself for Life, not Death, to the Eternal God or Gods, on behalf of one's breathren bound together by belief in the Holy Blood which united them. This was indeed a leap forward towards Light.

All the elaborate and hair-splitting theology devised by early Christians in the course of the following centuries related to this fundamental significance of sacrifice. Much of it was necessarily drawn from old sources and many codes of conduct. The Trinity Concept, for instance, was carefully paternalized to eliminate suggestions of a Feminine Deity. Reincarnation got hidden away because it was thought to encourage spiritual laziness and procrastination. A saying of the time was, "Though you may have as many incarnations as sands on the sea shore, yet live each one as if it were the only life you would ever have." Nevertheless, however these theologians twisted and turned the concepts of Christianity, none of them have ever yet managed to get rid of those vital words: *This is my body. This is my blood.* Without them, Christianity would have no more significance than any other ethical system.

This is not an attempt to convert you to Christianity, but only to show that it became the "Religion of the West" because it was an adaptation and modernization of a far older faith which has existed amongst us from time immemorial, and *still exists in principle* among us today as our Inner Tradition. It is most compatible with our studies and work. It has always been important in genuine spiritual systems that whatever is believed in at the deepest levels of awareness should never be named on objective levels because that would close off our open contacts with it on those inner lines of life. Hence the "Forbidden Name" practice, and concern with the Nil-concept* which relates us with the Great Universe. We have no name for our God in fact, because the word "God" is not a proper name, but an indicative term meaning: "That which is worshipped."

If you want to get some ideas about your own connection with antiquity, try this odd little experiment. See if you can find photographs or pictures of your parents and grandparents, great-grandparents, too, if you can. Otherwise write their names as far back as you can trace, on slips of paper. Arrange them in chronological order and contemplate your collection thinking something like this:

"People out of people out of people for Lord knows how long, and at the end of them all—*me*. How many human beings has it taken to make *me*?" Assuming you have a calculator, try figuring

*See *Concepts of Qabalah*, Volume 3 of this series.

a few generations back like the famous chessboard problem which was invented for this reason. One for the first square, meaning you. Two for the second, meaning your parents. Four for the third, meaning their parents, eight for the fourth to show theirs, and so on. You just keep doubling up. Allowing the modest average figure of three generations per century, your results should show you that a mere 500 years ago you must have descended from 32,768 ancestors! Try continuing that for 2,000 years and you may wonder if your calculator has gone wrong. Then remember that humans have been on this earth for several million years! Try pushing this idea around a bit. Take the very low average weight of an adult human body at 100 pounds to allow for early deaths and other factors. Calculate the bulk of human tissue from a thousand years back needed to produce your own weight at present. Oh yes, you *do* have plenty of connections with your past. Literally, tons upon tons of it! The mathematics of biology are that it takes two to make one. You *are* of the Blood Royal.

## Questions

1. How would you define "The Gods"?
2. Discuss the validity of exchanging animal in place of human sacrifice, and then vegetable in place of animal. Can you think of another extension yet?
3. Define and discuss a Sacred King.
4. What are the origins of human "resurrection"?
5. Why were Vestal Virgins sworn to chastity?
6. Why were geneologies so important in old times? Should they be considered important now?
7. How did the *droit de seigneur* custom arise, and what was its function?
8. Why did Christianity become a popular Western religion?
9. Discuss the custom of "God-eating" in relation to modern Holy Communion.
10. Choose the ten most important sentences in this Lesson.

# · 3 ·

# *Sacrificial Circles*

You should have realized by now what is at the bottom of our Western Inner Tradition: *self sacrifice.* Before you start jumping to any wrong conclusions let us be very clear what this means from an occult standpoint. Many people are apt to suppose it means making their lives more difficult so as to make other lives easier, a sort of spiritual masochism in which you inflict all kinds of hardship on yourself while others have a better time at your expense. That sort of notion is plain nonsense. Granted it is wrong to deliberately exploit others for the sake of your gain, but the converse act of intentionally disadvantaging yourself with the idea of pushing unasked profits on other people is equally wrong. So do get things straight in your mind what self-scrifice really is.

You only have one Self which is genuine, the entity you are, quite apart from any of your incarnate bodies or the temporary personalities attached thereto. What most people usually think of as "self" is the sense of identity being built up in their current Earth-bodies. This is what might be called a "pseudo-self" because it is no more immortal than the body, and should dissolve in its turn after physical death. It can be a considerable embarrasment and nuisance if it lingers on to a fresh incarnation and overshadows the new image being built up for that appearance.

So real self-sacrifice means getting your priorities right and setting a higher value on your Immoral Identity than the affairs of your pseudo-self, and living accordingly. In other words, you "sacrifice" the interests of your "Lower" Self to those of your "Higher" states of being; the purely human side of you to the God within you. Sometimes it does get terribly confusing to talk about Lower and Higher Selves as if they were two distinct beings, and hence the problems involved when the same ideas are termed so many different ways. For instance, Ego, Self, Identity, Lower Self, Higher Self, are all labels pinned on different parts of you by various terminologies struggling with spiritual concepts. For that reason we are trying to use the simplest and most straightforward wordings possible and to be explicit about meanings as we go along.

Do remember that the old Sacred King self-sacrifice had to be not only an absolutely willing one, but he had to be *joyously glad* he was so chosen. The slightest sign of unwillingness or reluctance at the last moment would be enough to disqualify and dismiss him disgracefully, while the next in line pressed forward to claim his place. Protocol was usually very strict on that. The death of a Sacred King must not only be honorable, but it must be *happy* also. Putting this in modern terms means that if the earthly, entitized, and egoic part of your Self is unhappy, discontented, or in the least disturbed about offering its abilities and agencies freely to the God within you, there can be no true sacrifice of any sort, and nothing you do could be considered as such until a state of harmony flows between both ends of your existence. The Divine end of you must *want and will* to accept what the human end of you *wills and wants* to offer.

*Now* can you see a little further into this mystery? Sacred Kingship in terms of today means that you must become both King and Priest, your "priestly" function being to offer the "kingly" side of yourself to the Deity of your Immortal Identity. Physical death is quite unnecessary before its due time. You are offering your life, your abilities, energies, and intentions to the God behind the whole of your being. You are also offering kinship with other humans attempting the same act "because of the Blood" which relates you all together in the "Family Circle of the Faith." Before you attempt any such thing however, do be reminded that this cannot be accomplished without your full comprehension and conscious awareness of what is happening throughout your entire being. Nothing will work until exactly the right factors coincide with each other through different dimensions. Therefore, just be content for the moment to keep in touch with these topics as they unfold and examine them for yourself as we go along.

There has been so much talk of "sacrifice," yet what does the word actually mean? Strictly speaking, it comes from two Latin words: *sacra*—holy, and *facere*—to make. The entire meaning; therefore is *to make holy*. Just that. All the implications of renunciation, blood-offerings, self-denial, and so forth, are accretions and attachments over the centuries of customs so described. Why not accept a perfectly good word in terms of its original value, and grant that when we talk about "self-sacrifice" what we mean at rock-bottom is "making ourselves holy." That is to say, *devoting our energies towards changing our characters and self-structures into a more "Godworthy" state.* From now on, let us be crystal clear that whenever we speak of "self-sacrifice" this is *exactly* what we mean.

Any ideas that we should renounce this in order to gain that or do something in return for specific Divine favors have nothing to do with genuine sacrifice, but would only be bargaining or putting our own prices on deals with Divinities. Any God prepared to haggle with humans on their terms would obviously not be worth the least real respect, let alone reverence from any sincere soul alive. A bribable God? An entire contradiction of concepts, yet some people supposed this possible once, or acted as if they did. The whole essence of sacrifice is that it must be done for its own sake or not at all, and it should not be felt as a duty, but a delight.

A most important part of this self-sacrifice belief at the base of our Inner Tradition is that the accent should fall on the first word—*self*. In other words, we are *not* entitled to attempt sacrificing anyone else or offering them to the Gods of our beliefs. This does not mean we should not set reasonable limits on their social (or anti-social) behavior in keeping with acceptable standards of human conduct. What we must *not* do is deliberately interfere with or impede their sincere searches for spiritual truths. This is quite foreign to our Western Inner Way and has brought untold misery among mankind when we have been invaded by those who ignore or deny such freedom of faith.

Although official oppression for reasons of conscientious and religious convictions has virtually ceased throughout the Western world in relatively recent history, it will still be possible for individuals to contravene the underlying spirit of our Tradition *in themselves*. For instance, you may disagree with, dislike, or otherwise reject different religious customs than your own. You are quite entitled to do this *within your own area of consciousness,* providing you recognize the right of others to hold equal ideas in theirs. In that way, energies are confined to relatively small circles and do no harm outside them. It is when you begin to circulate currents of consciousness *outside yourself* that trouble starts. That is one reason why the idea arose of making your own magical circle around yourself and *living within it.*

Most people have vague ideas of medieval magicians tracing chalk circles around themselves and raising demons outside it for all kinds of reasons. So long as the magician stayed strictly inside his circle he was safe, because the demons dared not cross the "Holy Names" inscribed on the perimeter. If the silly magic-maker in the middle stuck as much as one finger over the circle's edge—wham!— the demons had him just like that. Today we may laugh and think how stupid people could be a few hundred years back. Yet the Magic Circle performance is *symbolic of an absolute esoteric fact.*

We live in a sea of consciousness as real as the air we all breathe. We can only exist as individual, yet cooperating creatures, because we have built our own circles of consciousness around ourselves much like cells of living protoplasmic matter. *Very* like them in fact. so long as we live within the "wall" of that cell, exchanging energies through it by carefully designed channels, we shall be safe enough. If we carelessly extend the essence of ourselves beyond that protective perimeter, however, we risk encounters with energies which may well be hostile or harmful to us in our present condition. Additionally, the energies we extend may be harmful to others whether we intend so or not.

In a sense we are micro-organisms in the "Divine Body of God," but what sort? Are we helpful, healthful, and harmonious, or just the opposite, injurious and inimical? It all depends on what we make of ourselves, and how we determine the nature of our cell-structure. Either we become essential to Divine Life like corpuscles in Its bloodstream, or we become toxic to It until It eliminates or neutralizes us altogether. The same Laws of Life apply macro- or micro-cosmically. "As Above—so Below."

Hence, the reason for doing certain exercises with circles of consciousness around ourselves. They are to ensure the correct circulation of our inner energies so that we become healthy and useful spiritual organisms in the Great Body of God. That was the secret message which Jesus was imparting to his chosen disciples with the Body-Blood sacrament. He was symbolically telling them that they should strive to become as Blood within the Body of the Living God which is created Cosmos. That is the *Sangreal* or "Holy Grail"—becoming the Blood of God, the legendary Ichor of Immortality.

If each of us can become an operative cell of some kind in the Body of God, it follows that by association with each other we may build up into more important states of "spiritual solidity." So we can, but there is a maximum "adherence-factor" for human beings as ideal conglomerates of Cosmos in our scale of Life. This figure is *twelve* around a single central nucleus of another character. Anything much above that number tends to be disintegrative, breaking up the original circle or interfering with its efficient cycles of energy. The symbology of that is the twelve globes of equal size needed to enclose a central space of the same dimensions and contact each other simultaneously. Long experience has shown this is the best way for "Magic Circles" of more than one human being to combine and remain together in harmony.

Everyone should know the superstition about thirteen being an unlucky number, and many might wonder why. The story about Judas Iscariot being the thirteenth guest at the Last Supper is apocryphal, and a Christianized version of the "odd man out." The thirteenth around which the Twelve gathered was Jesus himself, and it was he who died a dreadful death as a Sacrificial King because he had personified the God and offered himself as mediator of the Divine Will. The old time circles around which twelve humans grouped themselves, had a nucleus in the center which was not human at all, but a concentration of entitized energy which was focussed among them from higher levels of Life altogether. To the humans it seemed like the Presence of God, from whom indeed it was a remote projection. They could all feel it, experience it in some way, and even "saw" it as a sort of Light. It seemed to speak in their heads with a "still, small voice" they had to listen for with great concentration. Often it "spoke" incomprehensibly, yet later on they found themselves understanding the gist of what it had meant. The entire affair had a profoundly uplifting effect on human participants, and they were convinced they had been in communication with a type of consciousness superior to their own which had raised theirs considerably and done them a great deal of good. Many thought it was the returned spirit of their last Sacred King who visited them.

Eventually, however, a lot of such circles just stopped working. There were plenty of reasons; wrong frames of mind, unbalanced membership, unworthy motivations, incorrect currents of consciousness, blocked channels of contact, dissentions and frictions among the people on personal levels, and a great many similar factors inhibiting the action of spiritual energies at earthly levels of living. No one knows when or where the practice first started, but someone got the idea of placing himself in the center of the circle and "personifying the God" who would then have a human medium through whom to speak.

This was very far from being an unqualified success. Though not entirely a failure, it opened up a fallibility-factor of considerable proportions. The character and personality of the medium was the most serious drawback, even when this was of excellent quality so far as human capabilities were concerned. When such qualities were of low or inadequate standards, results were correspondingly debased and circles deteriorated accordingly.

It became a common custom to "impersonate the God" by appearing in masks and costumes appropriate to the nature of the Deity invoked. Postures and voices were also stylized to suit, many of which have been retained to this day among folk-dancers and singers. Race-memory is strangely long where myth and legend are concerned. Even if external forms are forgotten, the characteristics and fundamentals of an idea persist for generations.

Where human mediums did become a central "thirteenth" of a circle and set themselves up as interpreters of "God-talk," they often paid the price in terms of sanity and what was thought to be "ill-luck." In trying to cope with consciousness on two or sometimes more levels, plus imposing their personal desires on a credulous human audience for a number of mundane motives, their balance frequently failed and the resulting bad consequences often shared by all in the circle. "God-possession" and madness soon became connected in men's minds, leading to a great deal of confusion for centuries to come and the famous saying, "Whom the Gods destroy, they first make mad."

Hence the reason today why thirteen is regarded as unlucky with more justification than many might suppose. Whoever usurps the rightful place of a God invites doom on his head. Here, too, the origin of so-called "Witches Sabbats," where primitive pagans throughout Europe tried to practice what was remotely remember-ed of their Old Religion in very debased and degraded forms. This was almost as if, in a few thousand years time, the only things people could remember of Christianity were that it involved multiple sexual intercourse with virgins, the death of young men by torture, and eating human flesh at banquets.

If forming circles of thirteen with a God-Figure and Twelve Companions is an unwise practice in general, many may wonder why Jesus should do such a thing. The only possible explanation is that he very well knew the risk involved, and being a Voluntary Victim invited his own immolation on behalf of those to whom he was bound by Blood. By inviting Judas to join (whom Jesus must have realized was the breakable link), he introduced the fatal factor on his own responsibility. There is a curious comparison here with the action of Gautama Buddha who was reputed to have died by eating infected meat which he had forbidden his intimate circle to touch. Each Avatar accepted death consequently to his own action so that the blame or "Karma" rested on his own spiritual shoulders.

Neither the circles of Jesus nor Gautama could be considered ideal, since they were all male, and therefore of unbalanced polarity. Granted it is the actual nature of a soul which is more

Figure 1. Family circles in the Western Inner Tradition

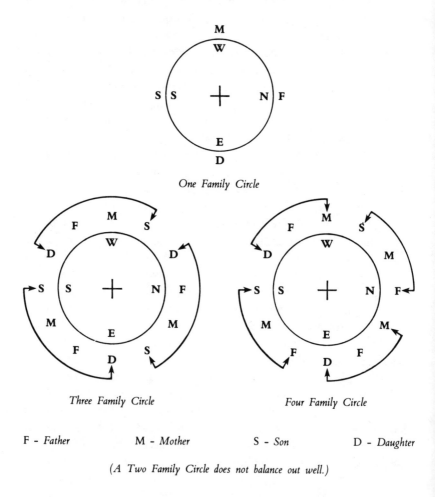

*One Family Circle*

*Three Family Circle*　　　　　　*Four Family Circle*

F - *Father*　　　　M - *Mother*　　　　S - *Son*　　　　D - *Daughter*

*(A Two Family Circle does not balance out well.)*

important than the sex of its physical body, but if the proportions of polarity are unbalanced beyond a certain degree, no circle of twelve human beings can function properly as a spiritual "cell system." Theoretically, a perfect spiritual circle of the Western Inner Way would be a "Family" one based on the combination of two males and two females, or Father, Mother, Son and Daughter. Between them they would mediate the Elemental Energies like this:

> **AIR:** Mediated by the younger woman who must assume the characteristics of Raphael symbolized by the Sword. She represents enthusiasm, keenness, flexibility of mind, idealism, and freshness of approach—all air qualities.

> **FIRE:** Mediated by the younger man who takes on attributes of Michael, representing radiant energy, strength of character, uprightness like his symbol the Lance or Rod, and willingness to act as champion and defender in his cause of righteousness.

> **WATER:** Mediated by the mature woman who becomes like Gabriel (or "Jivrael") the guardian of love and bearer of the Cup containing the Blood binding them together.

> **EARTH:** Mediated by the senior man who adopts the functions of Auriel, and shields the circle by his care and experience. It is he who "keeps their feet on the ground" and helps "solidify" their spiritual experiences.

That is the *minimum* basically balanced circle of combined human beings which will function as a "cell circle" of the Western Inner Way. If it has hopes of linking up with other similar combinations, it will need the services of an extra auxilliary capable of contacting at least one other such grouping, who is symbolized by the Cord because this "ties things together," like Suvuviel, the circling "Archangel of Truth," does.

This office of "Cord" is an odd and interesting one. It has no set place in a circle, and is really a "semi-member" since it connects with other circles. Yet whoever takes this office must be prepared to act as "stand-in" for any unexpectedly absent member, cope with emergencies, generally act as secretary, agent, and "dogsbody," and be the invaluable person of any team without whom it would quickly fall apart. Such is the real function of the "thirteenth" in connection with spiritual circles of the Western Tradition. He is not a central "God-personifying" individual attracting all the attention and applause, but a peripheral non-descript personage who attracts both risks and hard work usually without much appreciation. No wonder this office was considered unfortunate, but it was also recognized and respected as an essential of ordered existence.

Sometimes the thirteenth attachment to a complete Circle was considered to be a Doorkeeper, through whom communicative channels were kept going between the closed Circle and external human affairs. Thus it corresponded to the office of Herald or Keryx in Lodge or Temple systems. Although in theory every member of a Circle was supposed to have trained their replacements when death or other causes removed them, it was often the Cord who found likely candidates to fill vacancies and "presented them at the Portals" for initiation when opportunity came.

It should be very strongly stressed that there is really no need of physical relationship between members of any Circle, or even for the ages and sexes to be specified, providing the required abilities and polarities of members can be properly coordinated. The "Family Circle" is only described as an ideal example for emulation if humanly possible (which it seldom is). The important factor is that Circles should be as if they actually were such a family together, except that the Blood-bond between them is spiritual rather than physical.

Each individual should be a "Circle of One" in themselves, relating their own Elemental life-energy together. Here we are only seeing how Circles of up to twelve plus one people should interrelate themselves and link up with others in Western Inner Traditional style. If a Circle of this type can be properly constituted, it forms what could be termed in modern language a "spiritual cyclotron" in which Life-energies circulate freely and beneficially for all concerned.

In case you think it might be a wonderful scheme to get such a Circle going yourself, be assured that no one has any idea of the difficulties and problems involved except those who have tried for many years to do that very thing themselves with extremely limited and often most doubtful success. Unless each member of a Circle is not only well balanced in himself but is also in a similar state of harmony with all the others, the Circle simply *will not work* with any degree of accuracy or efficiency. You might just as well grab an armful of ill-assorted spare parts from a motor scrap yard and expect to assemble a perfectly working motor from them. Forming a Circle of the Western Inner Way is a *precision job* calling for the highest skill and capability. If you can imagine a complicated piece of electrical or mechanical apparatus *in which each single item had to engineer itself,* you might get some idea of what is needed.

Nevertheless there is no reason why you should not know how the spiritual Circles of the Western Inner Way tried to constitute themselves in keeping with the basic formula of our Tradition. Most of them were nowhere near the full complement of twelve plus a connector. Probably four, five, or six would be nearer the mark, and these were largely family affairs confined to a relatively small percentage of the population. At the same time it was among Circles of this kind that the essence of our Tradition reached earthly levels of expression and disseminated itself in various forms throughout the peoples of the Western world. Though such Circles may have diminished considerably in number and changed a great deal in construction, they have never become extinct altogether. The time is approaching when the system must reactivate itself, and the newest externals of our oldest Inner Tradition will circulate around us again like a revivifying stream of the Blessed Blood which is our Holiest Heritage.

You could start constructing your own self-circle around a nucleus of Pure Power which is unnameable and indescribable by human consciousness except as symbolized by Light, the Divine Spark within you. This was usually represented in old circles by the light and warmth of a friendly fire which drew the people around it. Sacred Circles are built just the same way on a multi-human scale. Hence the circulation therein is clockwise or "deosil" (with the Sun). If you could keep flying at a constant rate from East to West, you would remain in continual light. By reversing the process and circulating from West to East, the world would eventually be between you and the Sun and you would continue in darkness. That was why the circulation in debased gatherings was always "widdershins" or against the Sun.

All this has considerable bearing on why so-called "traditional" occultism in the West has such an apparently illogical aversion to spiritualistic meetings where a number of people form a circle around a human "medium" who makes contact with Inner intelligences for the information or interest of the sitters. This practice in modern dress seems too much like the "bad old times" when humans were bold enough to "personify the God," and most of the messages they gave out in the name of that God proved to be not much more than their personal opinions and interpolations. That was what first began to deteriorate the spiritual qualities of the Mysteries, and why it became so strictly forbidden later on. Additionally, it was considered quite wrong to "call back the dead" under the personal forms they had used when incarnate. Theoretically, they should be outgrowing these transitory appearances much as a child grows to adulthood. Past personalities ought normally to die or fade out naturally after physical death. Thus it was looked on as an entirely retrograde procedure to invoke a living entity under the guise of a personality it should be liberating itself from. This is still the view of many Western occult circles in our time.

Personalizing lesser aspects of Divinity, Archangels, and so forth, was considered permissable providing it was for the specific purpose of engendering such qualities and characteristics in the personifier or beholders. This is how "Divine dramas" and Mystery plays started, so that the Temple and the theater fulfilled combined functions, and actors were thought to be inspired by Divinities whose qualities they were representing to an audience. They were not purporting to *be* the God or Spirit they portrayed, but only symbolizing some of Its attributions as, say, another type of artist might sculpt or paint these. That made all the difference between them, and other imitators who expected people to worship them like Gods and reward them accordingly because of their pretensions. We have had our false claimants to Divinity from very early days indeed and always from the same motives—artificial aggrandisement by fanatical or foolish followers and personal profits derived therefrom.

We have to face the fact that being in contact with the "Blood" does not *automatically* guarantee that a soul will become an outstanding individual with wonderful virtues and of unimpeachable character. *Of itself* it brings the heavy responsibility of "living up to it," or disgracing it by fighting against all it stands for and breaking away from its spiritual stream. Remember the Blood does not compel or force allegiance to it. It never did. There have been many who "bore the Blood" and yet betrayed it for numerous reasons, mostly connected with short-term gains in terms of this world's advantages. So it is insufficient to *have* the Blood, it must also be *held,* and in order to do that, we must become Cups or Vessels capable of containing it. That is to say, we must literally make ourselves into "Holy Grails." Such is the meaning and mystery of the Sangreal.

This of course only applies to those who intend to offer themselves as "Bearers of the Blood" in the true sense of that term. For the majority of folk it usually suffices to feel that there is "something" behind them which seems to help them on their difficult way through incarnate life, and maybe one day it will become a lot closer and clearer. Then there are those who need to have some conscious knowledge of what Inner Life is all about so that they can approach it with at least a few clear cut and *shaped* ideas connecting normal rationality with a sense of inherent reverence for that "something" which lies beyond the boundaries of bodily being. Whichever you are, you may be sure your interests and intentions have not escaped notice on levels of awareness other than ordinary human ones.

You may have wondered why it should have been necessary for a genuinely spiritual system to "go underground" and confine itself to small and scattered families around the Western World. This may be what things look like on the *outside,* but you have to remember this is an *Inner* affair and can only be understood from such a viewpoint. This is *not* a spiritual world, and truly spiritual matters have a similar relationship to this physical world as the inside of your body has to its outside. Have you thought of that?

We stay alive in this world only because the *vital* part of our bodies remains *within* its outer protective shell of skin. Cut that open beyond a certain limit and we die. In the same way our Inner spiritual energies need to remain inside their equivalents of "skin" in this world if they are to enliven and animate us here on earth. Thus it is just as essential for our Inner Tradition to remain "secret" in the sense of being non-evident objectively, as it is for our internal organs to stay safely under our human hides. We can only observe our secret Traditions from external evidence of them while we examine them from worldly viewpoints. To feel and *experience* them, we must live *inside* them and let them look out of *us*.

There has always been among us, a sort of "Secret Church behind the Churches," influencing the inmost natures of establishments claiming connections with spiritual sources of energy. Admittedly, its influence may seem very slight if we judge by the behavior of human dogmatists and policy-directors responsible for the codes and conduct of such organizations. Nevertheless without its gentle and unobtrusive guidance through violent and perilous centuries, we should have been in even worse spiritual states than we are today. We must never forget the "No compulsion or coercion" rule. It must be *as we will* either way, and *all* the Way.

From time to time in our history, signs of this "Secret Church" appear in strong liberating guises affording us opportunities to free ourselves from spiritual shackles we have made with our own hands, mostly from sloth and stupidity. One of these signs which is still significant in the Western Tradition to this day, was the cultus of the Holy Grail which coincided with a low ebbing of the Church's concern with true spiritual values and a high point of its political power and temporal ambitions. We shall be taking a closer and unconventional look at this development in our next lesson.

## Questions

1. Define self-sacrifice.
2. How do you "stay in your own circle"?
3. Define the "Body of God."
4. What is the ideal number of a Magic Circle, and why?
5. Why is thirteen considered unlucky?
6. How are the Life-Elements best represented in a Magic circle?
7. Define a "circle of One."
8. Why does "orthodox" occultism disapprove of conventional spiritualism?
9. Choose the ten most important questions in this chapter.
10. What do you think of as your protective perimeter?

# ·4·

# *Greatness of the Grail*

**S**urely everyone even vaguely connected with the Western Tradition has heard in some way of the Holy Grail? In the loosest possible way, it is usually connected with idealistic unattainable objectives and it is also supposed to be something to do with the Kiddush Cup used by Jesus at his Last Supper or the Passover feast still celebrated by orthodox and semi-orthodox Jewry.

Not many people realize, however, that the cultus of the Grail or Greal, far from being of Christian origin was, and yet is, a survival of our oldest Western Folk-Faith. When it reached literate and publishable forms in the eleventh century A.D. the Grail concept had become a highly sophisticated and spiritualized version of the ancient Sacred King system. Though deriving from far older folk-myths and oral traditions of the past, the romanticized story of the Grail appealed to the intelligensia and the influential people of the period to remember the roots of their religion and to be less concerned with its superficialities.

This was not an anti-Christian ideology in any way, but was definitely "contra-Church" as the ecclesiastical establishment stood at the time. It was not *ostensibly* against the Church, for the Grail literature was written by brilliant minds who could claim the whole thing was a legitimate flight of poetic fancy and no more than imaginative fiction if pressed by heresy-hunters. Nevertheless, their hidden message certainly got out and around among the more literate parts of the population, and rustics more or less guessed the gist of it anyway.

Most modern people should know the rough outlines of the Grail Myth. The Grail is a fabled Dish, Cup, or sacred Vessel, once containing the Blessed Blood of Jesus, brought to Britain, most probably to Avalon or Glastonbury, by Joseph of Aramathea after the Crucifixion. Its custody was confined to "Keepers" who moved it from one secret place to another. Eventually, it was reputed to have left Earth altogether, but might still reveal itself to a very favored few after long and arduous questing for it. If ever found, it would bestow inestimable but unspecified blessings on that favored being.

The unidentified orginators of the Grail Legend were certainly very highly skilled myth-makers. Their central symbol of a feminine Cup or Dish being filled with Holy Blood dripping from a masculine Spear-Staff should scarcely need much interpretation. A receiver of the Blessed Blood *drop by drop* is most important symbology. The Spear is the sacrifice of old Sacred Kings. The *dropping* Blood is the descent of individual holders of "Blood Royal" from such sources. The Cup, or Vessel is the gathering or combining of these souls into a common "Pool of Power." In other words, the Grail symbol was, *and still is,* a Call for Bearers of the Blood to unite with each other for the "salvation" of themselves and their people.

The "salvation" theme is introduced by tales of "Waste Lands" belonging to a Maimed King who needed "healing from his grievous wound" before his kingdom could be restored to full fertility again. This King was sometimes called the Fisher King, once considered an allusion to the Papacy on account of the Christian "Fishers of Men" quotation. If so, this would definitely indicate the sad state of the Church in that era. The term could, however, be a mistranslation from the Gallic *pecheur*—sinner. Thus the Sinner-King and his castrated condition represented the falsity into which established royalty had fallen, and the spiritually desolate state of human kingdoms. In either case it made the Grail Mythos a *cri de coeur* for the righting of all human ills due to the usurpation of privileges and positions once held by blood-lines of Sacred Kingship, and a restoration of this ancient folk-function in a modern manner.

In its time, with echoes reaching ours, the Grail ideology was a version of the cry made in every age against its current socio-economic injustices, and a pious hope of bringing better conditions into this world for the benefit of humans as a whole, and for "Blood-bonded believers" in particular. Average humans may not have known this objectively but they recognized it instinctively because of the archetypal symbology tied in with their genetic inheritance.

Hence the linking of the Grail with Arthurian legend. The Folk Figure of Arthur is essentially one of a King fighting for the rights of his people against oppressive invaders. His "Round Table" company is of men prepared to die if need be in the cause of righting wrongs suffered by innocent and undeserving people who cannot defend themselves. That Round Table roughly equated with the old time Stone Circles which were supposed to be "freedom forums" for folk to come together and sort out their individual and collective troubles. Thus the Grail Ideal was really a continuation of the ancient Megalithic Mysteries into the Christian era, and on such ideological levels it survives very much into our times.

The implications of the Grail cultus are simple enough. It is a belief that humans may have begun along the right lines, but things went wrong when power got into unworthy hands. Since then the world has drifted into a sad condition from all angles. It can only be "saved" by selfless sacrifice devoted to Deity by the best blooded individuals alive on earth. We can accept this today as the devotion of a lifetime in the services of a cause intended to help humans a little higher up the Ladder of Life, culminating in a shared condition of consciousness. The Spirit of the Grail is the same in any century whatever its contemporary interpretation may be. There is little point speculating about its early history unless we are prepared to follow its projections through our times and beyond into the future.

One of the main points emphasized in the early Grail stories was that specific secrets were omitted from the official liturgy of the Christian Church. These were only known to "Keepers of the

Grail" and their appointees. The secrets, evidently told in very few words, had to be passed precisely from one generation to the next and repeated correctly by the recipient to confirm he had heard them correctly. In one account of Joseph of Aramathea delivering the secret to his son-in-law Bran (whose head was buried at London until removed by King Arthur), the tale remarks that Joseph received it from Jesus in person, and then proceeds, "He spoke the precious words, tender and precious, gracious and compassionate, that are correctly called and named "The Secret of the Greal." Elsewhere the mystic words are translated as being, "sweet, gracious, precious, and piteous." An interesting sentence follows, "From thenceforth he encountered scorn and imprisonment." This last presumably refers to Joseph.

Throughout Grail literature there are references to these vital words which appeared to be very few yet capable of containing the entire secret. Another account tells of Jesus appearing to a holy hermit with a small book no larger than the palm of his hand which was supposed to hold the entire secret of the Grail. The vision made it clear that Jesus had written this book himself. On its cover, these words were emblazoned:

> This is the Book of thy descent.
> Here begins the Book of the Sangreal.
> Here begin the terrors.
> Here begin the miracles.

This book is said to contain the "extra efficacious words" to be pronounced over the Sacramental elements in order to make them the "Archnatural Body and Blood of True God." The implication is that the Church offers only a substitute Sacrament rather than the real thing. That is to say, only those in the Grail Circle have access to the genuine Messianic meal.

Hereditary keepership of the Grail was so closely guarded that scarcely a hint of identities is given apart from legendary figures like Joseph. Other Keepers were reputed to be Alain, son of Bran, Carcelois, Manuiel, Lambor, Callifas of Terre Forrain, and then King Pelles. After that there is a mention by Merlin that the Keepers might be in Northumbria. Before any Keeper might die in peace, he had to pass on the secret with the all important Question, "Whom does the Grail serve?" That was the fatal Query which so startled knights during ceremonial Grail processions that they were struck silent until it was too late for the service to be of any use. The obvious inference here is the question demanded who was willing and anxious to die the old way as a sacrifice in the service of his Blood-kindred. If no knight present was so willing, then the misfortunes of his immediate world would continue unabated because nobody was brave enough to give his life gladly for such a cause.

There is no great strength of evidence to show that human sacrifice was commonly carried out among membership of the Grail cultus, though there is strong possibility it was practiced on very select and secret occasions. An early reference to this tells the story of Galahad gaining the Grail. He first attends a service at which Joseph of Aramathea is officiating. Since chronology makes this impossible, we may suppose the title "Joseph of Aramathea" was assumed by officiants of the cult much as Masonic titles are assumed in modern ceremonials. At any rate, on that rare occasion Jesus himself appeared and gave communion in person, afterwards asking Galahad if he knew what the Grail was. Then he gave the precious Vessel to Galahad, telling him to anoint the Sinner King with the contents. This was done and the Sinner King was indeed healed of his wounds and his lands were restored to full fertility. Subsequently, Galahad was elected King of a city, and at the year's end attended another Mass where Joseph again officiated. This time Galahad prayed to be taken out of this world and gave the Kiss of Peace to Percival and Bors who were present. Then, "Suddenly his soul departed for Heaven and was taken up by great multitudes of angels, after which a mysterious Hand came down from Heaven and bore the Cup and Lance away for ever."

This does seem a fair account of an immolative end at the appropriate Solstice when close companions were expected to hold the Victim steady on the altar awaiting the fatal stroke, so that no instinctive last moment flinching might result in a shamefully struggling death. It would be customary to give the Kiss of Peace and forgiveness beforehand to those offering such service. (Curiously enough, this practice extended to publicly pardoning an executioner on the scaffold before a beheading.)

Selection of sacrificial Victims must have been limited to a very small company of companions. Qualifications of personal purity and fitness for office seem to have been very strict. One proviso stated that only knights that knew not their parentage were eligible. This could refer to artificial insemination, since candidates must obviously have impeccable blood-links with an ancestry known to have Sacred King connections from times of antiquity. There is also a strong contact here with Melchizadek, the "King of Righteousness, who was without Father, without mother, owing descent from God alone." To this day, Melchizadek is a "Grand Master" figure in many Western versions of the Holy Mysteries.

In the Arthurian cycle of the Grail story, the test of fitness for the Quest was to try candidates by the "Siege Perilous" or Throne of Trial. The word "siege" derives from the Gallic *asseyage* or seating place. This dangerous seat was next to the King, and if the knight were unworthy when the moment came, it would open up under him and he would be precipitated into a most unpleasant pit. The story went that when Percival sat on it the trap duly opened but he was miraculously suspended over the gulf. All those caught before his time were forthwith released from bondage.

It is likely that this refers to some of the more stringent tests or ordeals which candidates for initiation had to face in earlier days and which were later done away with. With a diminishing number of candidates to choose from, the standards for acceptance into Mystery cults would have to be altered. The name Percival derives from *per les Vaux*—by the brave deeds. In one romance, this knight is credited with several nights spent in the bed of a lady Blanchfleur (White flower). Stories of knights sharing beds with virgins, with a drawn sword between them, are fairly common. Early Gnostic Churches were familiar with chastity trials of this kind, and Grail romances place higher importance on chastity and virginity than any other contemporary literature. It is interesting to note that in the end Percival retires to a religious life and a Divine Voice tells him to divide the Hallows between Hermits of the Forest, because the Grail itself will not appear any more, though he will learn later where it is.

It was said that when Merlin was asked who might achieve the Grail, he allowed that all good knights were eligible, whether Christian or not. He also said that three white bulls would achieve it, two being maiden and the other merely chaste. The two spotless bulls were Galahad and Percival, while the one with the single spot was Bors. Here we have a fine distinction drawn between purity and chastity, the latter taken to mean an honorable sex life of abstemious practice. There seems to be a touch of the Mithraic Mysteries about the bull simile. Sacrificial animals were always supposed to be unblemished, though odd minor marks were usually painted out or concealed in some way to cover up unintended insults to the Gods.

Not all knights were obligated to total chastity. Some of them had to pass the Blood Royal along normal physical lines. There is the story of Lancelot being deceived into spending the night with the daughter of King Pelles instead of Gwenifer, so that he will get a child on the girl with his blood in its veins. Lancelot was supposed to be the lineal descendent of the King of Sarras, and Pelles was Keeper of the Grail at that time, so needed to keep Blood Royal in his family. Many guesses about the identity of Sarras have been made, the most probable being that he was a Syrian king. Wherever he was from, it provided the Grail with a place of refuge from wrong-doing or desecration. Though Galahad's son gained the Grail, his father never did on account of his "sin" with Queen Gwenifer. He did once obtain a distant vision of it through an open chapel door, but when he attempted to enter he was blasted by a fiery breath from which it took him twenty-four days to recover. All he could remember was a priest at Mass with two servers placing a naked child in the priest's hands. Did this mean someone had once witnessed an actual human sacrifice in Christianized form? We shall never know.

A very old legend from the "Book of Adam,"an Ethiopian text from about the 7th century, has an odd linkage with the Grail story. After detailing Adam's expulsion from Paradise, it tells how he requested that his body be buried in the center of the earth with gold, frankincense and myrrh. He predicts that the Crucifixion will take place above his tomb and the Blood of Christ descending on his skull will recall him to life again. His words are very significant. "My priesthood, my gift of prophesy, and my Kingship will he restore unto me." Significantly again, Adam is buried by none other than Melchizadek. It may be coincidence, or more likely not, that in relatively recent times what is called the "Melchizadek Crucifix" has been quietly creeping into Christian Churches of the West. The figure thereon shows a risen Christ clothed and crowned as a Priest-King with his arms extended in the sign of blessing.

Another more than interesting item in a recondite source of oral tradition suggests that part of the Grail Secret was tied up with knowledge of a familial line descending directly from Jesus. The story went that his mother Mary, then a widow, accompanied her kinsman, Joseph of Aramathea, to Glastonbury after the Crucifixion, where she eventually died at a ripe old age, and both were buried there. This would certainly account for the so-called "Assumption into Paradise" since Paradise and Avalon mean the same thing—an apple orchard. Mary was said to have with her a grandson by Jesus whose mother's name was unknown, though naturally Mary Magdalen might be suspected. The bloodline begun by this unique immigrant was only known by Grail Keepers who handed the secret from one generation to another and presumably guarded the "passing on of the blood" with utmost care. There is nothing to tell of subsequent history, and beyond being a remote possibility, the story must remain an insoluble problem.

Nevertheless, this story does add some background to the odd words, "This is the book of thy descent" mentioned previously, and so does the tale of Joseph carrying two precious vessels with him to Avalon, one containing the blood and the other the sweat of Jesus collected at his Passion. If we can believe that these "vessels" were in fact living people, Mary being the Blood (Jews have always accepted the maternal bloodline) and the boy being born of Jesus' seed (sweat being an euphemism for this fluid), there could perhaps be a very slight foundation behind this belief.

As an additional point of interest to the foregoing, it might be remembered that Britain has been called the "Dowry of Mary" for many centuries by the Church. Jesus was said to have appeared to St. David (uncle of King Arthur) the night before he was supposed to consecrate a new church at Glastonbury, and told David this would be unnecessary, since he, Jesus, had already consecrated the primitive church there in honor of his mother. Whether David had that vision or not, there is still a stone near the south door of the Lady Chapel at Gastonbury Abbey inscribed:

| I | E | S | V | S |
|---|---|---|---|---|
| M | A | R | I | A |

It is tempting to think this might be a monastic cypher which might be translated as:

| I | E | S | V | S |
|---|---|---|---|---|
| n | c | e | i | a |
| i | c | p | r | n |
| t | l | u | g | c |
| i | e | l | i | t |
| u | s | t | n |   |
|   | i | u |   |   |
| M | A | R | I | A |

InitiuM EcclesiA SepultuR VirginI SanctA. The First Church was the Sepulchre of the Holy Virgin.

Monks were very fond of concealing information by cyphers of such kinds or by pictographic rebus. The floor of the Abbey (which has not survived) was reputed to have all sorts of riddles concealed in its designs. Still to be seen behind a modern gateway built before the Diocesan House back of the Abbey ruins are the "Arms of Joseph of Aramathea." This is a "ragged Cross" with a phial shaped vessel on each side. The rough-staffed Cross is meant to signify Joseph's pilgrim's staff which he is said to have stuck in the ground at Wearyall Hill where it took root and became the famous Holy Thorn. Trees growing from sacred Staffs are not uncommon in mythology, and usually represent the implantation of a family line in friendly foreign soil.

Like the Thorn, the roots of the Grail cultus do seem to stem from Celtic countries where the earliest Western Christian Church developed its own particular structure. There are links to be found mainly in Britain, Gaul, Germany and the Netherlands, with traces in Spain, Italy, and Portugal. As perhaps might be expected, the "centers" of the Grail story are countries where the Reformation had most influence when it started.

The Celtic Church had distinct differences of opinion and practice from the Roman branch of Christianity which had political ambitions for taking control of all European Churches including those of Britain and Ireland. We must remember the latent Druidic influence in those parts which came from a well-organized Celtic priesthood, a proportion of which conveniently converted to Christianity in its original form and interpreted its beliefs in their own way.

A noteworthy point of Celtic religious behavior was that its Church had its special version of the Liturgy. This included an "epiclesis" or "extra words of consecration" which invited the Holy Spirit to enter the elements of the sacramental bread and wine. Thus in the Roman Rite, the sacrament is regarded as the Body and Blood of Jesus specifically while in the Celtic Church it was that *plus* the "Holy Spirit," which in Roman eyes could have a suspiciously feminine angle to it. Utimately, Roman insistence got the Celtic Mass altered sometime around A.D. 750-820. The Eastern Orthodox Church retains an "epiclesis" clause in its consecration formula to this day.

Another important item of Celtic custom was that metal chalices were not introduced officially until about the time of King Arthur. Previously, it was usual to serve sacramental wine in rather bowl-shaped vessels, often of wood, pottery, glass, or other non-precious materials. In the Languedoc dialect, "Grasal" was such a shaped vessel, usually of clay, while in Anglo-Norman, "Graal" was a dish, often of silver, used at great feasts. Sometimes this is thought to mean "Gra-Sal" or a salt-server.

In the German cycle of the Grail, it is not referred to as a Cup or Dish at all, but a *stone,* the "Lapis Exilis" or Stone of Exile. No one could die for eight days after seeing it, and it was supposed to be borne around on a green cloth, that being the color of the Holy Spirit. Now in Hebrew, the word GVRL—Goral—specifically means a rounded stone used for casting lots often from an urn or cup. This could indicate a practice of casting lots to choose the next Sacrificial Victim. The selectee would not die for eight days because he would be granted that much grace to settle up his affairs. Making fatal decisions by casting lots reaches far beyond historical time, and we have to remember the custom in Nordic countries of throwing "rune-stones" on the ground to decide how the Finger of Fate pointed.

Another Celtic connection with the Grail was the magic Cauldron in which the God Kernunnos was cooked and regenerated. He was the antlered archetype of vegetation and Death whose name means "The Horned One." He is shown as presiding over a magical communion meal during which an intoxicating drink is served which allows partakers to make contact with the "Otherworld." In other words, he symbolizes the spirit of the meat and vegetables which afford life to consumers after being cooked in a communal pot. It is interesting to think that the rare modern custom of saying "Grace" before meals descends from early gratitude to the once living food which had to die so that humans might live.

Celtic mythology is full of cauldron-regeneration episodes, and the Spear which once killed Sacred Kings was later turned to the Lance of Longinus at the Crucifixion. When we think of the Grail "Hallows" or Holy Things as being the Cup, Sword, Lance, and Dish, it is easy to see how the Tarot suits were invented, and why they became so quickly popular among the cognoscenti. It is well to bear in mind that the Tarot appeared on the heels of the Grail story and seemed to cross Europe on the same stream that bore the Troubadours, Qabalism, and a series of "occult underground" movements leading eventually to Rosicrucianism and Free Masonry. All these were connected with ideas of spiritual liberation and emancipation from official establishments which enforced compulsory doctrines and dogmas.

That was why the Grail was considered as a panacea or cure for all ills of body, mind and soul. Maybe this was the reason why the Grail was reputed to serve everyone with whatever food or drink they liked best. Some saw it one way, and some another. It was very seldom seen in the same shape by any collective group awaiting its coming. Most Grail appearances are recorded as being entirely visionary, though there are instances of feasts being served from it accompanied by wonderful music and perfumes. There is one story of the Grail appearing at Camelot during a thunderstorm, when all the assembled knights saw each other in the kindest possible light.

The original "Knights of the Grail" were vigorous young people of good birth and ability, "blood-bonded" together in a common cause of spiritual ambition aiming at ideals above human limitations and restrictions. They were wholeheartedly against injustice, unfairness, persecutions, or any such inflictions on the helpless fellow-folk who struggled against low levels of living on earth. Those Knights were ready to risk their lives to defend their beliefs and their weaker bretheren. Fortunately, we have plenty of such Knights in our time. If only they were able to see the Grail in a clearer light they would be able to help their kindred much more easily.

This is where the Hermit figures come into the story. Throughout Grail literature odd hermits keep cropping up, usually attached to chapels in wild surroundings. These solitary figures reveal or indicate some useful information to Grail-Questers who visit them in the course of their travels. Sometimes they warn of dangers, or offer positive inspiration. Though none of them seem to have attained the Grail themselves, they were said to hold its Hallows among them, and were therefore able to offer assistance and advice to all seekers of the Grail. These Hermits, of course, are what might be termed "Elder Brethern," concerned with saving younger generations from making the same mistakes as themselves in their early lives. In time, eager young Knights become elderly Hermits themselves, encouraging others in their turn, and so the story steadily unfolds, each episode in its proper place.

No reference to the Grail could ever be complete without mentioning its mysterious Castle. This is actually a structure made of pure consciousness for the protection of an individual's most precious and important spiritual beliefs, without which he is in danger of his whole identity disintegrating. The Grail was said to have been kept in the Castle chapel. The Castle itself is described as being at the head of a great valley and surrounded by water. There are three bridges to cross. The first is a bowshot long and a foot wide which broadens out when a brave man begins to cross it. The second is of ice (sometimes glass), highly arched and brittle. The third is solidly built on marble pillars. One way or another, we all have to learn how to build "Grail Castles" in ourselves in order to protect our Holiest Heritage. Later on we shall attempt exactly that.

While there remains a wrong to right on earth, the Grail must inspire Knight-hearted souls to seek solutions to the problem. It might even inspire King-sized souls to sacrifice themselves willingly if real need arises. Faced with the Question: "Whom does the Grail serve?" there can be only one answer. It serves the needs of our salvation, this much misunderstood word to be taken in its full sense of rescuing from ruin and restoring to pristine condition. The Grail is not some legendary luxury, but an absolute necessity to anyone working the Western Mysteries, and anyone else seeking spiritual liberation. In one Western system of initiation, a candidate is asked a question during the initial ceremony which often puzzles and sometimes irritates him behind his blindfold. That question is, "What do you seek?" and his formal reply must be, "I seek to serve." Just that. No hint of service to whom or what. Many assume it is a vague acknowledgement of willingness to serve God and Man alike in some scheme for spiritual welfare. No one unfamiliar with the Grail story would guess this is the dreaded Question from another angle. The respondent is put in place of the Grail and answers with its voice inside himself. That is the Grail Secret. It seeks to *serve.*

To serve. Not impose, demand, or put the slightest pressure on anyone. The symbolic Grail is shown as a serving dish, and so indeed it *is,* on much higher than literal levels. The word *servus* means a slave, the humblest officiant in ordinary human society of any epoch. The Sacred Kings sought to serve their people through their sacrificial deaths. Kings voluntarily reduced themselves to slaves so that slaves might eventually become Kings in their own right. This is the meaning of the first being last, and the last being first, the meeting of Alpha and Omega in the magical closing of our conscious Circle in Cosmos.

Our Grail is a spiritual service which seeks to enliven those who should awaken to inner realities while yet on earth. The closer one looks into the Grail Tradition, the more obvious it becomes that the entire ideology stems from the single reality of a Westworking struggle to achieve individual independence for souls seeking such relationship with spiritual solidities rather than accept without question whatever they are told by establishments opposed to spiritual, and possibly, temporal liberty. The Western, and particularly the Celtic soul has always fought instinctively for what it believes to be true Freedom. One might call this the "Idealism of Individuation." Only slaves who know their status place the highest value on liberty, while those unaware of their own spiritual bondage are unlikely to accept unwanted freedom thrust upon them unwillingly. The Grail itself knows better than that. It knows that it will remain in servitude until the very last of its line on earth become liberated into Light forever, and takes an Empty Cup with him for company on his Cosmic Quest toward Eternal Truth.

## Questions

1. What do you understand by the Holy Grail or Sangreal.
2. Describe the concept of "Blood Royal."
3. What was the vital "Grail Question"?
4. What are the "extra-efficacious words"?
5. What was the "Siege Perilous"?
6. Mention some distinct features of the Celtic Church.
7. Draw a parallel between the Grail and the Cauldron.
8. How do Hermits figure in the Grail legend?
9. Choose the ten most important sentences in this Chapter.
10. Do you believe the "Blood" exists in yourself, and why so?

# · 5 ·

# *Individual Identity*

**A**lthough it is a good thing to know what is at the back of our Inner Tradition and how it came down the ages to us, it is much more important for any active member of it to see how it extends into *our* time and what each of us may do with it in order to make our modern lives significant and valuable as contributions to Cosmos in general and ourselves in particular. Without a sense of "I know where I came from, what I'm doing here, and where I'm going next," human lives get rather pointless and frustrating.

There is not much use telling youself you are in this world to make a lot of money, gratify every whim, satisfy worldly ambitions to the full, attract a lot of favorable attention, live a long and lucky life then float out of it at the end in a happy haze of hallucinogens. You may do all of this, some of it, or none of it. Such are the incidentals of Life, not the *fundamentals*. Those are the really important things you may be missing out on all the time. Until you realize you are in this world for the same reason as the rest of us, to *find your Self*, and apply what there is of you in this world to that task, you will never know any real satisfaction as a human being.

You have probably heard that the inscription over the sanctuary of an ancient Greek Mystery Temple read "Know Thy Self." Inside the sanctuary was—nothing. Nothing visible, anyway, except bare walls. Those who entered, wondered, and left without understanding, usually missed all they were meant to encounter—themselves. The whole meaning behind a human life lay in those three words. That *is* what we are here for. To *know* our True Selves. That is to say, be conscious not merely *of* but more importantly *as* the Individual Identity behind our mortal beings.

*You* (in the highest meaning of the word) are your own "Holy Grail." That was the important message the Grail cultus was trying to convey. The orthodox Christian Church at that time was almost totally concerned with showing humans the worst side of their natures, telling them what terrible sinners they were, utterly dependant on God's mercy and tolerance of their wickedness for which they deserved nothing more than eternal Hell. If it were not for the intervention of Jesus on behalf of degenerate man, born in the deepest sin, his Divine Father would wipe humanity out without a qualm. Moreover, it was the Church alone which controlled the Grace of God on earth, and without the Church there was no hope of salvation anywhere. All outside it were undoubtedly doomed. The Church controlled its congregation with a very old whip and carrot—fear of Hell and greed of Heaven. A very unsatisfactory state of spiritual slavery.

A lot of this was true enough, but the trouble lay in the fact it was only a small fraction of the truth and badly garbled at that. There is no denying humans have a bad side to them. Sometimes very much so. But they also have amazing, if often undeveloped, possibilities for perfecting themselves as a life-species far beyond bodily limitations on this poor old planet. Everything depends on how they construct the spiritual side of themselves with intentional consciousness from one incarnation to another.

Only a relatively small part of the "Real You" is actually incarnate at a time, but it is a vitally important part since it is the contact-point between that "Inner Identity" and the energies of life on these early levels which have to be "converted back" to their sources of spiritual supply. We as humans are essential links in the ecology of existence and our specific function is the conversion of consciousness from this Life-level back along its "lines of Light" towards the Consciousness of Cosmos Itself. In other words, each of us are "cells" of some kind in the "Body of God," intended to enable the Omniscient Intelligence to experience Existence in this particular part of Creation.

The point is that we are autonomous or self-governing cells to quite a large extent. Although we are limited by birth, hereditary, and circumstantial factors of life, those limits are *capable of extention or contraction,* and our intentional behavior within them determines our degree of value and relationship to the Creative Consciousness which constructed us in the first place.

Put in child-easy terms, "God" uses you (and the rest of us) to experience Life through your *awareness of* it and your *reactions with* it. Granted that "God" uses all other humans, animals, plants and minerals for the same purpose along different lines, but as a unit of awareness among these, *you are unique,* and *only you* can act as a channel of communication between "God" and Life as you know it here on earth *in your particular way.*

Everything depends on how you interpret Life as it happens to you with your share of creative consciousness. Suppose something happens which affects your awareness in some very marked way. You can simply react instinctively and unintelligently with it like millions of other humans, or you can do something much better. Put it through a process of your own consciousness so that it makes a complete and comprehensible production forming your particular pattern of perception. Symbolize it if you can. When you have summed everything up in your own terms, "Pass it back along the line" for Deity to deal with at levels of your "Highest Self." Whether your findings are factually right or wrong makes no difference so long as you have put things *as you feel and believe them because of your experience.* This has the effect of "informing God" of something He or It *wants to know* about Life-conditions in the here-now, and *that has value* in the construction and evolution of our Cosmos.

"God" is reputed to be Omniscient or All-knowing. That is only because *you* in your miniscule sphere of consciousness are acting as an agency for that Omniscience. Look at things this way. Shut your eyes and pick up any object you like. What do your fingers and hand tell you about it? Quite a lot, even to identification. Now how do you suppose your brain got the message? Through untold numbers of individual nerve cells, *each single one* passing its own fraction of experience along the main channels to the brain, where all have to be combined, compared and interpreted in a split second. That is comparably how Cosmic Consciousness extends through Existence, and *you* are a single link in that incredible chain. Most importantly, what you think and do within it *does* matter so far as all are concerned.

Let us suppose again that you encounter another Life-event, but this time you encode it badly, muddling all the issues involved and making a thorough mess of impressions and evaluations. Then you "shove this along the line" through your subconsciousness. Eventually of course it will all get sorted out, but in the meantime you have only caused confusion and complications which will have to be clarified. *Now* can you see some of the purpose behind "thinking patterns" like the Tree of Life and other "consciousness constructing" symbols you are being trained to use? These are for "awareness arrangement" so that you and your consciousness will become of best possible value to "God" or whatever you care to call the Supreme Being, and therefore to your True Self.

Bear in mind the part of yourself we have been thinking and talking about is the incarnate aspect of your intelligence as a human being living on this Earth, sometimes called the "Lower Self," but this is a very unsatisfactory nomenclature if it implies anything derogatory or devaluating. There is a useful and important job of work in this world to be done through that section of the Self, by making it a finer and fitter means of mediating Cosmic Consciousness on these levels of Life which are only "low" when compared with the heights we hope to scale through subsequent evolution.

It was once the fashion to disparage or denigrate anything to do with our "Lower Selves" and the "lusts of the flesh" lumped together with them as if anything of an animal nature were offensive to a pure (and seemingly easily shocked) God. That was not only ridiculous, but absurdly insulting to the Intelligence of a Creative Spirit capable of living consciousness. As humans we live in animal bodies for the simple reason that these were specifically designed for living on this planet. Our bodies *are* animals, and they have the right to be treated decently and looked after for the sake of the service they afford us during our incarnations.

Have you ever thought of your body as an animal you happen to be living in, which has a nature of its own and characteristics to match? It is only yours to borrow for a single incarnation, do the best you can with during its lifetime, then leave with maybe gratitude but no regrets when the time comes. That is the normal mystical way of looking at it. The abnormal way is to despise the poor thing because it is not better than its nature and is apt to act accordingly. Some so-called spiritual schools of thought believe in ill-treating their bodies disgracefully, inflicting vicious "punishments" on them to "purify them from base desires" and the rest of all such rubbish which is nothing but concealed cruelty and sadomasochism. Thankfully, we have far less of this now than formerly, but some stigmas stick a lot longer than they should.

No one has a right to ill-treat his body or to cause deliberate suffering to other animal creatures on Earth. Nevertheless, we do have an obligation to *train* our bodies and make them behave properly just as in the case of children or domestic pets. The important thing from a mystical viewpint is not to *identify* with your body, but see it in the light of a living creature you have been entrusted with to care for, educate, and train as well as you can while it serves your purpose in this world. Never think of your body as *you* any more than you would identify with your clothes. For instance, do not say things like, "*I* feel sick today" instead of "My stomach is upset," or whatever it is. Always make a conscious distinction between your bodily bits and *you* to whom they belong. Get things straight in your consciousness as to who owns what.

It was once aptly said that the Life-Spirit sleeps in the mineral kingdom, dreams in the vegetable, stirs in the animal, wakes in humanity and lives in the Divine. Not a bad analogy at all and well worth remembering. These are divisions of Divine Consciousness through the whole of Nature. Maybe you wonder why "God" would want to be a snake, a rat, a flea, or any other creature you think horrid. *All* forms of Life fit into Creation somehow because their specific types of consciousness approach it from some needed angle at a particular period or place. Nowadays we think our ancestors were stupid enough to worship animals, but did they? There is a difference between worshipping or adoring anything and *respecting it* as representative of something higher. Why should they not have respected the Life-Spirit in other orders of Creation than ours? Especially in different types of animals helpful to us in some way.

For instance, in ancient Egypt people recognized the actions of a Deity in the behavior of hawks, dung-beetles, crocodiles and jackals, among other Life-forms. Those all have one important factor in common. They are scavengers, helping to keep the environment healthy by disposing of corpses and reducing vermin. Cats, in particular, apart from decimating rats and mice, were good at killing small snakes. So the Egyptians honored and protected these and other creatures with religious recognition, and they were not a primitive or uncultured people but highly civilized in their day. The devaluation of animal life by Judeo-Christianity has been a great pity for many reasons, particularly because it deprives us of a fellowship-sense with Life.

There is no reason why we in the West should re-establish the old animal cults in their original forms, but every reason why we ought to encourage our modern concerns with animal welfare. From a religious sense of duty, we owe them, because of the way our species have treated theirs. Why some humans should expect kindly treatment from a Life-Spirt which they have treated so badly in other Life-forms than their own is one of the anomalies of this odd world.

So don't let anyone sell you the idea that "Lower Selves" are depraved or regrettable things to have *as such*. Their primal purpose is to keep Cosmic Consciousness in touch with Life on these levels, and while we are humans here we might as well make as good a job of this as we can until we evolve above and beyond the self-stages confined to this earthly existence. That is what all forms of spiritual training should be aimed at, otherwise they are no more than calisthenics of consciousness.

What so many occultists have been calling a "Lower Self" is really no more than the "Earth-end" of the same Self which reaches as high as "Heaven." It is like the "Sandalaphon-Metatron" combination of Archangels, which is the same archetype with its feet on Earth and its head in Heaven. It just depends on where your focus of consciousness is. So long as this is through the "Earth-end" of yourself, then you are using this "body-based" form of being to express the essential energies of Life on these levels probably because you have not yet learned how to focus higher up the scale of Self. Also you probably have some useful function to fulfil for the Cosmic Consciousness right here on this Earth among your present circumstances.

A number of mystics from all spiritual systems have firm convictions that the best thing they can do is "turn their backs on the world' as much as they can, isolate themselves in solitary surroundings, then focus their attention on the Absolute in the hope it will absorb them completely and that it will be the end of their worries forever. Is this a good idea or not? All depends on motivation and self-status. If they have almost concluded their span of service as incarnating entities and have nearly reached the point of rising above incarnation anyway, this pratice might be quite valid. So it could be for the last few years of any life providing there are no outstanding responsibilities on Earth still awaiting fulfilment. Again it would be justified for the sake of recuperation or special spiritual training for definite periods. Nevertheless the inescapable fact remains that while there is redemptive work to be done in this world, each soul aware of that obligation should accept its fair share of the burden. Anyone presumptuous enough to "claim Cosmos" before It claims them will only be pushed back into service again.

There is a lovely legend of Michael Archangel which may be unknown enough to be worth telling here. The story went that God was so disgusted by human behavior, he determined to wipe out all humans and try his hand at some other kind of creature. Michael at his right hand (the Sword hand) said more or less, "Please don't, they could improve in time. Give them a longer chance. I'll tell you what, let *me* try to help them and see what I can do. They're not *all* bad. I'll make you this promise. So long as there is as much as one single spark of good among the lot of them, I'll stand by and do my best for them. If the time ever comes when the last spark of good is extinguished forever, then I'll give up and help you annihilate them." Michael is reputed to be still on our side when we need him, and is yet the symbol of fire and Light.

Western estoeric lore tells of souls that have actually advanced beyond any obligation to incarnate in human bodies who still do so voluntarily in order to help others. While embodied, they may not be objectively conscious of this because they have to accept the limitations of a human brain in addition to those of the body. They may not necessarily become famous or outstanding in any way, but they just come here for perhaps one particular purpose which might not seem important to anyone at that time, yet neverthless could be of vital significance in the future for a great many people. There are "spiritual seeds" of this sort being planted among us here and now which may not "come up" for a very long time, yet when they do, their flowering forms are likely to alter human Life-courses in many strange ways.

Never make the mistake of supposing that because nothing observable by physical senses happens immediately or soon after some special "consciousness-working" that it must have been ineffective or negligible. Time is a factor far from easy to bend by any form of consciousness available to normal human minds or wills. All "special workings" of Cosmically connected conscious-ness achieve results *eventually,* but many of them may be lifetimes later. Which does *not* mean they are not worth doing now. If you have been looking at mystical matters with an ordinary human time-sense, then you *have* been using the wrong end of the telescope.

Most people find that time seems to get a lot faster as they get older, yet cannot see exactly why it should. The answer is very simple—proportional progression. Suppose for instance we take an ordinary solar year as a standard and apply it fractionally to our lives. Say that we are two years old. That year is half, or 50 percent of our lives. At ten, it becomes a tenth, or 10 percent . At fifty, the year is a fiftieth or 2 percent of a life. If we ever lived a century, it would be down to 1 percent and so on. It is exactly the same time getting shorter and shorter in proportion to our total time-sense. So the longer we live the faster it does go. If we saw this same year from a life-span of one million years it would seem about half a minute long.

Conversely, a few seconds may seem like ages in moments of exceptional stress or danger when life expectancy is shortened to those moments. Everything which would normally seem rapid is slowed down to a crawl, because consciousness has speeded up so much. We may be reminded of Dr. Johnson's remark that nothing concentrates a man's mind quite so much as knowing he is going to hang at eight o'clock next morning. Time is really the rate at which we relate our consciousness with Cosmos, and in this world it has a definite range within a top and bottom limit outside of which we could not be conscious here at all.

Imagine a film passing through a projector at about twenty frames per second so that movement looks normal on the screen. Now speed to a thousand a second. It would be nothing but a blank on the screen. Go the opposite way till the speed is one frame a year. Though a static picture is perceptible, there is no movement to engage attention and interest and therefore nothing with which to modulate consciousness. This should illustrate that unless we are able to adapt awareness with very different rates of existence, we need not expect to be actively aware of energy effects outside ordinary limits.

This is a distinct weakness in our Western Tradition that we have yet to overcome—a lack of patience. We are frequently too restless and unable to lay out our time-tracks properly. Patience is not just sitting around aimlessly and waiting for something to happen. It is (or should be) a correct calculation of event-liklihood so that energies may be switched into other channels during the interval between cause and effect. Who would be so stupid as to plant an apple pip then stand and wait for the expected tree to produce ripe apples? Yet some people will do almost the spiritual equivalent of such idiocy due to a complete lack of understanding as regards causes in consciousness resulting in effects upon earth-levels.

There was an old magical saying, "work without lust of result." That is to say to do the Willworking or magical operation, push it in the right direction, and then get on with something else instead of constantly worrying and impatiently demanding results and responses from Inner Powers. Very good advice, too. The word "lust" implies greed, unreasonable demands, ignoble motivations, and probably insatiability. Nothing very commendable, anyway. Apart from moral issues, it is contra-productive to keep sending anxious, querulous, irritable, and prodding thoughts after some originally adequate inner operation of consciousness. Far from helping it along, this actually interferes with its working on higher levels, and in the end may negate or divert its action into insignificance. Any afterthinkings sent in the wake of specific Willworkings should be calm, steady, and non-insistently contributive to the original intention.

For instance, you may have set up a particular Willworking (to be disucssed later) with an objective in mind. It is best not to specify a deadline date in ordinary human time such as, "I want so and so by the 24th of this month." Those terms are meaningless when translated into inner language. The way to phrase it is to consider the function or application of whatever it is *in relation to yourself and your consciousness,* stress a sense of imminent need, codify this symbolically, then "send it up" inside yourself for the higher Self to deal with. Does this mean that one end of you doesn't know what the other end is talking about? Not exactly, but they do *not* speak the same language. The Earth-end of you understands ordinary English and whatever other tongues you have mastered, but the "Heaven end" of you uses a different kind of communicative consciousness altogether. The common *lingua franca* of the Inner World is *symbology,* hence, its importance in mystical work and the usage of special symbolism for spiritual purposes.

Once you gain the habit of almost automatically translating your thoughts and intentions into "Inner" forms of symbolic speech, a great many things will become a lot clearer to your normal consciousness because it will be in *operative* contact with your awareness on much higher levels of life which do not communicate much in the ordinary course of events. This is what all those little "magical exercises" are about, and why you should keep pegging away at them. By rhythmic reiteration they are helping you open up lines of communication between your Earth-end and a lot higher up your Self-scale.

Maybe you have sometimes wondered exactly what is the difference between those "magical practices" and ordinary common or garden-variety prayer as advocated by Christian or any other religion. Why, for instance, should official religions insist upon approach to Deity by supplicatory prayers, yet make such a frightful fuss if the same Deity is approached by alternative channels? Where does religion stop and magic start or vice versa? It's a good question which might as well be tackled here instead of anywhere else.

The bedrock bottom of the matter is that so-called "magic" is a do-it-yourself kind of religion as distinct from an organizational do-what-we-tell-you one. The word "religion" in the dictionary sense comes from the Latin *religio* meaning to bind fast, or tie up, re-tie, and keep tying over that. Figuratively, a religious person is one who binds himself tightly to specific beliefs, or is so bound by any other means. When we think of the ancient custom of binding Sacred King sacrificial Victims, this makes the meaning of religion a lot more interesting. Metaphorically, it signifies that a sincerely religious soul is voluntarily binding himself by adopted beliefs into a state of self-sacrifice acceptable to its own Divinity. No more. No less.

As we know, organized and official religions are all characterized by dogmas, doctrines, and specific formularies laid out for observance by humans holding such beliefs, beyond which they are not supposed to stray. There is no denying this is very sound spiritual discipline for many millions of people who are incapable of self-supportive spiritual action. Nevertheless there could be good grounds for suspecting that well-established priesthoods of any sort would be very much against individualists seeking self-liberation apart from their authority. In fact, we have historical evidence of anti-heresy campaigns to prove the point.

Our Inner or "Magical" Tradition of the West has always been individualistic in character. It does not have an official hierarchy, no fixed formularies, no "believe-or-be-damned" creeds. Essentially it is a "find it yourself" sort of faith which only very strong or sturdy souls can follow. Where, then, you may ask, have all the "occult practices" and such formularies as the Tree of Life come from, and why should anyone regard them as integrals of our Tradition? These are no more than legacies from past experience which previous workers have passed down to us because they found help from such things in their time, and supposed we might find them useful today. All we are expected to do is study them, adapt and improve them according to contemporary consciousness, and hand over the results to our successors in hope they will continue the process.

So what you are being given from the Inner Tradition is not the dead and mummified remains of previous superstitions, but a living, active, and authentic spiritual survival from our earliest existence on earth, which has been quietly growing and changing through the centuries because it has been cared for and nourished by many generations of humans who realized the value of what they were entrusted with, and did their very best to ensure you receive it in a fit condition for furthering.

In one way perhaps, our Inner Tradition could be described as a "Religion without a Church" insofar as it automatically implies belief in some "Supreme Spirit of Life" and the need for making human relationships with that Spirit and Its available aspects by all possible Paths of approach. If some of these Paths are described as "Magical" because they align with what the alchemists termed the "Great Work" or Magnum Opus, then this description has to be acceptable. The only sensible interpretation of the word "Magic" is that it derives from the old root Maj meaning "great" in the sense of importance or priority. If you can think of anything greater or more important than ensuring the best Humano-Divine relationships, then you must be missing everything that Life on Earth was meant for.

If you would really claim conscious connection with the Inner Way of the West, what you are expected to do is pick up whatever pieces of it you encounter, then *make something of these for yourself* which connects with what others have accomplished. Supplies may reach you from quite surprising sources, but *you will have to do* the work yourself. There is no other way, regardless of what you may have heard. You cannot cheat your own consciousness or live effectively by lying to yourself. Sooner or later you have to learn how to tie yourself to Truth with knots of your own making. This is what the "Consciousness of the Cord" means.

With the old Circle-workings of the Western Way, it meant that the same central concept could be seen from twelve different viewpoints by as many different souls. It also meant that the concept should be seen by each soul from at least four distinct angles. With all these combined observations, a much more accurate impression of the concept can be reached than by anyone staying still and looking at it from one side only. This is a most important point in the Western Circle Cross method of working "Magic." Set up any central spiritual concept, then *circumambulate* it with a ring of consciousness, and view it through every possible point of the 360 degree circle. In other words, don't just *encounter* concepts with consciousness, *encompass* them with it. Run rings round them. If you can't do this by yourself get others to help you make a Magic Circle.

Try this experiment for yourself. Set up a symbolic circle which need not be more than a few feet across. Take up a position anywhere on the perimeter, but know where you are supposed to be in relation to it, for example in the East or elsewhere. Face center. Imagine some definite spiritual concept there, for example, one of the Spheres on the Tree or perhaps a Path. See it *only* from the viewpoint of where you are. If you are Sword-East, look at the concept from an angle of keenness, flexibility and so forth as if you were the Raphael archetype of that Quarter. Consider the concept carefully and steadily in an East-Light. Shift slowly to the Southern Quarter, changing your consciousness to a "Michaelian" one. Regard the concept in that Light. Continue the exercise until you have gone right round the circle. Do this several times if you like, then stop and think it all out.

What you should have done was look at the concept with four different aspects of *yourself*, thus obtaining the best balanced viewpoint of it possible for *you*. As you might easily see, if you could share this with eleven other people doing the same thing, there ought to be a pretty clear idea of the concept between all of you. This is why in any sound circle of the Western Way it is not a case of everyone seeing Inner Life from the same uniform angle as if it were a flat picture, but each reacting with it individually in combination with others doing the same so that the total production is far better and wider than any single member could achieve alone. It is not our agreements with each other that are so vital as our variations.

This does not mean *dis*agreement, which implies refusal to examine other viewpoints, rigidity of opinions, and so forth, which often happens when many humans are involved in coming to conclusions on any given subject. Its advantage lies in having alternative angles of awareness from which to compose a more complete picture of any belief. When you come to think of it, this is no more than the jury system which has served Western justice for so long a time. You have only to apply its principle to a spiritual instead of a legal standpoint, except that spiritually you are looking for a lot more than a simple "Yes-or-No" decision.

## Questions

1. Define "Know Thyself."
2. Describe your function as an agent of Divine Consciousness.
3. Why should we regard our bodies as animals for which we are responsible to a Higher Power?
4. Define "Lower" and "Higher" Self, and say why these terms are unsatisfactory.
5. Why does time seem to get faster as we get older?
6. Define patience.
7. What does "Work without lust of result" mean to you?
8. What is the *lingua franca* of the Inner worlds?
9. Choose the eight most important sentences in this chapter?
10. What is the root-meaning of the word "Magic"?

# The Art of Abra-Melim

$\mathbf{A}$re you now beginning to understand how the Western Inner Tradition comes into being? There is no "High and Mighty Authority" laying down long lists of rules and regulations with shalts and shalt nots to be obeyed by an unquestioning membership. Everyone has to "go inside" for themselves, get what they can in their own way, then try to fit that in wherever it seems to link up with what others have found. In a way, it is like a lot of people picking up pieces of a huge jig-saw puzzle which some passing God has dropped on this world, and then trying to assemble the puzzle by matching up the bits as best they can. Unlike the God, however, none of them has the complete picture on the lid as an overall guide, so they have to work by trial and error methods.

This may sound to you like a crazy way of assembling any Tradition, but the whole essence is that everything has to be compounded by free and individual efforts. That is what makes it uniquely Western. Any authority with adequate power can enforce rules on a body of people by sheer oppressive and punitive legislation, so that a standard behavior among them is almost guaranteed. As we know, this has been tried many times in the course of our world's history, but somehow the "Western Soul" manages to slip free eventually, and evades all attempts to enslave it entirely. That has only been possible because its directive drive is not concentrated in one vulnerable point and it is so disseminated among millions of souls that they cannot *all* be adversely influenced at the same time. One might say the "Torch of Inner Freedom" gets passed from hand to hand so to speak, as it may be endangered in any particular section.

Do you remember in the Grail legend, the Grail itself was said to be "removed to Heaven" while its Hallows were left on earth divided among the "Hermits of the Forest" who lived in remote and difficult terrain? The real meaning of this is that because our Tradition became threatened on earth, the only sensible thing to do was secure its "Command Post" well out of "enemy range" but leave its "Contact Units" where they could be found by loyal "Knights of the Grail" when necessary. If one or the other of these got overrun or eliminated, there could always be an eventual replacement from elsewhere. The Hallows were replaceable, whereas the Grail Itself was *not*.

Have you realized we are a threatened Tradition on earth? You may ask by whom or what, and why we should not easily be able to overcome any possible opposition from anywhere. Although these are not simple questions, you should be able to answer them for yourself without too much soul-searching. First, ask yourself what sort of sectional interests in this world might be likely to oppose and discourage individualism most strongly. You could come up with a number of answers which are all different yet all correct. So that makes supporters of such interests automatically antagonistic to Western Traditionalism. Then again, how many people do you suppose *really* care enough about Inner Freedom to "become Themselves" that they would be prepared to sacrifice *something* in order to uphold their inherited spiritual birthright? If you are anything of a realist, you will have to admit few are willing to do more than drift with the tides of thought directed at them by whichever type of media moves them most. That is plain old human nature.

The legend of the Grail *is* the story of the Western Inner Tradition. The Grail was *not* some kind of All-Powerful compelling force which eliminated everything in its way and imposed itself everywhere on earth. To the contrary; it was a retiring, reticent, and one might almost say, extremely delicate and intangible concept altogether. It needed constant protection in strong Castles defended by its champions against unspecified enemies or antagonists. Of itself, the Grail was entirely non-aggressive, its only defence being disappearance in the face of danger. If anyone got hurt during a Grail Quest, that might have been due to action on the part of its guardians, but never the Grail directly.

It should be seen by all these implications that the Grail is analogous of one particular thing—the human heart, which is defenseless in itself, of supreme importance to life, needing constant protection in the "Castle" of a strong body, having many environmental enemies, and symbolically the center of Love, Compassion, and "Life-Feeling." It is also the "Cup of the Blood" within us. Just as our ordinary hearts are the main vessels of Life in our physical bodies, so is the Grail (or Greal) *the heart of our Western Soul.* If our physical hearts are stopped we die as embodied humans. If our Grail ceased action we would die as a type of spirituality on earth. That is how important it is, and why it has to be kept going from one generation to the next under a great variety of names and appearances, but having the same concept throughout. Call it what you will, describe it any way you like, but the Grail continues to be what it always has been—*the very heart and blood of the Western Spiritual Tradition.*

By itself, the Grail is neither Christian, Pagan, nor belonging exclusively to any definite culture or creed. It is the Life-drive of our need for Spirit in all forms of faith. Creeds, codes, or conventions are external expressions liable to alter from lifetime to lifetime. The main drive behind them remains essentially unchanged throughout our progress as souls working our way through humanity toward an ultimate state of *Perfect Peace Profound.* If we in the West choose to call this concentration of energy the Holy Grail or Greal, why should we not? It will Christianize, Paganize, or express itself in whatever way opens up your heart to the Life-Spirit it stands for. A pious Hindu might call it Yoga, because it *yokes* humans to their concepts of Divinity. So do feel free to think of it as you think best. We shall continue to term it the Grail in these lessons, partly because that is a simple and straightforward word, and also because it will always remain our G-reatest *Reali*ty. Think of it that way by all means.

Our Western Inner Tradition is not so much a spiritual system in itself, as an entire collection of systems gathered into a corporate whole linked by a single "Blessed Bond"—the concept of Individualization conjoining Liberty, Light, Life, and Law. The Liberty of everyone to seek the same Light through their own Lives and the Laws thereof. Granted this is more of an ideal than an accomplished reality, but it is one to be worked for by everyone believing in the Western Way of Life as something to value and uphold in this world. Looked at superficially, we might seem to be a mess of spiritual systems, with cults, creeds, codes, and bizarre beliefs apparently running riot everywhere. These do not threaten our Tradition in the least except to the extent they deliberately restrict or inhibit spiritual freedom among their followers. What would be far more serious would be if some absolute authority forbade them all and imposed its own code of consciousness on everyone while inflicting penalties for non-compliance. Do not make the fatal mistake of dismissing this as an utter impossibility. Improbable and highly unlikely, yes, but *not* impossible altogether. You know quite well there are areas in this world today where freedom of thought is strongly supervised, to say the very least. Besides, there are cleverer ways of working by permitting apparent liberty on the surface, while subverting it most effectively and imperceptibly underneath. Your spiritual liberties could very well be seriously threatened without your knowledge unless you look extremely closely and carefully for concealed signs.

Don't forget that we in the West have a history of religious and allied persecutions. You may suppose that was all very long ago and ceased several centuries back, but *did it?* Was it a case of not so much ceasing as changing its appearance and methods, then continuing unrecognizably on far more subtle than physical levels? Had you thought of that possibility? If not, then think about it for a while and see what comes to you. Not a nice or comforting thought at all, is it? Nevertheless, it could be a *needed* thought to prevent you from becoming too dangerously complacent. It is not intended to *alarm* you needlessly, but to *alert* you, if necessary.

For a revealing sidelight on our Tradition, let us go back into those times of open persecution in Western Europe when thinking was dangerous and convinced opinions could be fatal. We will focus our attention on Wurtzburg, Germany, in 1458. First note that this is roughly the area and era where the "backlash" against *official* Christian Church corruption and compulsions of conscience began to emerge. Lutheranism and other schisms on the continent followed by the reformation of the Anglican Church, plus "breakouts" in many directions from hitherto hidden groups like the Rosicrucians and other "occult" organizations which had been quietly influencing events "from Inside" challenged ecclesiastical authority on all sides. What we are going to look at is a truly remarkable book of that period written for anyone brave enough to seek a lifetime of spiritual guidance entirely by themselves through making direct contact with their individual sources of supply. The idea was to make this vital link-up not through the mediation of any Church, Synagogue, or official body of belief, but to obtain it directly from spiritual agencies entrusted with helping human evolution.

This book was ostensibly of Hebrew authorship attributed to "Abraham the Jew" and purported to be a special spiritual legacy to his second son Lamech. He remarks that it consists of an ancient Magical Science which he himself had gained from an old Egyptian sage who lived near a place called "Arachi" close to the Nile. Though this is not locatable on any map, the name in Hebrew means "Strong Life" and that is probably what the real author had in mind. The sage's name was Abra-Melim, which we shall interpret shortly.

It is likely that this may have been the first "modern" occult handbook ever written, and more importantly *it is not yet out of date.* Insofar as it can be called a system, it is *still in use* among the most dependable "Occult Schools" of the West today. Though its practices have been considerably brought up to date, its principles are fundamental to them however they may be arranged. If you have not read the book, you should do so, but be warned there is not much use reading it if you do not know how to interpret its implications. The literal wording can be most misleading if you do not read between the lines to find the meaning in the material. It was written in the form of a "Magical" work, which it truly is in the genuine sense of the word, providing you realize where the magic lies. You have to be on the look out for meanings behind meanings to a great depth.

Intrinsically, the system is one of individual approach to Divinity extended over a prolonged period graded into easy, harder, and intensive stages. It was a highly disciplined method of living which had to be fully experienced and passed through the psyche. The aim was to obtain Life-linkage with one's own "Higher Identity" consciously personified as a "Holy Guardian Angel." After such a contact was obtained, it seemed reasonable to suppose that one's spiritual future might be assured under this "Divine Guidance." Furthermore, the worst side of human nature could be controlled beneficially and energies which might otherwise have evil or injurious results could be directed into good and peaceful paths. This was symbolized by a ceremonial "Summoning of Devils" and ordering them to obey the Divine Will within the words of the Magus. We have the same problem now, except we call it "Deliverance or Destruction by Nuclear Energy." This is the ancient "Good over Evil equals Peace" formula in our times.

Actual authorship of this book, *The Sacred Magic of Abramelim the Mage,* is highly speculative. Though it is reputedly a translation from the Hebrew into French, no Hebrew original has yet been found, nor was the translator's name mentioned. In fact, the only copy known is in the Bibliotheque de l'Arsenal at Paris and it is a *handwritten* manuscript. McGregor Mathers of the Golden Dawn found it and translated it to English in 1897. Throughout the book there are references which make it read more like Christian than Jewish workmanship. It mentions Latin Bibles, "mortal sin," etc. and the 90th Psalm being quoted as *Qui habitat in adjutorio Altissime.* This would be correct in the Catholic version, but both Hebrew and Protestant Bibles list this as Psalm 91. Coincidence or not, the date of the manuscript was given as 1458, and the "Chemical Nuptials of

Christian Rosencreutz" is attributed to 1459, though it was not printed until over a century later.

Another interesting point is that "Abraham" termed his system the "Abra-Melim" type of Sacred Magic after his own "Great Egyptian Master." Now this comes from two Hebrew roots, ABR—to be strong and mighty, also to fly aloft, and MLAIM—consecratory sacrifices. The name for his son is Lamech, which means an ox-goad for controlling the courses of oxen, which in those days provided all the power for cultivation. It should not need a very keen intelligence to see the message here is something like, "Be strong. Raise yourself to the Highest. Make the right sacrifices to God, and control your animal nature with a firm hand so that it will supply you with power for cultivating your soul." All that admonition and more lies in the title alone.

That was only the beginning. After this, our author really lays down his laws. He does say that aspirants might be of any religion at all including "Pagans," but insists they must have the highest moral qualifications, be of a devout nature and well educated. (Remember Merlin made similar remarks about who might undertake the Grail Quest). Abraham's candidates, however, must obviously have some independent means of livelihood, because they had to subsist for at least a year in secure seclusion from human interference, living a calm and carefully controlled existence. This factor of insulation from inimical influences was absolutely essential to the whole operation. Should that be impossible or even unlikely, would-be practitioners were strongly advised against starting the process at all. Furthermore, they must be healthy with no hereditary diseases, of legitimate birth only, and between twenty-five and fifty years of age.

On the face of this, it seems that only wealthy or independent people had any hopes from this system. Cynics these days could suppose recipients of State Welfare might qualify equally well and, given the right attitudes of mind and souls, this could be true enough. Abraham was only insistent that the operation must be motivated *solely* by the highest altruistic intentions and undertaken "for the glory of God, the good of the practitioner, and the benefit of all humanity." He did go on to say, however, that it made no difference whether a man were married or not, so long as his wife or family did not interefere in any way.

Our Abraham was very forthright concerning chicanery or pretensions of any kind. He pours overall scorn on the whole field of "charms, conjurations, sorceries, letter and number twisters, stargazers, prognostigation and like, deceivers working with the aid of the Devil." For him, Magic has only one meaning—the purest and most direct means for humans to deal with Divinity. Nothing less. To him, all else has an element of fraud and deception in it, not to mention suspicions of diabolism. By modern standards he might seem absurdly puritanical, but there can be no doubt whatever of his sincerity and uprightness. He remains resolutely uncompromising about the principle of Evil, though he sees value in it when its energies are converted into channels controlled by "good Angels" and the "Powers of Right and Light." At least he knew where he stood in Life and how he intended adapating with it. How many moderns have the same confidence in Cosmos?

Any "new boy" to this system was strongly advised not to attempt the practical part of the exercise before the whole book had been read and re-read for at least six months. In other words, get a good theoretical grounding, before trying to project anything into practice. This should seem obvious enough, but it is absolutely incredible how people in our times who would not dream of the least material venture without adequate preparation are likely to attempt the most ambitious and improbable spiritual schemes with less than remote chances of the slightest success. Abraham always advises common sense, moderation, and "Middle of the Way" procedures in all things. He reads like an ideal Father-Figure speaking to an eager and well-meaning son who lacks experience of life and needs kindly paternal guidance.

It is worth noting that Abraham speaks of his system as being "Holy Wisdom" and *not* Qabalah. He says he has already passed on his Qabalistic knowledge to his first-born son Joseph, which name means "addition" in the sense of "increase." He evidently regards Qabalah *per se* as a tradition limited to lines of primogeniture, or else this is another indication of non-Jewish authorship, because this "Sacred Magic," as he sometimes calls it, may be attained by all who are able and determined to do so. He is more or less saying that humans have two mainstream chances of salvation in Life. One is whatever "Holy Heritage" they are born with from efforts presumably made in previous incarnations, their "addition and increase." The second opportunity is that made entirely by individual efforts at approaching Divinity during a single lifetime. This is due to the "goadings" or promptings of Spirit in us, prodding our slow and ox-like Earth-natures along our Paths of progression. Hence the "Lamech" cover-name.

Candidates for the Abra-Melim system are supposed to be even-tempered, abstemious, charitable, and sincerely devout without being in the least fanatical or biased against other beliefs. Tolerance of religious opinions is a must with Abraham, who seemed entirely unorthodox in his views. He also insisted it was essential to have at least a bedroom and a small Temple or Oratory specially dedicated for the last six months of the "Magical Retirement." This is vital to success with the Operation. Everything had to be very simple but of good taste and quality, the accent being on cleanliness, good order, economy, and practicality. The Temple must contain nothing superfluous or flamboyant whatever. All had to be accomplished with quiet dignity and the deepest sincerity of purpose.

The Temple itself was quite austere by some standards: clean scrubbed pinewood walls and floor having a central altar with a hanging lamp above it and a censer on its top. The altar was the usual "double-cube" shape which, in effect, was a wooden cupboard where spare incense, oils and so forth were kept. The Temple should preferably have a window or access to an outside terrace or area where the "Evil Spirits" may appear without daring to enter the consecrated area. If possible, this must be on the North side. Robes were a plain white alb and a scarlet overtunic of silk with no ornaments. (Is one reminded here of the phrase, "Through your sins are as scarlet yet I will make them as white as snow"?) A girdle of silk was also worn, and a headsquare or nemyss had to be held in place with a silk or metal fillet. The only weapon was a slender staff of almond wood with the bark peeled off. This was traditionally of the operator's own height, or the "measure of a man." There might also be a small plate of burnished silver on the altar to act as a "scrying-mirror" for an assistant child-clairvoyant if one could be found who was suitable.

Although Abraham gives most meticulous details about such purely material matters, he is absolutely adamant that the candidate must "play by ear" the entire spiritual side of the operation. He resolutely refuses to lay down any set prayers or formulae, other than a single example. He says that everyone should speak his own language with God and His Holy Angels. He insists that all invocations must be made in the natural terms of one's mother-tongue. Not even a single word should be used unless its meaning is fully *understood*. A rather sensible admonishment! Moreover the praying and ceremonial moves must be conducted in a controlled and moderate fashion. No shouting barbarous names. No wild prancing or bad language. Put plainly, behave like a gentleman and treat God in a civilized fashion, then perhaps He might return the compliment graciously. *Toujours la politesse!*

The best time to begin the operation, says Abraham, is just after Easter. (Strange he does not say Passover until later in the book as a kind of afterthought.) This is presumably because of increasing light and fertility throughout Nature, and also because warm summer days and nights are helpful to peaceful meditation. Therefore, the six months season would be roughly from sowing to harvest time, which is symbolically sound as well.

Training begins by early rising just before sun-up, ablutions, than a prayer-meditation session in the Temple. The lamp is lit and perfumes burned in the censer. Abraham's formula for incense is the straightfoward one used in churches today, and the same incense is burned throughout the whole operation. No hallucinogenic additives of any kind are incorporated. Just plain olibanum, storax, aloes wood or cedar, rose, and citron are all that Abraham thinks necessary, though he does suggest burning rather large quantities of it. He also believes in using "Holy Anointing Oil" as body perfume associated with sanctity and dedication. This oil must be of the same formula as that which in olden times was used to mark out Priest-Kings from the rest of humanity. The recipe will be found in Exodus 30. Abraham here specifies a mixture of myrrh, cinnamon, galangal, and olive oil. It is interesting to note that this is employed to this day in anointment of English monarchs, and *it is this anointment* which is considered to bestow the monarchy upon them and proclaim their Royal Blood. The subsequent coronation is purely a civil law public confirmation of this fact.

For the two months of April and May, the candidate had to start taking his life seriously in hand, organizing it in what used to be called an "edifying manner." Everything had to be done in strict moderation, and a semi-retirement made from "the World." All forms of anger or argument had to be scrupulously avoided and temper kept well under control. Occasional sex was permitted during this period, but only between legally married couples, and not during the banned time of menstruation. Any unusual form of sexual intercourse was entirely forbidden.

The two months of June and July called for a real tightening up of spiritual security: Stop sex entirely. Give up going to business. See only few and very carefully selected close friends on rare occasions. Pray and meditate in the Temple three hours a day, at sunrise, noon, and evening. In between times, study scriptures or write suitable material. Take moderate exercise in a secluded garden. Eat ascetically, though moderate amounts of wine are permitted. No sleep during the day and rise before dawn. Regular bathing and extreme cleanliness. Almsgiving and works of charity are recommended.

The last two months of August and September demanded a maximum of really devoted discipline. Abraham does admit in general terms that one has to accomodate to the era and locality lived in. For example, if one lived in the country, the Temple could be in the middle of a wood where a stone altar might be raised of natural stones "without use of hammer" in the old way. A hut had to be built over this altar for shelter. However it was done, the really important factor was the privacy and spiritual selectivity during the "approach period," otherwise the operation would have little or no hope of success. During these final months, prolonged periods of prayer and some fasting is ordered, and it might be mentioned that rhythmic rocking back and forth from the waist is part of Hebrew mystical practice. It is called "dovening," and helps induce a very light state of hypnosis, especially if geared to the breathing cycles and chant beat.

Now we come to the climax of the whole affair—contact with the "Holy Guardian Angel" or higher part of one's own identity. This will be made some time around the Autumn Equinox or harvest time, and it begins with a three-day solemn fast. The initial approach is made by adopting a humbly sincere attitude in a sort of "Domine non sum dignus" spirit, admissions being freely made of the operator's shortcomings and fallibilities as a human being, then asking Divine permission to continue the action to a successful conclusion. A kind of "Prayer of humble access" petition.

This is where the mediumistic child-assistant comes into the picture. He is supposed to be no more than eight years old, a child of discreet parents, and suitably trained by the operator. He must not be the operator's own son, probably because such a child would be likely to say anything his father suggested for the sake of some hoped-for reward, or maybe because blood-relatives are seldom if ever suitable psychic reactors. The function of this child is to objectify the "Holy Presence" invoked by the operator, and confirm by clairvoyance or inner impressions that contact has indeed been made. It is not suggested for one moment that anything we might call psychic phenomena is likely to happen. No materializations, apports, telekinesis or other unusual events are promised. Everything remains on subjective and inwardly experienced levels, and has to be translated into terms of conventional consciousness. There are certainly no visual observations expected from the operator who wears a black silk veil over his face like a mask hanging below eye level and reducing visibility to almost nothing. The child on the other hand wears a light gauzy white veil producing an effect of somewhat unreal surroundings on the mind. Against such a fuzzy background enhanced by thick incense fumes, it is easy for a suggestive child to visualize imaginative pictures.

The psychodramatic action of the final stage in the Abra-Melim sequence, begins with the operator praying and prostrating himself at great length and with full emotional fervor. He is supposed to be negating his "Lower Self" aspects, so that the "Higher Self" or HGA (Holy Guardian Angel) will take control of his living. Meanwhile, the child should be watching the silver mirror on the altar and reporting audibly whatever he senses may be happening of spiritual significance. His job is to tell his hearer's ordinary consciousness what seems to be happening along inner lines, thus making a confirming link with both angles of awareness. Being technically "innocent" the child is presumed to speak truth put into his mouth by "God's Holy Angels" and theoretically he cannot be used by any evil entity. (Do we get an echo here of "Out of the mouths of babes and sucklings," etc.?)

These prayers and child interpretations go on for three days, during at least three hourly sessions per day. The operator's first humble attitude gradually changes as the HGA influence takes over, and finally the services of the child can be dispensed with altogether. In the end, a triumphant and transfigured operator should stand in a state of altered consciousness, alone and semi-ecstatic, holding direct communion with Divinity via the HGA linkage. In Abraham's own words,

> "You shall see your Guardian Angel appear to you in unequalled beauty, who will also converse with you and speak in words so full of affection and goodness that no human tongue could express the same. He will show you the True Wisdom and Holy Magic, and also wherein you have erred in your operation, and how henceforth you should proceed to overcome the evil spirits and finally arrive at your desired ends. He will promise never to abandon you, and to defend and assist you during the whole period of your life on condition that you should obey his commands and not voluntarily offend your Creator."

This is the obvious summit and highlight of the whole proceedings. The operator is supposed to spend a whole day in the company of his HGA. For the next three days he summons up "Evil Spirits" and demons, making them all promise to work with him for good purposes only which may be authorized by God for the benefit of humanity. In other words, he identifies his own worst and lowest propensities, personifies them, then says in positive terms that he intends to alter their energies into better courses of action and behavior. As a "Higher Magician," he means to accomplish the most spectacular change possible on this earth—the transmutation of Evil into Good. Beside that amazing alteration, the alchemical change of lead into gold would pale into insignificance. A mortal human being converting the nastiness in his own nature into sheer goodness and benificence altogether? Nothing else except *real* Magic could work that effect.

This "dealing with Demons" might seem something of an anti-climax, but it is the logical conclusion of an operation expressly designed for the purpose of human identification with the Divine Spirit of Life which animates our mortal manifestations and inspires us to seek such unification. If we ever hold the slightest hope of achieving this spiritual status, we shall have to harness and re-deploy all energies which might interfere with its process of perfection in ourselves. Whether or not we personify these adverse influences as "Devils" or anything else makes no difference to the fact we have to deal with them effectively and lastingly.

The important thing about this Abra-Melim system is whether or not it may be used in our times as a fundamental formula for finding our Divine Life-drive. Can it really be adapted as Abraham suggests? Principles are principles, and may be applied universally through their field of reference. Two and two makes four in any century and every language. There *are* such things as "universalities" which are sound through the whole of human experience. Presently, we shall come to analyzing the system and discovering if a spiritual process described in the fifteenth century may still be of service to we who are rapidly approaching the twenty-first.

Despite all that has been said, the Abra-Melim system has an odd reputation in our times. Many stories of failures with it abound, and warnings not to meddle with it are prevalent in some occult circles. This is scarcely surprising, and no one could have given more warnings to that effect than old Abraham himself. Again and again he kept stressing the ill-advisability of attempting his system unless it can be carried through as he specifies from one end to the other. So what seems to happen with modern people who make a mess of it? Tales vary from mental breakdowns and unaccountable "ill-luck" to bad health following failures with the Abra-Melim system. It is doubtful whether any dedicated occultist of modern times has fully and faithfully carried out *all* the conditions of this system to the last letter. Many have carried out *some* of it with mixed, if interesting, results. Some have been glad they did it, and others sorry. A few wish they had never started. Most are very reticent about effects on the process on themselves. All seem convinced of its authenticity, whether they got results from it or not. This is interesting because, as previously noted, most of the "solid" occult organizations of the West today are using adaptions or extensions of this Abra-Melim system insofar as they are encouraging students to make their own inner contacts rather than rely on someone else supplying them. In the next chapter we shall look at some of the basics behind these methods in our times.

## *Questions*

1. What is the essence of our Western Inner Tradition?
2. What constitutes the greatest threat to our Tradition?
3. What is the derivation of the name Abra-Melim?
4. What was the specification for suitable followers of the Abra-melim System?
5. What is the distinction between Qabalah and "Holy wisdom"?
6. Describe the oratory and vestments mentioned and comment thereon.
7. How are the months of the year allotted in the Abra-melim System?
8. Why was a child medium advised and how used?
9. Choose the nine most important sentences in this chapter.
10. How do you suppose that the Abra-melim system might apply in modern life?

# · 7 ·

# *Abra-Melim Again*

It may be puzzling you a little that if the Abra-Melim system seemed to produce such varied results, apparently not all of them good, why should reputable "Occult Schools" in the West adopt it as a basis for their training schemes? The reason was, and still is, because the method of self-training in the *outer* world while under supervision from the *Inner* levels of Life, *is* typical of the Western Way whatever the system is called. It always was. Ours is *not* an easy, effortless, and non-demanding way of Inner Life at all, and it never has been. That uncompromising fact has to be faced quite squarely. If our Inner Tradition was a sort of do-as-you-like, and have-what-you-please affair, with no need for discipline or control of conduct, *it would not be worth bothering with for a single instant.*

The plain facts of the case are that the only sort of souls really worth considering as active members and conscious partici- pators in the mainstream section of the Western Inner Tradition, are those who are capable of "taking themselves in hand" and conducting their own spiritual training with help received directly from Inner sources. This help is available to whoever earns it by making the right efforts. So what responsible "Occult Schools" of the West do, is supply students with materials for "making their own Magic," give them some starting guidance and moral support, perhaps provide a certain amount of fellowship, and then let them develop along their own lines. A good proportion will "drop out" for a wide variety of reasons, others will struggle along in a desultory way for a while before losing interest altogether, while a *very small minority* will continue working with determination, sometimes against considerable difficulties, until maybe after many unrewarding years they "come into the clear" and "glimpse the Grail" they have been seeking so long.

That is just the normal, run-of-the-mill expectation of average human behavior. The main thing is that all have gained *something* from their experiences to take out of this world with them. If some have hurt themselves in the process it could only have been those who deliberately disregarded the guidelines given or ignored the advice and warnings with a contemptuous conviction that such could not apply to *them.* In which case they taught themselves a lesson the hard way which could be better than all those offered them otherwise. Even those who supposed they "got nothing out of the Occult" were wrong. Had they said they got nothing they *wanted,* that might have been nearer the truth, but what *did* they want? If they expected to be given material advantages gratis and failed to find them on their doorsteps next day, then they deserved no more than that. Motivation is always something to check carefully before making any judgements on spiritual affairs.

The system outlined by Abra-Melim is admittedly hard, demanding, and challenging to the last degree. It is really a *ne plus ultra* in Western esoteric practice. Christian mystics would describe it as a frontal assault on the "Citadel of God." One could compare it with the sojourn of Jesus in the desert, or Gautama's retreat beneath his Bo-tree. A kind of "kill-or-cure" approach to Divinity. An "all-out" attempt to find one's own spiritual Self by applied stress-techniques. Mysticism in general has employed such methods for a great many centuries. Prolonged prayer, fasting, carefully applied physical and mental pain, oxygen deprivation, all these and other more dangerous methods are well known to modern psychologists as inducers of what are now called "altered states of consciousness" or just ASC's. It is well known that the most feared punishment in prisons today is solitary confinement in which a troublesome prisoner is locked in a small darkened cell and left alone with nothing but his own thoughts for prolonged periods on a minimum diet. Being confined *within the Hell of his own mind* is a terrifying experience for such a man. Conversely, hermits, or "solitaries" as they used to be called, have sought parallel conditions in caves or cells and lived blissfully in the tranquillity and peace of their "Interior Heavens." Could anything show more convincingly that "Heaven" or "Hell" are opposite ends of the same consciousness depending on the user, while what we term "Truth" must transcend them both?

To be confronted with one's own nature in an objective manner can be alarming in the extreme. That is what old time occultists used to call the "Dweller on the Threshold," a sort of fabulous and hideous monster which had to be faced and overcome before progress might be made towards higher spheres of the spiritual world. The "Dweller" was in fact a personification of all the very worst and nastiest side of one's own character summed up as an entity. It was the very opposite of the "Holy Guardian Angel." Put in simple language, we know that no human is entirely "good" or "bad" but a mixture of both in various proportions. Old mystics postulated that if you could put all the good together in one lump, so to speak, you would have what they termed an "Angel," while the "bad lump" would look like a "Devil." Simplistic maybe, but a convenience of consciousness nevertheless. What is wrong with trying to simplify confusing and pointless complications?

Even today in our most liberal frames of mind, we cannot deny that there *is* an undesirable side to human nature which we would alter if we could. Moreover, you will have to admit (if only to yourself) that there must be some degree of this in your own character. Otherwise, you would not be in *this* world at all. It may not be a nasty looking devil in the least, but something you might consider a lot worse—just a naughty and tiresome little imp. Whatever it may be, the thing *is* your "Dweller" and will have to be dealt with accordingly. Somehow it seems more shame-making and a lot less glamourous to put an imp in its place rather than "draw the Sword of Spirit" and fight the most fearsome Fiend threatening your very existence. Luckily for humanity, most of our Fiends turn out to be only imps in the end.

With the Abra-Melim system, a human soul is asked to personify the best side of its being as a Holy Guardian, then turn around and summon up the worst of its characteristics under the form of "Devils," all specified as faults, failings, and vices of human nature itself. Lastly these "Devils" are consciously commanded to obey the Angelic part of oneself in future, and carry out the "Will of God" acting through you. In other words, Do what *thou* wilt, or more simply, "God's will be done." That is the whole essence of the scheme. Make the worst in you serve the best in you and dedicate yourself to Divinity alone.

That precisely is what every ethical and religious system in the whole world has been trying to persuade humans to do since they first appeared among us. Whether it is called "Magic" or anything else makes no difference at all to the fundamental idea of improving our species towards a standard of perfection which can only be called spiritual because there is no physical equivalent. The Abra-Melim system is purely religious, devotional, and mystical to a very high degree. It is an intensely individual affair, however, and belongs to no Orthodox or conventional faith whatever, being an immediate and intimate relationship between creature and Creator on an "I-Thou" basis, using the "Guardian Angel" archetype as a symbol of consciousness common to both states of Being. Whoever "Abraham the Jew" was his book was a brilliant piece of psychology throughout. As religion, it stood no chance then, because thinking people had had enough of religion in those times. Religion then only stood for persecution, prejudice, and a lot of other wrongs on this earth. Call the system "Magic," however, and it might appeal to a number of independent and opportunity-seeking individuals looking for Light among inner lines. Perhaps it was a pity it never found its way into print before the nineteenth century. However, it had parallels elsewhere, and twentieth century occultists have found it useful.

What the system amounts to is living entirely towards a single Life-aim and negating everything likely to hinder or prevent that purpose. This means putting all power into one point and focussing every force in oneself at a single target, becoming, as it were, a laser for Divine Light and concentrating a cone of Consciousness into one concept. It was once put, "Seek first the Kingdom of God and His rightness, so that all else necessary might be added." Those able to live something along those lines might be able to work the Abra-Melim type of Magic, and others would certainly fail. That is the decisive factor. Do we, or do we not have such a need for Divinity in our own natures that we are willing to live solely for that one end during half a single year of one incarnation? That is the "Abra-Melim Question" to be answered before the system should even be considered.

Taking an average lifetime as maybe fifty years, six months would be one per cent. Is anyone prepared to devote one solitary percent of their lives entirely, wholeheartedly, and exclusively for the sole purpose of coming to conscious contact with their own Immortal Identity? That is what the Abra-Melim system implies. Surely, however, it might be "spread out" over a number of years on a simpler and easier scale providing its principles are observed throughout. That is what some of the Western Occult Schools have tried to do, and it would seem successfully on the whole. One percent of a day is slightly less than 15 minutes. Dedicate that much exclusively to spiritual ends, and it would work out over a lifetime if the organizational lay-out is effectively managed.

After all, the requirements are simple enough in themselves, too simple, in fact, to attract much attention from unsuitable people. Only those likely to make good with them will recognize instinctively their solid spiritual value. First, the candidate has to measure up to quality standards which most people have to some degree, but there is an important proviso. This is a determination to continue with this system in principle for at least the remainder of this incarnation once it has been commenced. There must be no thought of abandonment or desertion in favor of maybe more flamboyant procedures or exotic and alien attractions. Whatever else may be undertaken in addition, the basics of this system have to be persevered with, no matter how unrewarding they may seem during dull or adverse periods of living. So what is the least a candidate for the Abra-Melim system can commit himself to apart from other interests in Life? Let us list the requirements and see:

1. Regular and constant periods of prayer-meditation at morning, noon, and night. This need only take seconds if deeply sincere enough.

2. Develop and practice the ability of thinking and acting directed at Divinity straight from the heart in simplest and fullest terms.

3. Learn how to insulate one's sense of identity from all adverse and distracting influences. Stay entirely within the "Magic Circle" of one's self-selected system and reject temptations to wander aimlessly or wildly outside it.

4. Dedicate even a minimum of personally controlled space entirely and solely to HGA aims. This may be anything from a whole room as a Temple, to the smallest corner, or the space of a thumb nail on one hand. Use of such space should be made only for its dedicated reason.

With only these few factors quite a lot is accomplished. Time-Space-Event components of Cosmos are intentionally linked in line with the highest Life-aims, perhaps only to a small degree, but enlargements can always be made. Next, the good habit of dealing with Divinity in oneself clearly and comprehendingly is formed. Then comes a steadily improving type of "screening," giving spiritual protection in this world while we work on inner levels developing awareness and a sense of identity as more than a mere mortal human.

Carl Jung describes this as the "individuation process" but it was described a lot earlier and more succinctly at Delphi as "Know Thy Self." All the privacies and procedures of this system are designed solely for the purpose of approaching individual spiritual status by one's own particular Path. They were the limitations which make manifestation possible in the midst of them as it were. To use Tree of Life phraseology, they are the skilled pruning resulting in good fruition and healthy seeds for future planting.

Modern youngsters might describe this as "doing your own thing," but they would be well advised to take notice of what old

Abraham has to say about hallucinogens which were prevalent in those days, too. He makes disparaging and dismissive remarks concerning an experience of his own which he had when he was young at Lintz. He admitted trying the effects of "witch-balm" or "flying-ointment" which he got from a girl "pusher," but remarked that he had what would now be called a "bad trip" and "felt as if I were waking from a profound sleep with great pain in my head and deep melancholy." He noted that he and the girl had entirely different visions, and was not impressed when he made a veracity test on her, so he concluded, "This was but a simple dream and the ungent merely caused phantastic sleep. Later she told me it was given her by the Devil." That is to say the girl got it from her "coven leader" who sometimes assumes that title today.

All accomplishments in the Abra-Melim system have to be made entirely by individual efforts and intentions. Apart from the spiritual stronghold of the Temple, the only significant artificial aid is an incense-laden atmosphere and a pungent body-perfume. Scent of any kind is a basic liberator of our deepest instincts and oldest reactions. Moreover, it is the "Sacred King" scent which was utterly forbidden to any other than a consecrated priest or someone whose life was totally dedicated to Divinity. There were very strict rules about this in Exodus 30, which makes one again doubt the entirely Jewish provenance of this manuscript. Genuine Jews would have regarded it as blasphemous to prepare and use such an oil on their own persons in defiance of the Scriptures. Anointment with the special "Sacred King" oil was a drastic dedication to make. It meant placing one's entire life unreservedly in the hands of God as an absolutely willing sacrifice. *It still does* if accompanied by sincere intention.

As an aid to concentration, only a simple reflecting surface of silver is used, though of course any other such device would serve. Be it noted that though the light spot would tend to concentrate attention, the drifting clouds of incense would have the opposite effect of dispersing it. Between those extremities a "central clearway" has to be sought. All Abra-Melim practice comes back to "Middle Way" procedures in the end, and has to be done by pure control of consciousness itself.

A major discrepancy we should note between original and modern "Abra-Melimism" is the employment of a child psychic. That would not be encouraged by any reputable organization today because of possible effects on the child's developing mentality. Therefore if any independant observation of the actual operation is positively needed, it would have to be made by some adult associate of suitable ability, and they are more than difficult to find. The presence of such a person does *not* assist the spiritual side of the process at all, but only supplies confirmatory support of what the operator should be feeling in himself anyway. In any case, the child-companion was only supposed to be there long enough to recognize the actual "Presence" of a "Higher Intelligence." He was dismissed before the operator met his "Angel," and of course was not present at any of the "binding of Devils" which followed the ceremony during subsequent days. There the modern mage is on his own entirely.

As regards spontaneity of practice and "making up one's own Rites," modern people are very much in agreement with Abraham. Given a general sort of pattern, occult students today are strongly encouraged to design their own psychodramas. In fact, it is difficult to obtain workable ritual scripts other than those intended for formal usage among members of definite organizations. These are of no value at all to non-members of such bodies, and besides which, what Abra-Melim calls for is *original creative effort,* invoking very deep levels of awareness within practitioners. Every single thought has to be dredged from the very bottom of one's being and not just skimmed off the top of one's mind as is so often the case with routine rituals.

Withdrawal from the world and insulation from ordinary human contacts needs careful evaluating in our times. It is obvious that spiritually sensitive people should have some kind of built-in protection against the adversities of modern psychic atmospheres. Without protection of that nature, a really sensitive soul would be driven stark raving mad through intense suffering. Full exposure to radiation from certain kinds of humans can be just as damaging as an overdose of gamma or any other lethal rays. Had you realized that? Yet we cannot live permanently in a lead-lined shelter. Nor can most of us shut ourselves up in the seclusion of some cosy little sanctuary cowering behind battalions of convenient Guardian Angels. There has to be a compromise enabling us to live in this world while enjoying the same spiritual security as if we were elsewhere. This most important ability is something to be acquired and developed within the framework of "Abra-Melim up to date."

Actually, it can be quite helpful to live without a lot of the pressures coming from the mass-media of TV, radio, newsprint, and the other intrusions directed at us from questionably motivated sources. If we really mean to open up inner lines leading to higher levels of Life, then we must be prepared to close down much of the useless and harmful cacaphony which deafens and depresses us during our ordinary earth-experience. Dealing with this problem is a high priority matter for modern practitioners of the sacred magic of Abra-Melim. Not everyone is in a position to live in a secluded and secure place, and modern magical methodology is much needed for safeguarding those who cannot very well avoid exposure to the harmful effects of our mechanized pseudo-civilization.

Once the practitioner of this system has reached a point where he feels reasonably certain that the Good Angels of God are indeed on his side, and he can have some confidence in guidance from spiritual sources, his last job is to confront the demons of his own nature and subdue them with an intention of "True Will." We hear a lot about exorcism in these days with publicity-seeking priests boldly banishing reported evil entities from various localities, but how many people are prepared to banish the devils from the depths of their own natures? Nobody likes admitting they keep demons in their basements, and would much prefer to think they got in there accidentally or were sent by an ill-wisher. That would supply an unjustified ego-boost they would secretly enjoy. Now, however, the magical worker who has had the courage to face his inner realities and find that he *does* have something God-like in him, has also to realize that if this is true, he must also have present its complementary opposite or what used to be called "the Devil."

Modern people do seem to have a singular fear or dislike of admitting a nasty side to their natures, which is really ridiculous, because all humans must have *some* element of the undesirable in them. A modern Abra-Melim worker has to put himself through the same process as his predecessors. He must identify and call up his "Inner Demons" one by one, then objectify them and make it clear and conscious which side of himself he means to be the master of his life from that point on. He can think of this any way he pleases, but there is no denying it is a first class piece of psychotherapy if properly carried out.

The method by which Abra-Melim advised practitioners to summon the "Evil Spirits" and obtain their "Oath of Obedience to the Divine Will" was most interesting. The Demons were supposed to approach the door or window of the Temple but remain outside on the terrace or place reserved for them. The Temple itself was regarded as a Magical Circle. When summoned, the Demons had to wait until the magician extended his Rod or Staff toward them through the opening, then they were to touch the end of it and make their oath or promise thereon. What is particularly significant about this is that it was an ancient custom, particularly among Semites, to swear the most binding promises to someone while placing the right hand on or above the man's phallus. Here we have a symbolic substitute for that act.

Abra-Melim (or Abraham or whoever) believed in summoning the worst Devils first, then working down through the Hierarchy of Hell to the lowest grades of merely irritating imps. In his book, the Four Chiefs of Hell were: LUCIFER (The Light-Bearer, i.e. Darkness), LEVIATHAN (Crooked Serpent), SATAN (Adversary), and BELIAL (Wicked One). These are all general classifications of ignorance, malice and evil. Medieval magicians made enormously long lists of demons, each specializing in a particular type of nastiness just as their opposite numbers, the Angels, specialized in specific types of goodness. Nowadays our psychiatrists do much the same thing without clarifying the problem any better than the magi who described devils in terms of their ill-effects on humans.

The author does not imply for one moment that contact with the HGA alone will be sufficient to keep all the devils docile and amenable forever afterwards. To the contrary, he warns that one has to be constantly alert for signs of disobedience or insurrection later on. He makes a very telling comment about keeping the firmest control of one's own affairs, and never allowing such spirits to influence individual judgement and responsible decisions. He puts it this way: "Command them never to say anything to thee themselves, but only speak when thou shalt interrogate them, unless it be to warn thee of matters concerning thine advantage or hurt. *For if thou dost not limit their liberty of speech they will tell thee so many things that they will completely overcloud thine understanding and thou wilt not know what to believe so they could make thee fall into irretrievable error.*"

He goes on to warn readers that this type of spirit will find all the weak points of human nature and use them for hurting or ruining people if possible. As an example he says, "If they know that a man is given to vanity and pride, they will humiliate themselves before him and push that humility into excess and even idolatry. Such a man will glory herein and become intoxicated by conceit, and the matter will not end without his commanding them some pernicious thing of such a nature that untimely therefrom will be derived that sin which will make man the slave of that demon."

The mainstream influence of modern Western Occultism would agree with this 100 percent if rephrased in the psychological jargon of our times. It is only too easy for one part of the psyche to deceive another with the full collusion of the latter. There is a fatal part of ourselves that *wants* to be deceived all the time by enjoyable or entertaining deceptions. A lot of that is harmless enough and does little damage, but if malicious motivation is involved that is a different matter entirely. Most of the malice in this world reaches us from other humans, but there *are* such things as "Evil Spirits" in the sense that certain classes of non-incarnate Intelligence are "anti-human" mostly because our respective Life-energies conflict when brought into contact. If they are a danger to us, so are we to them if we but knew how to enforce our energies properly. That is something for us to learn from our "Guardian Angels." However, there is no need to start worrying unduly about "Devils from Outer Space." The ordinary Inner ones we have to deal with by the Abra-Melim or any other Magical systems will be quite sufficient for a normal human consicousness.

The last section of the manuscript is the "sprat to catch the mackerel." This is a series of "Magic Squares" of the acrostic type like early crossword puzzles. They were, in fact, the forerunners of modern ones. They had a great reputation in the Middle Ages as talismans, and the Abra-Melim ones were said to attract wealth, power, good fortune, etc., in addition to repelling ill-luck, destroying enemies, and working other wonders at will. Owners were told on no account to use them without permission from the HGA, and they would be worthless without the six month preliminary work anyway. If rashly employed they would only bring bad luck instead of good. Heavy warnings about this were given.

Here the hidden implications are that if such unworthy motivations can persuade anybody to live for a whole six months in what would once have been described as a saintly manner in order to achieve those particular ends, *then the entire point behind the Abra-Melim operation would be demonstrated beyond doubt.* Our worst "Devils," (in this case greed and lust for power) can co-operate in letting us live a life dedicated to Divinity *and* supply us with the energy to do it, providing *we* pay *them* off in "Fool's Gold" in the end. We have to learn how to "be-Devil the Devil," as it were, in other words, play their own games back at them and win.

The author has a somewhat sobering thought to say at the end of his magical operation. It is this: "Often the secret judgements of God permit disgraces, hinderances, infirmities, and other vexing incidents to happen to mortals, either to wake them from lethargy wherein they do not know their Creator, or to give them opportunity by affliction of increasing their merits. Therefore it is always best to govern yourself by counsel of your Holy Guardian Angel. If thou considerest maturely what are the essential parts of this operation, it is first needed to live in a truly edifying condition of modesty and retirement from this world. Solitude is the source of many blessings such as opportunities for prayer and avoiding evil conversations and occasions of sin, to *live in oneself,* and become accustomed to continue a life of such regularity. The pleasure and contentment thou shalt enjoy when thou art possesor of this Science will be so great that thou wilt despise all amusements, excursions, riches, and every other thing however attractive such may be. There is nothing more in this world we should desire so much as this true Science, neither is any more difficult to achieve, because one often dieth before attaining its entirety."

A surprising devaluation of merely material pleasures by an authorship which has been previously promising powers over all of them! Again one questions that authorship on account of the phrase "occasions of sin" which was a typically Catholic Christian theological expression. The old theory that God permitted the Devil to tempt and test humans to the extremity of their endurance in order to bring out the best or worst in them is a familiar theme. Old time initiatory Temples put their candidates through very severe ordeals for the same reason. Hence the clause in the Lord's prayer "Do not put us to the test" (lead us not into temptation). Those Temple tests were real ones and not just symbolic as they are today. Candidates who failed, *died,* and their deaths were considered as part of their Life-experience to be continued another time. Modern people who live as if death were the end of *everything* find this almost impossible to comprehend. They can believe that other people may have thought that way once, but they somehow cannot accept their own immortality to such an extent. One wonders why not. Can it be because they do not want to exist any longer than they have to, and if so, again, why?

You should be able to see by now why most of the "rationalistic" modern Western occult teaching schemes are adaptions of the Abra-Melim system. They more or less make you face yourself *and then do something about what you see if you don't like it.* They encourage you to exorcise your own devils, and discover in the process that you *do* have an immortal side to yourself which will and does survive the death of every mortal body you may ever inhabit. They don't lie to you and pretend that everything in your garden is going to be wonderful, and you are going to be so rich and successful you won't know what to do with it all. If they are genuine, they tell you nothing but the truth. Life is *not* easy. It is hard and difficult, but it is worthwhile and has a definite purpose which lies between God and yourself. It is *death* which is easy, but you are needed to *live* in this world and engage in the "Great Work" if you are to be of the slightest use to God, your fellow-men, or yourself.

It is so easy today to laugh at the ideas of medieval magicians, but surely no serious soul can laugh dismissively at the Abra-Melim spiritual system which proposes that human souls should confront their stark selves stripped naked in the Light of Truth and live to tell the tale (to themselves only) afterwards. No one *dare* laugh at such a revelation. It is too significant for any sort of flippancy. Only a God could truly see anything funny about humans as they are now. Nothing but the *God in yourself* has the ability to be amused at human antics because *only* that Divine type of consciousness is able to look from one life to another, see the connection through them all, and enjoy what can only be described as a "Cosmic Joke."

It has often been said that the Path of an Initiate in the Holy Mysteries is the loneliest on earth. That is true because it is an individuation process during which you become increasingly conscious of your own uniqueness and responsiblity *as a participator* in the Divine Plan for Perfection. It was once said that "unless a man be born again he cannot enter the Kingdom of God." Real initiation has always been described as a "second birth," for that is literally what it amounts to. You have to leave the close comfort of a womb which is symbolized by your being "part of the mass" among other humans, thinking their shared thoughts, and needing no particular efforts to support yourself on spiritual levels because you are no more conscious of them than the embryo in its mother's womb knows what is happening in the external world. Eventually however, there comes a point where you need to be "born" by pulling yourself free from dependence on all this and stand (if somewhat shakily) on your spiritual equivalents of feet and learn how to *be your Self* as a soul and spirit in your own right. Sooner or later you have to hear a summons which amounts in modern language to, "Come out of that womb, and help us get on with the Work." It needs a lot of courage to answer that call, and even more to become one of the chosen few survivors from the many who risk a reply.

What is this mysterious "Great Work" or Magnum Opus which occultists mention quite casually without always realizing its full implications? It was originally an alchemical expression meaning the process of perfecting base metals into gold. It means a lot more. The word "Great" stems back to the root "Maj" from which Magic or the "Great Art" derives. So the real "Work" is the greatest transmutation of all time—a microbe into a Man, and Man into a Magnaspirit; Macrocosm and Microcosm interacting through a common Life-consciousness. That is the "Magic" not only of Abra-Melim, but of everyone consciously participating in the Perfection-process of our human species in particular, and all other Life forms in general. So let us learn a little further how to continue this Greatest of Works in the Western Inner Way.

## Questions

1. How do reputable training systems of our Secret Tradition work today?
2. What do you understand by an ASC?
3. What is the "Dweller on the Threshold"?
4. Sum up the Abra-melim system in short and comment.
5. What do you understand by the HGA?
6. What is the significance of anointment?
7. How would you attempt a self-exorcism?
8. What were the "Four Chiefs of Hell"?
9. Choose the ten most important sentences in this chapter.
10. Comment on the "Path of an Initiate"?

# · 8 ·

# *The Mysteries of Melchizadek*

$\mathbf{Y}$ou should realize by now that the end-aim of the "Secret Spiritual Tradition" of the West is to promote you through a long system of training and experience into becoming your own "Priest-King" mediator of the Mysteries. This is often known as the "Melchizadek" process, because of an early scriptural reference to a Priest-King of that name. It comes from two Hebrew roots MLKI TzDQ (Melki Tzaddiq), meaning King (or Ruler) of Righteousness. To this day Hebrew "holy men" are known as Zaddikim—those living rightly. It signifies one who rules himself rightly, since right was associated with the principle of Good, and the left with Evil on account of the Solar Path of Light around this planet. There is very little in the Bible about this legendary figure. The first reference is Genesis 14:18:

> "And Melchizadek king of Salem brought forth bread and wine, and he was the priest of the most high God. And he blessed him and said: Blessed be Abram of the most high God, possessor of heaven and earth. And blessed be the most high God which hath delivered thine enemies into thine hand; and he gave him tithes of all."

Then there is the verse from Psalm 110 which says:

> "The Lord hath sworn, and he will not forswear, thou art a priest forever according to the order of Melchizadek."

Finally a few cryptic verses from Hebrews 7:

"1. For this Melchizadek, king of Salem, priest of the most high God who met Abraham returning from the slaughter of the kings and blessed him;

2. To whom Abraham gave the tenth part of all, first being by interpretation King of righteousness and also of Salem, which is King of peace;

3. Without father, without mother, without descent, having neither beginning of days, nor end of life, but made like unto the Son of God; abideth a priest continually.

4. Now consider how great this man was, unto whom even the patriarch Abraham gave the tenth of the spoils.

15. And yet it is far more evident: for that after the similitude of Melchizadek there ariseth another priest,

16. Who is made, not after the law of a carnal commandment, but after the power of an endless life."

Another name for Melchizadek was Adonai Zedek, meaning "righteous Lord," and he was supposed to have given Abraham the "coats of skin" made for Adam and Eve which were once stolen by Ham. Esoteric tradition also links him with the symbolism of the beehive and asbestos. He has become a "Grand Master" figure in several schools of Western Mystery practice much as Hiram Abiff, chief mason-designer and metal worker of King Solomon's Temple, has become a Grand Master personification for modern Free Masonry. The Melchizadek Archetype is chosen by those schools which follow the ideas of the "Sacred King" and Sang-Real system. In some Christian churches, the old "Agony" type of crucifix depicting a tormented and dying or dead Jesus, is being replaced by the "Melchizadek" cross, which has the *resurrected* Christ robed like a Priest-King with crown and stole, his arms outstretched with hands in the blessing attitude.

Now why should this particular character be chosen rather than another, and what is a "Grand Master" (or Mistress) *for* in any Mystery? It is specifically an *exemplar* image for presenting symbolic suggestions as to character or behavior on which to model one's own self-structure. It is a type rather than a personage, which is supposed to be representative of the sort of soul which humans who are aiming in a particular direction of spirit would like to become. There is no implication at all that people should attempt to make themselves into rubber-stamp copies of such an image, but only model themselves along the lines of whatever principles are being typified.

For instance, Hiram Abiff was chosen as a Grand Master figure in Freemasonry because he was a master-craftsman in metal-casting and construction, and what we might now call an "ideal boss" type. It was he who supervised the casting of the two Pillars. In Masonic tradition he was murdered by three blows from three assassins in truly symbolic style. The first blow was to the throat with a two-foot rule, the second with a square across the heart, and the final one with a gavel on the head. In other words, first prevent free speech with rules and regulations, then strike a blow against sentiment and feelings by rigid conformity, and finally suppress original thinking by sheer force of compulsion! After the evildoers have been duly detected and executed, Hiram's body was dug up and resuscitated by the Grand Master King Solomon aided by twelve brethren. So here we have a traditional Victim, a good man, slain by wicked ones but restored to life by a superior spiritual power in order to continue serving the Cosmic Cause for which he was willing to die. A straightforward Life-Death-Rebirth drama.

We can see perhaps why Hiram Abiff was chosen by the Masonic system as a "Master" figure. He was not himself a king, being the clever son of an ordinary widow of the tribe of Napthali, but he was described as being "filled with wisdom and under-standing" which it should be noted are the heads of the Pillars on the Tree of Life. His two associate Grand Masters, however, were both Kings in their own rights, one being Solomon, and the other Hiram of Tyre. Thus, Hiram Abiff typifies the hard-working craftsman who by diligence and his own developed intelligence was worthy to rank with Kings and become an acceptable Sacrifice on behalf of his brethren in their common cause of spiritual freedom. He represented the type of man which the Masonic movement was trying to encourage—men of strong and sound principles who were prepared to become leaders in their professions, help their fellow-men, and sacrifice themselves if necessary in support of their beliefs, thus making themselves the equals of Kings.

The Melchizadek-figure of other Western Mystery movements is seen differently. He did not die and resurrect in a traditional Sacred King manner at all. He did not die because he had never been born in the normal sense, being "Without father and mother, without descent, neither beginning nor end." Consider this in conjunction with the text, "Before Abraham was, I AM." Also remember the quote about the Grail being attainable only by knights who knew not their own parents nor lines of descents. Melchizadek was therefore an Eternal Life concept of a constantly living Spirit, personifying or typifying the principles of priesthood and kingship in human nature. His death is not needed because he transcends it.

Thus the mythical Melchizedek represents the sort of soul that members of the Western Mysteries are expected to emulate, a soul who is right-living, can rule itself correctly, and serve as a priest for the "most high God." This is a broad category which looks as if it could cover many ordinary decent people until it is realized that the essentials of combined priesthood and kingship fused into a focus of consciousness are not exactly very common qualities.

How do we define "priest"? The dictionary definition is "one who officiates at sacred services; especially at sacrifices." It is in fact the element of sacrifice to Deity which constitutes the function of priesthood per se. Without such an element, no priesthood can possibly be valid. People may be described as "ministers," "pastors," or anything else, but never truly as *priests* unless they are capable of making dedicated sacrifices on behalf of their fellow-men in the service of Divinity.

Why should a Deity *need* sacrifices in any case? If a Deity *was* Omnipotent, then by implication It could take whatever It wanted at any time, therefore it would be technically impossible for humans to have anything a God could not take for Itself whenever It wanted. Except *one* thing (if it can be called a "thing"), the "Free Will" constitutent of human character. In esoteric doctrine, Man was "created in the likeness of God" by virtue of the gift of independent will in his own natural "Kingdom." Theologically, that was something God could not take from Man without automatically denying his own pledged Word—which would be unthinkable—*but,* there was nothing to prevent a human from using that very free-will to offer itself as a willing sacrifice to the Creator from whence it originated. *That* was the sacrifice expected of all who aspired to priesthood of the Melchizadekian order.

A primary question is *why* should a Creative Consciousness invent the idea of "free will"? There can be but one conclusion—in order to experience Its own Existence through all the individual "lesser lives" involved; for exactly the same reason we are alive at this moment—to become *ourselves.* Put in child-easy terms, the Great Consciousness or Macro-Cosmos, diversifies Itself through all orders of Life into uncountable units of Micro-Cosmos, so that by re-combinations of consciousness on their part, It expresses Itself as an Eternal Entity. As the *One* willed Itself to become *Many,* so must the *Many* will themselves to become *One* in order that Consciousness should circulate around Cosmos, and Life continue Its own Creation.

Now taking an ordinary soul of our species to be a mixture of human and Divine consciousness, the human part of this combination provides the Priest-component which is willing to sacrifice its ordinary will to that of Divinity. The Divine Life-factor offers the Kingship-element which wills that humans should be rightly ruled. Thus "Kingship" (or the Blood Royal—GREAL) is of God, and the "Priesthood" is of Man. When *that part of ourselves in God which is "priestly"* encounters *that part of God which is "Kingly" in us,* and the offering or sacrifice is exchanged between these extremities of Existence, then *the Grail is being gained.*

Put simply again, we as humans have to approach the "Presence of God" as priests with something to offer (our human "free will"), while the Divine Presence comes to us as a King or spiritual sense of Right Rulership in our lives. The action has to be reciprocal in order to work properly. This *is* the "Melchizadek process" of the Western Holy Mysteries. It is symbolically depicted in Figure 2, by the sign of the Macrocosm associated with special significance. At the apex of the Symbol is God, seen as diversifying until the base of Its triangle represents all humanity. At the nadir is to be found Man as *one* of those souls (in this case, *you*). By

Figure 2. The Sign of the Macrocosm

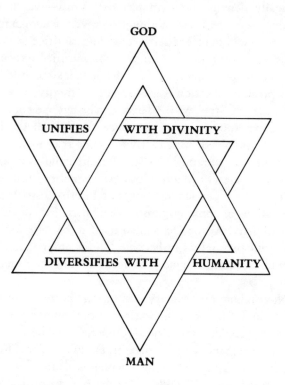

extending yourself toward Divinity in a *truly* priestly fashion, you are uniting with the Divine Will ruling the lives of *all* for the sake of a Single Consciousness. It will pay you to study this symbol carefully and meditate on its meaning.

Do note above all else that the "Mechizadek Principle" is not simply rulership per se, but *Rightful Rulership.* That makes all the difference and must always be clearly specified in your consciousness. Never think only about your "ruler-principle" because humans can be "ruled" in a sense by very *bad* principles. It is more correct to think about this as being *dominated* or *governed* by wrong direction and associate "rulership" with "Rightness" only, but we have to remember purely human interpretation of words which often confuses their once clear meanings. It was for that reason that Hebrews and others when referring to the "Kingdom of God," always qualified the principle of Kingship by saying "Faithful King," "Holy King," or simply "King of the Universe." It is very important to specify *what* Power we are inviting to rule our lives on earth.

We usually think of priests as offering sacrifices on behalf of other humans unable to do this for themselves. This, of course, happened all the time in ancient or modern Temples where sacrifices of some kind is the central feature of worship. Responsibility for such assumption of office rests on the shoulders of organized priesthoods who appropriated for their own convenience and aggrandisement what rightly belongs to whoever becomes capable of functioning on these levels by themselves. Establishment of exclusive, eclectic, and highly privileged priesthoods among official Churches in the West led to historical abuses of authority too well known for comment. It remained to what was left of the Mystery Schools to perpetuate the tradition of Priest-Kingship wherein ordination has to be earned through actual experience of the Melchizadek process as a fact of mystical life.

Let us be quite clear that there *is* a need in this world for an officiating priesthood on behalf of all who are incapable of fulfilling this function for themselves but would gladly do so if they were able. A true priest of any faith should be there to help and guide them into such an ability if he can, while making it perfectly plain what the spiritual situation is on inner levels. Even when a priest may be ceremonially officiating at a ritual presentation of a sacrificial act, participants should be uniformly engaged in following the entire action of inner levels exactly as if they were at the altar themselves. That is the only real way to work such a rite. Nevertheless, it has to be plainly understood that both priesthood and kingship are fundamentally natural abilities of a developing human soul and it is only through their practice that we shall ever attain anything like perfection as a Life-species.

Going back to the Melchizadek figure, consider the symbolic bread and wine factor. These are the sacrificial symbols of our Inner Tradition, signifying that we accept the rulership of Divinity within us and thereby "belong with the Blood." In the Christian interpretation of these Mysteries, bread and wine symbolize the body and blood of Jesus Christ, but in the Melchizadekian sense, *they symbolize the body and blood of whoever is freely offering themselves as a sacrifice to Deity.* It is the Priest part of a human being which is saying, "This is *my* body and *my* blood which I am offering entirely to God." It makes no difference how many participators there may be in this act, the fundaments are always the same. A human does not "eat a God," the God "eats a human."

Understanding this is absolutely vital in order to comprehend what lies behind the Mystery Tradition of the West. Everything else is interesting and incidental, but this is the central key to the whole spiritual structure, the Grail Factor, if you like. If you can grasp even an inkling of what is involved, it will lead you inevitably, if slowly, toward your Life-aim as a Western Soul. If you cannot follow the implications of this concept, or they do not invoke recognition responses from your inner depths, then you will have to continue prowling around the "Outer Paths" again until you *do* "pick up the scent" and point yourself in the right direction once more.

At a casual glance there does not seem much to understand. An ordinary psychologist might say, "This only means letting the more experienced part of your mind control the normal basic instincts of your body." An alchemist could phrase it, "This is the transmutation of your base lower nature into the Pure Gold of Spirit." Gold is God if you take the L away, and possibly speculate on the chemistry of such an operation. A fundamentalist could suggest "subjugation of Evil by Good." A Christian would explain it as "letting Jesus take charge of your life." A Theosophist might sum it up as "Higher Self controlling Lower Self." Perhaps a Buddhist would term it "absorbtion of Self by Not-Self." It is an alteration of human character and consciousness which is *one and the same thing* whatever it is called.

All faiths, systems, creeds, and codes which are concerned with helping humanity a little higher up the Ladder of Life have this Magical Change as their central theme in one form or another. Even the rankest and grossest materialist believes that he should be better off at the end of his life than the beginning of it, and if he isn't, then he has failed to achieve an objective. That may be the bottom rung of the Ladder, but it is a rung nevertheless. The overall summing up of every belief system in the world is that we are here to *change.* The hows, whats, whens, and other considerations are matters of speculation and experiment, but the solitary factor on which there is virtually universal agreement is that Life and Change go together as essentials of existence.

It is generally hoped that any alterations we make in ourselves will be for the better, but it is admitted that changes could also be for the worse. There are only two courses open for humanity, regeneration, or degeneration. Ultimately, comes Perfect Peace for the former, and extinction for the latter. While we live, we cannot stay still, but have to continue moving one way or the other. In the Holy Mysteries of the West, all encouragement is given to steady progression up the Tree of Life, according to the manner of Melchizadek, or by learning how to become a Priest-King by accepting responsibility for both functions in your own nature.

You should see by now that the Melchizadek approach is really the same one as the Abra-Melim system extended another way. It is merely a matter of terminology and variation of ritual. What will suit one type of developing soul is unlikely to suit another, so it is only a question of adaption to match necessities. Whether we make our archetype figure into a "Holy Guardian Angel" or "Melchizadek," or for that matter into their female equivalents, should make no difference at all to the issue at stake. It is always the underlying principles involved which are of the greatest importance, and the deciding factor in differing contingencies should be how those principles are best served. It should be noted, though, that the "Holy Guardian Angel" concept is a sexless one, although there is an esoteric teaching that these "Angels" are always of the opposite sex to the human they guide, and are projections of the female part of the psyche that is within each man, or the male part of the psyche that is within each woman.

There is no real reason, however, why the Melchizadek concept could not be equally accepted as an archetype by either human sex. Royalty and Priesthood are not the exclusive perogatives of males or females, but common to both. In early times, the Blood Royal always descended through the *female* line which is why there were sometimes brother and sister marriages such as in the case of Cleopatra and Ptolemy, so as to "keep it in the family." Despite the paternalism of the Semites, bloodlines to this day are transmitted through the mother. It was probable that the office of priesthood devolved mainly on men because it involved killing victims, and women were regarded as givers of life rather than takers. Also, in the case of large animals it needed masculine strength to make it a neat, quick, and effective act. If the sacrifice were human, it seemed more appropriate at the hands of men than women. None of this applies now, and in the case of ancient religions such as in Egypt where vegetable and floral offerings had supplanted animal sacrifice, priestesses officiated equally with their male colleagues.

Apart from these considerations, the "sacrifice" made in the Mysteries of Melchizadek, as they are sometimes called, is the same for any human being of whichever sex. Indeed, physical sex has nothing to do with a soul's offering the human side of its nature to the Divine Intention within it. Such an offering is technically made by anyone saying or thinking, "God's Will be done," but it is not *factually* made unless accompanied by an act of inner intention which authenticates it. In a way, the sacrifice is a complete act of "spiritual sex" by itself. The human "priest-part" of anyone may be likened to a feminine principle which freely offers itself to the masculine "king-part" as a act of pure Love. Symbolically, it is the Cup offering itself to the Lance in order to be filled with Royal Blood.

Orthodox Christianity has lost a great deal of force and significance by trying to conceal the old symbolisms of sex beneath pretty petticoats supposed to "cover decently" the facts of fertility and Nature beneath them. The older and so-called Pagan faiths which accepted biological behavior as an normal act of life, and saw Cosmos as the result of a gigantic sex relationship between the polarities of the Life-Spirit in Itself, were far more honest and credible. They did not make any mysteries of this, but took it for granted that it must be so. How Christianity expects followers to accept a "God-the-Father" concept without a complementary "God-the-Mother," and then affirm "God is Love," is a mystery in itself! Not unsurprisingly, the feminine side of religion in the West had to "go underground" and continue through some of the Mystery cults which did not always preserve it very faithfully.

Looking back at Melchizadek again, we note that he was described as King of Salem or Peace. This is about the oldest friendly greeting on earth. In the East, Salaam or Shalom, with a gesture to forehead and heart is an assurance of non-aggression. In the West it became *Pax* and the extension of a weaponless hand. More, it was adopted as the Western equivalent of Nirvana or Ultimate Life-aim as Perfect Peace Profound, sometimes shortened to P.P.P. especially by Rosicrucians. So Melchizadek as Ruler of Peace does represent the end-aim of existence—humanity and peace together at last forever more.

His odd symbols of the beehive and asbestos are apocryphal attributes. The beehive has always been associated with royalty and industry, and the symbiosis between Ruler (the Queen), and People (the workers), is surely a sign of One and All sharing a common consciousness for the sake of Life-continuance. Bees are also symbolic of Love, partly because they combine pleasure (the honey) with pain (the sting) and also because the honey was regarded as a "fertility food." Hence the word "honey-moon" or the month after marriage when honey was eaten mostly by the male to ensure his fecundity. We have to remember, too, that in old times before sugar was discovered, wild honey was the only natural form of sweetness. In many areas it became a "royal perogative" claimed by tribal rulers for themselves. Once it became known how to breed and keep bees, an important attribute of "old Royalty" had reached ordinary people.

The symbol of asbestos is not so straightforward. In olden times this was supposed to be the wool of salamanders or Fire-elementals and, of course, was fireproof. There was also a legend that it was a stone which was amazingly difficult to light, but if it once caught fire, no natural means could extinguish it. It could scarcely be both things at once. Since the word is derived from the Greek and signifies unquenchable or "un-put-downable," let us assume the symbology indicates the undauntable spirit needed to supply us with illumination throughout our Quest in Life seeking Eternal Peace. It represents the ever-burning Torch of Truth we are entrusted to bear through the "darkened Caverns of the Earth-

Mysteries" which will guide us to the Light of Deliverance at last. Then, too, there is the factor that asbestos is purified from any clinging dirt by fire, and the legend that sins staining our souls since they were washed white by baptism in water, must be purged by fire after death until we are clean enough to enter Heaven. The truly immortal part of us survives this "ordeal by Fire," and only the dross perishes. That is what the asbestos symbol is saying here.

These symbols are sound enough. We must indeed be industrious like bees, which once symbolized the coming and going of thoughts in and out of the mind, each busy on its appointed task of bringing back "food for thought" to store in the cells of the brain against later need. Moreover, it has to be "thought-food" capable of sustaining the Rulership of the "God-Spirit" within us so that It in turn will keep us fertile and active. Then, once we have kindled the "Sacred Flame" in our hearts, it must never be extinguished by the Darkness directed against it. It is all we have to guide us through that Darkness, and our spiritual lives depend on it utterly. If we can obtain the spiritual equivalents of those two symbols from the Melchizadek concept in our consciousness, we shall survive and learn how to live rightly.

The "tithes" or tenths connected with Melchizedek which he reputedly claimed from Abraham are more easily explained. Devoting only ten per cent of our lives to what Melchizadek represents, would be sufficient to secure our spiritual future. This works out at about two hours twenty minutes a day, which is a lot more than most people are prepared to spend in "soul-service," even if split into three sessions of forty-five minutes at dawn, noon, and dusk. Nevertheless that is the figure laid down. Still, there are other ways of soul-service than by prayers, meditations, and sitting still in silent contemplation. It can be extended easily into the ordinary affairs of everyday life and it need not be continuous but may be at intervals. So if three ten-minute sessions are spent at the morning, noon and night periods, that would leave one hundred and ten minutes to account for during the rest of the day. Or put things another way: ten percent of a minute is six seconds. That means we would need to devote six seconds out of every minute to the God-Concept within us. Can that possibly be done? Let us think about this a moment.

Look at your watch. When the second-hand or numeral comes to a mark, say slowly in your mind, "My Lord, and my God!" or anything of that length you would prefer. You will find this takes just about those six seconds. Now do some simple automatic action you would normally accomplish without thinking of anything in particular. Open a door, sit in a chair, pour out a drink, anything you usually "do without thinking." A lot of those things take you *more* than six seconds. Now do them again, while thinking of the Melchizadek-idea concerning the principles of Priesthood and Kingship *in yourself*. Do you feel the difference? If you didn't, keep practicing until you *do*. At first, you will find it helps to "make a formula" for the job, by reducing the idea to the *fewest possible words*. Maybe something like, "God Be: All Me." Anything like that which concentrates consciousness into a focus aimed at the Melchizadek concept. Eventually you should be able to use the same consciousness without any words at all.

Do you see where we are getting to? We are aiming at employing spare time which would be unused for anything else, as opportunities for making contacts with your highest Life-aims, that is to say, superimposing spiritual significance on the trivia of ordinary living, and thus converting them into symbols for the Livng God all around you. There is nothing new in this: most religions and philosophical systems have advocated it for centuries, though none have explained it fully, and it has become mostly a pious but pointless custom done without the special inner concentration which gives it any spiritual value. It is not worth doing at all unless you can put this into the practice whenever you do it.

It is possible that this mystical practice fell into disuse because of the cumbersome formula connected with it by various faiths. For instance, a pious Muslim is asked to say mentally, "In the Name of God, the Compassionate and the Merciful," a Buddhist, "I take refuge in the Norm," a Jew, "Blessed be God, King of the Universe," a Christian, "In the name of the Father, Son, and Holy Spirit." Each case uses up a few seconds of time devoted to Divinity. This may be very praiseworthy, but it is by no means always practical for modern people living in contemporary Western "civilization."

What seems to be needed is a "split second intensity"

concentration of consciousness which can be *focussed in a flash at fairly frequent intervals during normal waking hours at a constant rate.* This could be likened to the constancy of Inner Light needed to illuminate our Path of Progress towards Perfect Peace Profound, and that is indeed what it amounts to. Somewhere, some too easily shocked soul is possibly saying to himself, "But that would mean I should be thinking of God at most embarrasing moments. When I am emptying my bowels, for instance, or maybe during sexual sessions, or if I am laughing at a dirty joke or doing something ridiculous or anything else I wouldn't do in church." There is only one real answer to this kind of short-fall thinking, *why not?*

If the consciousness of the Life-Spirit is operative through you to *any* degree, then it has to operate *the whole time you are alive,* and not merely at special times and occasions when you feel like it. Though this consciousness will vary in focus and intensity according to natural rhythms, you cannot hide from it, turn it off, lock yourself behind lavatory doors, or pull the bedclothes over your head and pretend it doesn't exist. In any case, why on earth should you? It shares *all* your life, good, bad, or indifferent, and every experience you undergo is passed back to the "Universal Mind" for consideration. So why not simply allow your ordinary awareness to be not so much conscious *of* this Spriti, as *with* it? We shall be dealing with some of these implications in our next lesson.

## Questions

1. Define the word Melchizadek and comment on its significance.
2. How was Hiram Abiff supposedly slain?
3. What is the essential function of a priest?
4. What is the Melchizadekian sacrifice?
5. What does the bread and wine sacrifice mean?
6. Why was a mainly masculine priesthood instituted?
7. Define P.P.P.
8. Discuss the symbolic attributes of Melchizadek.
9. Choose the eight most important sentences in this chapter.
10. What percentage of your life do you think you should devote to your "Ultimate Idea," whatever that may be?

# · 9 ·

# *The Simplicity of Brother Lawrence*

$\mathbf{P}$ossibly one of the worst and most unjustified fears instilled into children of previous generations was that an easily provoked God watched them invisibly every moment of their lives, observing them mostly with disapproval. Early feelings of guilt and shame must have warped many lives. Yet if the teaching of an Omniscient Spirit had any truth in it, how was it possible for such a Spirit *not* to know what was going on everywhere in Its Existence? Any misunderstandings about this arose from the fact that humans constructed their God-concepts in the light of their own fallible opinions and prejudices rather than allow themselves to grow naturally by the Light of that Actuality Itself illuminating their consciousness from within.

They visualized an invisible God looking *at* them constantly as some kind of "spy-in-the-sky" might. They saw God as an objective Entity outside themselves with views of Its own about human behavior which might or might not be favorable to them. In very old times, the Sun and Moon were often thought of as the "Eyes of Heaven" keeping a perpetual watch over people on earth except during the dark of the moon, when evil might be worked on earth without the God (or Gods) noticing. Hence early Black Magic was mostly practiced during that period.

What they found difficult or even impossible to understand was that Divinity would have at least three ways of contacting them with Its consciousness. It could be aware *of* them through the eyes of other humans and agencies of inner observation. It could be conscious *as* them through their individual consciousness, and It could be conscious *for* them in terms of Its own Omniscience. The combination of these is beyond ordinary human comprehension altogether. As should be realized, the first two lines of consciousness are limited as viewpoints, but the last is not, because therein the Life-Spirit is being aware of humans *as integral to Itself*.

Are you capable of selecting any cell in your body, uniting your consciousness with it apart from all the others, and relating with it in a way that you might want it to relate with you, not as a huge lump of meat, but as a being like itself, which is part of a Great Whole? Could you confine your consciousness to the terms of its life spent in living and working for you? How would you like to be changed into one of your body cells for a while? If, for example, you changed to one of your own red blood corpuscles, you would live about five weeks of our time from birth to death. Allowing for averages, that would be some thirty-two days of our Sun-Moon time. Can you see some connection with the Tree of Life here? Do you see any comparison between the relationship of yourself to a body cell, and the Life-Spirit with you? There does seem to be some similitude, doesn't there?

Had you ever thought that what you are to the living cells of your body structure, the Life-Spirit of our Universe is to *you?* A "God" in each case. If you had never thought anything like this, then you had better start thinking of it *now*. That is why you are supposed to be "in the image and likeness of God." In this respect, you *are*. The Life-Spirit has a larger and differently constructed body than you have, but you (like God) are the Life-Spirit of countless lesser lives composing your body and sharing Life with you as you should be sharing your life with God, and who can guess if this is an infinite process? Your human body *is* a Universe of which you may consider yourself a sort of "apprentice God" inhabiting that body in order to "learn the trade," as it were, before you will be fit to live otherwise.

As mentioned in an earlier chapter, many of the old mystics claimed to despise their bodies as "sinful flesh" and ill-treated the poor things shamefully. They had utterly failed to realize their responsibility to look after and cultivate the "cell-consciousness" they had been entrusted with, or act in any kind of a Godlike manner. Missing the mark entirely, they believed their bodies were nothing but awkward animals and should be treated badly. Man, they said, had sinned the original sin, and so was condemned by God to birth and death in fleshly bodies. So what was the "original sin"? It was *the will to gain knowledge of how to become a God.* There was only one way to do that—*learn from experience.* Again, only one method lay open to us. That was to incarnate as the Life-Spirit in an animal body composed of individual living corpuscles, then learn how to behave with that as we would have *our* collective Life-Spirit treat us. If we ever wanted to "rise" in Life, we would have to "fall" first. There was no other way to Godhood except the hard way of beginning at the bottom and slowly working our way up. So here we are.

Perhaps you are going to say something like, "But what about all the perfectly horrible humans who behave brutally, badly, and savagely, destroying each other, pillaging the planet, and all the rest of it? Are they Gods, or could any God be like that? No human is a God, but all are "trainee Gods" to *some* degree. Who knows how many of those millions make the grade? Of the millions of sperms ejaculated during sex, only *one* develops into a human body. Out of millions of human souls, how many continue steadily from one incarnation to another, developing themselves a little more each time until they are ready to reach higher levels of Life and go on with the God-job from there? It seems fairly obvious that a very considerable number do nothing of the sort. Not that any life is ever wasted, because its energies are re-cycled through reclamation channels, but the entity which might have otherwise evolved is simply taken out of circulation and ceases existence as itself altogether.

There is nothing very extraordinary about this. No soul is ever wiped out of existence against its own True Will. It just does not intend or want to exist any more, so there is nothing the Life-Spirit *can* do except cancel it. That used to be called the "Sin against the Holy Spirit" for which there was no forgiveness. Well, not even the Holy Spirit can forgive what does not exist any longer. Are many souls likely to eliminate themselves from existence? Untold quantities for multiple reasons. It needs "Cosmic courage" to continue existing from one incarnation to another faced with the Ultimate Responsibility at the end of them. It is so much easier not to be, than to be.

Do you ever think about the incalculable millions of cells in your body which die out all the time and are replaced in order to keep you alive? They are part of the same Life-process you share with the Supreme Spirit. Why should you, or any other human, expect a Deity to concern Itself so closely with your affairs on earth if you (or anyone else) are utterly indifferent to the fate of millions of lesser lives supporting *your* Selfstate? Is it reasonable?

Here is something to think about. If you are allowed your measure of free will as a human soul, then so are the cells of your body on *their* level of Life. If they refuse to accept your will and "set up in opposition" to it, disease and malfunction result. What else is a cancer, but a "take over bid" by cells which refuse to recognize your rightful rulership over their tissue-territory and invade it with malicious intentions of grabbing it all for themselves entirely? True, they destroy themselves in the process, since you die and leave them with a disintegrating body which will not support them for very long as *we* reckon time, but for them it seems like many generations of living. It may seem a strange thing to say, but your health as a human is entirely dependent on how the cells of your own body accept you as their "God," and how loyally they will resist invaders and other adversaries entering their areas of life.

There is a great deal more of an analogy relating you and your body with the Life Spirit and Its Universe than you might think. If you have an elementary knowledge of biology this comparison should be clear enough. In a far fetched imaginative way, it might be as if a small spirit stood before God and said, "Please, Sir, I want to be a God too," and the benevolent but amused Deity replied, "Oh, do you? Very well then, let me see what sort of a job you can make of it. Here's a lot of little tiny lives for you to learn with, so it won't exactly wreck the whole Universe if you don't succeed, but for their sakes I hope you won't do too badly. Just remember one thing before you go. *Treat them the same way you think I ought to treat you,* but don't blame me for the way other humans treat you. Good luck!"

Looking around this world, we can easily see what humans are doing with their physical Universes. On the average most people do the best they can, but so many are behaving worse than badly. Apart from poisoning their systems with overloads of drink, drugs, and totally unsuitable foods, they unbalance their brains and unstabilize its emotional system until its constitution breaks down, and it rebels against such an incompetent and inconsiderate "God." Could any reasonable intelligence blame it? On the opposite side, there are those who treat their bodies with kindness and consideration, yet these still give trouble due to non-cooperation from cells refusing to harmonize with the "God-Will" of the whole organization.

It is obvious that no type of Universal Life can truly be called healthy or harmonious unless the True Wills of its individual units are able to relate rightly with the Single True Will of its Supreme Spirit. This state of balance should not exist through compulsion, but solely through what can only be described as Love because we have no other word to symbolize the condition of consciousness needed to establish the symbiosis of Human and Divine Life. The only possible relationship between Man and God which makes Life worth living for both is one of pure Love in the real sense of the word.

It is sad that our English word "love" has become so devalued in recent times as to signify little more than physical sex. The word had much greater meaning formerly, and indicated the deepest and truest union between human souls whether male or female. It was perfectly normal for men (or women) to say they loved each other without the slightest implication of homosexuality whatever. Love then meant a state of harmony, Life-sharing, soul-sharing, and a condition of common consciousness giving rise to the greatest sense of joy and increased identity a human could reach. Physical sex was only a reflection of this on Earth-levels like the light of the Moon is a much lesser reflection of the Sun, but welcome during the hours of darkness.

There is a nice illustration of this at the end of St. John's Gospel which often puzzles people who do not know the nuances of the text. The risen Christ asks St. Peter three times if Peter loves him, and Peter, who also seems to misunderstand, is a little hurt, but replies, "You know I love you." The point is that Jesus on the first two occasions uses the term "agape," meaning love in the deep sense just described. Peter replies with "philo," signifying love also, but in a much more mundane way as we might say admiration, friendship, or sincere respect. So the last time, Jesus appears to realize what is happening and uses the word "philo" himself, whereupon poor old Peter faithfully replies with his "philo" again.

Early Hellenic Christians were naturally familiar with the significance of this term and called their most intimate gatherings "Agapae" or Love Feasts, during which they were supposed to demonstrate their love for God and each other. As might be guessed, these got very much out of hand, and finished up more like a Witches Sabbat than a Christian congregation, so they dropped into disrepute. Nothing, however, can diminish the value of genuine Love rightly understood, and that Power or Energy alone is capable of uniting God and Man as a combined consciousness.

Thus, as a "Deputy God" you have to establish a Love-relationship with the Micro-Cosmic Universe of your body, as a "Fellow God" you have to love the "God-part" of other humans, and as a human being you have to relate with Love to the Macro-Cosmic Life-Spirit offering you Identity in Itself. There is nothing particularly complicated about this if you learn how to recognize the "Presence of God" wherever you direct your consciousness, and relate with that by releasing the Energy of Love from your inner depths. You might very well say that some people are unlovable, and so they may be—by you. Do bear in mind that you do not have to love tham *as people* at all. In fact, you could loathe them *personally* providing you are able to exchange Love with the Deity awaiting their attention. Remember also that you are supposed to be mediating Deity yourself in their direction. That is where your Melchizadekian "priest-part" comes into the picture.

Possibly one of the most notable attempts in the West to make this "Practice of the Presence of God" into a workable system was formulated by one Brother Lawrence of the Resurrection, an Alsatian Carmelite lay-brother whose real name was Nicolas Herman. He lived in the seventeenth century, and although he only wrote a few letters, and some notes were made of conversations with him, these are still well worth reading for the sake of their natural simplicity and sheer fundamental faith with no trimmings attached.

Most mystics are initiated on their particular Paths by some vision or revelation which gives them the impetus to continue thereon for the rest of an incarnation. In the case of Herman, nothing could have been simpler. At the age of eighteen, a leafless tree in winter attracted his attention and drew his thoughts to the amazing power behind Nature (God, to him) which would eventually reclothe that tree with leaves, flowers, and fruit every year for the rest of its life. In the words of his commentator, "This view perfectly set him loose from the world, and kindled in him such a love for GOD that he could not tell whether it had increased in above forty years that he had lived since."

Brother Lawrence was an ex-soldier who became an ordinary monk, and for a while he was acting as cook for the community, a traditional "bottom of the ladder" type of job then. Though he disliked doing kitchen work, he converted it into a means of "meeting God" through every menial movement and action. In his own words, "The time of business does not differ from the time of prayer, and the noise and clutter of my kitchen while several persons are calling for different things does not diminish my posession of GOD in as great tranquillity as if I were on my knees before the Blessed Sacrament." His commentator said, "His example was a stronger inducement than any arguments he could propose. His very countenance was edifying; such a sweet and calm devotion appearing in it as could not but affect the beholders. And it was observed that in the greatest hurry of business in the kitchen, he still preserved his recollection and heavenly mindedness. He was never hasty nor loitering, but did each thing in its season with an even uninterupted composure and tranquillity of spirit." A very good description of a man able to mediate a Divine influence for the benefit of those in contact with him.

In the course of his life, Brother Lawrence discovered that everything and anything encountered in this world could be used as a symbol which connected the consciousness of the user or beholder with the concept of Deity. To him, the utensils of his kitchen were sacred like the Church vessels, and he felt he was in contact with his God whatever he did, night or day. It may seem a little strange to non-Christian mystics, but Lawrence did not seem to see the God-Element of Life in himself very clearly, and he identified with his so-called Lower Self. At that period it was customary for Christians to regard themselves as very inferior beings confronted with the awesome might and majesty of their Creator, who was nevertheless merciful, and graciously generous through the Power of Love.

Typically, Lawrence says of himself, "I consider myself the most wretched of men, full of sores and corruptions, and who has committed all sorts of crimes against his King; touched with a very sensible regret I confess to him all my wickedness, I ask his forgiveness, I abandon myself in his hands that he may do what he pleases with me. This King, full of mercy and goodness, very far from chastising me, embraces me with love and treats me in all respects as his favourite. It is thus I consider myself from time to time in his holy presence."

Lawrence believed himself the utterly unworthy and totally undeserving recipient of Divine Grace from a King-concept he visualized as apart from himself, but whom he dared to approach with reverential love. He did not see a priestly part to his own nature because he had not been ordained as such by his Church. A very interesting point is that he never once claimed to have received any "special messages" from God as so many mystics do. His language is simplicity itself, and all he says repeatedly is that an almost constant sense of a Divine Presence in close contact with him is everything in Life so far as he is concerned, and he honestly advises others to try this for themselves. There is no doubt whatever about the man's absolute sincerity and integrity.

He does say that he "conversed" with God, though the term seems to be used in its older sense—to be conversant or on familiar acquaintance with, not necessarily verbal communication at all. If Lawrence did verbalize his inner contacts with Deity, he kept these entirely private and personal, *which is the correct procedure with any such mystical practice.* Spiritual intimacies are *not* for casual discussion or display and should be regarded as confidential. Brother Lawrence gives a rather revealing hint of this when he writes, "I find myself often attached to GOD with greater sweetness and delight than that of an infant at the mother's breast; so that if I dare use the expression I should choose to call this state the bosom of GOD for the inexpressible sweetness which I taste and experience there. If sometimes my thoughts wander from it by necessity or infirmity, I am presently recalled by inward motions so charming and delicious that I am ashamed to mention them."

When Lawrenece was nearly eighty, he had sifted his spiritual life down to its essential basics and wrote to another elderly friend, "GOD requires no great matters from us. A little remembrance of him from time to time. Lift up your hearts to him even at meals and when you are in company, the least little remembrance will always be acceptable to him. You need not cry very loud, he is nearer to us than we are aware of. It is not always necessary for being with GOD to be always at church. We may make an oratory of our hearts wherein to retire from time to time to converse with him in meekness, humility and love. Everyone is capable of familiar conversation with GOD, some more, some less." A few days before he died, he summed up his whole Life-view and wrote, "Let all our employment be to *know* GOD; the more one *knows* him the more one desires to know him. And as *knowledge* is commonly the measure of *love,* the deeper and more extensive our *knowledge* shall be, the greater will be our *love* and if our *love* of GOD were great we would love him equally in pains and pleasures. Let us seek him often by faith; he is within us; seek him not elsewhere."

This truly remarkable man had approached the very heart of the Holy Mysteries by a simple, straightforward, and perfectly plain Path. It would be greatly above the reach of average mortals in our times. The thing that mainly concerns us is his pointing out that people can make equally good contact with inner realities by means of the most commonplace things and circumstances as by the most sanctified sort of symbology. True, but what Lawrence failed to realize is that because *he* could do this did not necessarily mean that anybody else should find it just as easy. He greatly undervalued his rare ability. It takes an extraordinary type of soul to make so much of ordinary facilities. Most people seem to need very specialized conditions of consciousness and spiritual symbolism in order to establish any degree of relationship with Divintiy in themselves. Otherwise there would be no necessity for any magical exercises or workings at all. It takes a fair amount of work over many incarnations before souls are able to sail through Life above them all like Brother Lawrence. Still, it will do not harm and may bring a lot of enlightenment if we try some of his suggestions in the light of later knowledge.

We would suggest that you start by considering yourself a sort of "trainee God" undergoing a practical testing program. The first awkward question is, have you been treating your Micro-Cosmos as you hope a real God would treat you? Don't be stupidly severe with yourself and invent a lot of wickedness you haven't really got, but if you *know* that you have been ill-treating your little Universe or neglecting ordinary health routines or otherwise endangering your physical and mental welfare unnecessarily, then you really will have to take yourself to task on this account. The least you can do is apologize to your "mini-cosmos." Send currents of consciousness down through your bloodstream and cellular tissue with the message that you *do* care what happens to them all and will try to look after them better in the future.

Talk to the Life-Force circulating through your body in simple "Brother Lawrence" language. All you have to do is formulate the consciousness in your head, and your bodily bloodstream and nervous system will take it from there right on down to every cell, translated into terms they can comprehend on their own level of living. If you like, think of yourself as being the commander of an enormous vessel speaking to all crew members through the P/A system. However you would like God to communicate with you, speak to the cells of your human tissue in the same ways. Assure them of your concern on their behalf. Thank them for what they are trying to do for you or what they have done in the past. Chasten them if they are giving you trouble, but at the same time tell them that you are trying to help by following medical advice or whatever else you may be doing. What matters most is that you communicate *consciously* with your Micro-Cosmos, realizing that your will for it is analogously what the "Will of God" is to *you*.

The beauty of this exercise is that you need not take up any kind of contemplative position or shut yourself up in silence anywhere. It is something you do while you are engaged in the ordinary business of living. Walking around, eating, drinking, doing housework, even when going to the toilet or having a bath. Why should you hesitate to think of God when your body is acting in the natural ways it was designed to do? Surely you can think something like, "If I could get rid of my spiritual detrius as easily as I am voiding this physical waste, I might be in a better state of spiritual health altogether." Writing to a soldier friend, Lawrence remarked, "Think of him as often as you can, especially in the greatest dangers. A little lifting up of the heart suffices. One act of inward worship though upon a march with sword in hand, are prayers which however short are nevertheless very acceptable to GOD and far from lessening a soldier's courage in occasions of danger, they best serve to fortify it. Think of GOD the most you can and accustom yourself to this small but holy exercise, nobody perceives it and nothing is easier in the day than to repeat often these little internal adorations."

Earlier non-Christians or mystics saw nothing wrong with thinking of Deity during sexual intercourse. In fact they believed this enhanced the act to the height of its possible enjoyment, lifting its inner content into an experience of Deity Itself. For them it became an entirely sacramental act of the highest order, completely transcending the purely physical and reproductive side of the process. Though the Gnostics had ideas of Christianizing this practice, they were condemned by the opposing opinions of the primitive Church and sex was demoted to functional levels for continuance of the species alone. The sacred side of sex was maintained in secret by many Mystery Temples, but it remains to this day a difficult and easily misused doctrine to teach unprepared and irresponsible souls who are unable to understand its aspects above ordinary levels, so it is therefore either avoided as a topic altogther, or else left open for individual discovery.

Once you can feel some sort of rapport developing between yourself and your Micro-Cosmos, try the experience of looking for any signs of Divinity in or among other humans. It is best to seek this in total strangers. Do no more than walk about the streets of any city or large town during busy periods and examine the faces of those you encounter in the streets. A pair of dark glasses will help hide the fact that you are staring at them, but may obscure details which could be meaningful. It is better to keep observation discreet by moving the eyes alone and maintaining the head steady. Quite apart from physical appearances, try to get the feel of the people from interior angles, but *be careful* how far you open yourself up for this experience. If you find it getting unbearable, "shut down" at once and assume a "normal" state of awareness again. When you have had enough of this for one occasion, find somewhere relatively quiet (if you can) and think carefully about this experience.

Humans in the mass can be an absolutely *horrifying* experience for sensitive souls to encounter. You might well wonder what could possibly be "God-like" about any of them, except maybe an odd one here or there. None of them may have reminded you of *your* God-concept at all, but are you prepared to accept that there must be *some* degree of Divinity in whatever lives, whether human or not, however minor or fractional? If so, would you agree that there must be a percentage-factor of relationship between Divinity and Humanity? This is something we can only take theoretically without attempting to calculate each human. Suppose for instance, the percentage factor in one case was only .0000000000000000000000000000001. By comparison with another human that figure might be more or less in value, and although you might guess which, it would be futile to pretend you knew exactly how much. At least you would have realized that humans would vary considerably as to their Divinity factor, taking the Life-Spirit alone as one hundred percent. Humans are *not* "all equal in the eyes of God," and never were. That saying does not occur in any known

Scriptures. There may be an average among any given mass of them, but that is all.

This brings you back to yourself and the ten per cent of you needed to achieve the Melchizadek-status in spiritual dimensions. Had Brother Lawreence known of this concept, he would probably have said that was very easy to offer by his "little and often" method. This does not mean that you could be ten per cent Divine yourself, but only that a *minimum* of one tenth of your whole being offered to the Will of Divinity within you is sufficient to ensure your eventual "salvation" in the sense that you will be preserved and prosper on your particular Path to Perfect Peace Profound.

Do something extremely simple this very minute. Look around you and choose anything convenient, then say to yourself, "I...(whatever your name is) will pick up this...(whatever) and put it back again." Do just that. Say again, "I...(name) am asking the God-in-me to repeat this action and make me aware of this." All you have to do then is allow your body to obey this request while you *notice the difference.* If you have any doubts, do it again until you *can* detect a difference between the actions. You may not feel anything very marked, but if you sense any difference *at all,* then work out ways of improving this exercise and follow it up on deeper lines. It could lead you a long way.

When you can sit down in a noisy crowded restaurant and remain with inner peace while you wield the Four Magical Instruments in the shape of your plate for a Shield, your knife for a Sword, your fork for a Rod, and your spoon or water-glass for a Cup as if you were working in your own Temple, *then* you may understand something of what the real magic of our Western Inner Tradition means. It means making a Grail of *yourself* for the Life-Spirit by using the Hallows available to your own hands. That is what they are for. Employ them properly and the Grail will manifest in the midst of them.

Do you see how Brother Lawrence's system worked? He took everything he encountered in Life as some kind of a symbol relating him with a single central concept which he conceived to be God. That was his "Magic Circle." He saw his Supreme Ideal reflected from everywhere he looked though in a somewhat varied fashion at every angle. Yet he saw only a God he could love and trust absolutely, moreover a Deity he could be friendly with on familiar terms. In his day, witches and wizards all over the place were claiming "familiar spirits" of every description. Lawrence was satisfied with the "spirit of Spirits" as *his* familiar. Once he says, "We must accustom ourselves to a familiar, humble, and affectionate conversation with him." Another time, "Get the habit of entertaining yourself often with GOD." Again, "Think often of GOD by day and night, in your business and even in your diversions." For Lawrence, his God-concept was no distant and possibly disapproving Deity, but the closest possible Companion with whom to share Life, "in sickness and health, for better or worse, until death do us *unite.*"

It is interesting to note that Lawrence uses the term GOD, (in capitals, just like that) throughout all his few communications, yet never once mentions the name Jesus or the title Christ, although he does sometimes refer to Christians. He was an Alsatian and a Carmelite, and he remained an unordained lay-brother till the end of his days at over eighty. Could he have been secretly a Cathar, or a Rosicrucian living in an orthodox Christian community for the sake of convenience, or what we would now call "cover"? It is tempting to suppose so, but it does not matter in the least now. He did a good job then by setting out a Western spiritual system so well worth following up in principle and practice by those able to appreciate its fundamental significance from an esoteric standpoint.

In fact, there is less difference between Christian and so called "Pagan" religious and magical beliefs than most people might suppose. The majority of "Christian" practices and customs are now well recognized as being "taken over" or inherited from much older faiths, and altered to suit the requirements of revised moralities and opinions. For the next Chapter or so we shall be examining this idea in connection with a type of "Nature Faith" which survived into recent times. This is purely for the sake of comparison with the mainline stream of Western occultism we have been following so far, but there is a lot to be learned thereby.

No one should be afraid to examine *all* forms of inner experience leading anywhere in the direction of Ultimate Light.

## Questions

1. Do you feel like a "God" to your own body cells, and how?
2. What was "Original Sin"?
3. What is the "Sin against the Holy Spirit"?
4. Define the word "Love."
5. Discuss the nature of Brother Lawrence from evidence of his teaching.
6. What is so special about his practices?
7. Define a "Trainee God."
8. Describe your reactions with "humans in the mass."
9. Choose the ten most important sentences in this Chapter.
10. Describe some of your own exercises of the "Brother Lawrence" type.

# · 10 ·

# *Paganistic Principles*

So far, we have been looking at the best side of the Western Inner Tradition but there is another, much older and some would say a "darker" element to it which needs to be known in order to appreciate the growth and developments that have arisen since earlier times. It is by contrast with primitive practices that we can measure our present position and estimate what may be needed to take us into a more favorable future.

Our concepts of the Gods in early times would be frightening by modern standards, almost as terrifying as the present threat of nuclear power. There is a strange parallel between the "old Gods" personifying the forces of natural elemental energy, and our "new Gods" typifying the invocation of that energy we have aroused by our intelligent consciousness. This means that the circle of our civilization is coming closer to closure when old and new will meet to decide the fate of Mankind.

Old time humans did not see their Gods as being purely benevolent, gracious, loving or merciful. They conceived of these aspects of existent Energy according to the way they encountered It or Them in the course of living. Life could be comfortable enough when the sun shone, fruits and food were plentiful, and there were no external threats. It could be horrifying beyond belief when natural disasters struck without mercy and destroyed humans, or they perished from diseases and poisonings they believed were sent from the same source. To them, God and the Devil were one and the same Power in opposite action. It could be either good, bad, both, or neutral. To early man, these concepts were inseparable.

As civilization became more sophisticated, and thinking systems evolved into more clearly defined religions and philosophies, there was always a residue of "hard-core" believers who were convinced that "old ways were best ways" and so they resisted the innovations of new thinking approaches to Deity. Through these approaches, people were beginning to visualize the characteristics of Divine consciousness in a more advanced Light. Since the reluctance to change remained mainly in rural areas, cultured Romans coined the word "Pagans," which referred purely to the *pagi* or fortified places around Rome in the countryside where peasants and agricultural workers were supposed to retreat if hostile invasions occurred. Each *pagus* had its own sacred rites and was quite well organized. They had their own annual festivals called *Paganalia* which often ended up in what we might cheerfully call "fertility frolics." When Christianity became the ruling religion in Rome, the word "Pagan" became a term of disapproval for those who preferred to worship the Gods in their old way, and it remains so to this day. Strictly speaking, it means no more than "rustic" or "countryman," specifically one who was not liable to military service. Only misuse of the word has given it a derogatory significance.

Throughout Europe, despite increasing culture and improving standards, a firm core of these "Old Believers" continued to defy the increasing influence of Christianity. Eventually they became diffused and disorganized, their children lost interest, and they gradually decreased to a relatively few "faithful," gathering round in small family groups as an "underground" type of movement which was more or less in opposition to officialdom, or what later became known as "the Establishment." Yet these groups, were not "Mystery Schools," which were apt to be advanced beyond the norm. They were "reversionists," concerned with preserving early concepts and customs which were almost of Stone

Age. They were the fore-runners to the now reviving "Pagan" cults in Western Europe.

As might be expected, they acquired some kind of sophistication and development as the centuries passed, and some of the groups "cultured themselves up" as their membership became better educated. Nor were they entirely confined to the agricultural classes in Europe. Members of the nobility here and there encouraged the clandestine continuation of the "Old Religion," and it is reasonable to suppose that the Royal Angevin House of Plantagenet, in particular, had strong connections with Paganism. However, the Christian Church did its impressive best to eliminate all traces of what it termed Paganity among the people, sometimes condemning practitioners as "witches" (or "workers of wickedness"), "heretics" if they had been nominal Christians, or finally "Satanists," since the Church pronounced all pre-Christian Gods to be "Devils." Athough devil-worship is very ancient, Satanism, as it developed in the West was entirely an invention of the Church, and did not really become practiced as such much before the seventeenth century.

Unluckily for most Pagans, they had characterized their favorite "God concepts" as a *horned* figure, frequently the Celtic Cernnunnos Deity with stags horns, but sometimes as a Goat, or very occasionally as a Bull—all *sacrificial* animals of the "herding" type, the ancient substitutes for a "Sacred King." Christians were already accepting their version of the horned and hooved image of the Devil, their avowed adversary and author of all Evil. So they had no difficulty in identifying the Pagan Deity as their Satan concept. There was also an awkward old word still in use among Romany Gypsies, "Duval," derived from the Sanskrit, and meaning "God." Modern gypsies say, "Boro Duval," meaning "Good God." This caused a lot of confusion through similarity of pronunciation, and many Christian authorities unaware of the etymological derivations became more convinced than ever that "Devil worship" was rife among the rural population.

Since following these "Old Gods" was quite unofficial, banned by civil and ecclesiastical authorities, and had become disseminated over wide and remote areas of Europe and Britain with no overall control by a centralized hierarchy, it collected into relatively small autonomous groups, and remained a matter of local practice, largely in the hands of whoever became hereditary leaders in the sense that they were personally concerned with keeping the fundamental ideas going, and passing on these primitive beliefs to their immediate kin or whoever they considered worthy of receiving such oral tradition. Like Qabalah, the "Old Religion" was always handed on from "mouth to ear," partly because of illiteracy, partly because of an inherited Druidic dislike for writing down what they considered sacred matter, but mainly because of the risk to life if caught by the authorities with such damning evidence in their possession.

Nevertheless oral tradition can be amazingly tenacious, if subject to local variations, and considerable fragments of the "Old" religion descended into our times. It was less persecuted in Britain than on the continent of Europe, so the probability is that it survived there in a somewhat better state of preservation than elsewhere. So we shall summarize the principal beliefs and practices honored by one of the now extinct branches of rural Paganism in Britain. Emigrants, mostly in the seventeenth, eighteenth, and nineteenth centuries took it with them chiefly to America, where variations of it survive to this day, and imitations of it are springing up almost everywhere. If one branch withers, another soon appears to take its place, and might be an improvement on the previous one. The branch which we shall examine here is of West-country origin, but representative of Paganism in general throughout early twentieth-century Britain. It has to be remembered that not until after World War Two would anything like this dare to emerge in "daylight" where there was the slightest possibility of "outsiders" realizing what lay beneath the surface of human hearts still firmly attached to the roots of religion in an continually changing age.

These particular Pagans were of the "small family group" type like others, though they preferred to call themselves a "clan" consisting of thirteen members with the sexes divided as equally as possible around the leader who might be male or female. The leaders were never referred to as "High Priest" or "Priestess" (which is purely modern) but simply as "Master" or "Mistress." That leader *sometimes* personified the God and was considered "God-possessed" by the others, but usually the "God" was represented by a plain staff with a bifurcated end stuck in the ground in the center of their circle which was traced around it with a knife and a looped cord. Their ceremonial gatherings were normally held in the open air at remote spots on hill-tops if possible, and their workings were "widdershins" or counter-clockwise, often at the dark of moon.

This was not because they regarded their Old Gods as Evil, per se, though these capricious Deities could work Evil or Good as they Willed. It was because these people regarded themselves as belonging more to the Night than the Day, and to Lunar rather than the later Solar cults behind so many more orthodox religions of the West. Though their principal officer was occasionally termed the "Duval" of their group, this had nothing whatever to do with the "Satan" concept behind Christian ideas of Evil. These Pagans despised this "Satan" which could *only* work Evil. Their "Over-God" figure was sheer, raw Power, working Good and Evil alike, indifferent to either principle or to human opinions about them.

Like their Deity concept, these folk regarded their religion as a means of working Good or Ill according to intentions. They did not think of themselves as "Black Magicians" devoted solely to the practice of Evil on earth, and they were no more concerned with ill-intentions than most other humans. On the other hand, they did *not* believe in "returning good for evil." They felt that if they were ill-treated by others, then they had a God-given right to retaliate appropriately, and their Deity would back them up to the hilt. They also believed that if their curses were unjustified, these would certainly "bounce back" on themselves, so they were always very careful before they held any "cursing sessions," which were usually considered to be a group responsibility after a lot of discussion among themselves.

If they cursed people, they also blessed others and practiced what is now called "absent healing." This was done by one of them (usually the Master) inviting the disease of the absent person to transfer itself to his body from which it was "banished" by the others through ceremonial procedures. They believed that if they could not get rid of the disease, then their Master might die from it. His solemn duty was to take the ills of others, if they were closely connected with the "clan," on his own shoulders. If need be, he might have to die on behalf of his people like the old Sacred Kings.

They did not practice ritual nudity or wear any special costume except ordinary country clothing. There was a custom that the men wore braces crossed at the back, and the women wore aprons with the strings tied behind them in a peculiar type of knot. Both sexes alike had knotted cords with a loop at one end and a tassel at the other. The loop was symbolic of the female sex and the tassel of the male. When one was put through the other a noose was formed, and they usually wore these cords round their necks with the tassel dangling in front of the body. The cords were ordinary hemp and not colored in any way, but the knottings carried considerable symbology.

These particular Pagans were extremely versatile people. They claimed to have inherited what are now known as "Psi-powers," and to be acquainted with the old "leaf-language," herbal secrets, "horse-whispering," and other recondite rural lore, yet intermixed with this was philosophy and esoteric arcana from intellectual schools of mysticism prevalent in medieval times. Questioned on this point they naturally claimed theirs was the older culture from which all else derived but eventually they had to admit that a great deal of influence from sources behind other systems had indeed altered a lot of their style since the Middle Ages.

A most intriguing factor behind their practice was that their "mythos" became backed by the "Castle concept" similar to the Grail Legend, except that they termed theirs the "Castle of Arianrhod" (a Celtic Goddess of Magic), and linked it with the very early hill-forts or equivalents of *pagi* on which early Western survival depended on so greatly. This was also known in Christian mysticism as the "Interior Castle," and consisted of a conscious structure in the psyche symbolized by an actual physical fortress. Building this "Castle" constituted a series of spiritual exercises as an "approach system" to one's own inner reality, and was said to afford access to whatever "group consciousness" one shared with others of the same persuasion. We shall be coming to this topic presently apart from this lesson, because it is a leading idea in most Western types of esotericism.

The Christian version of the "Castle" comes in seven stages: first, ordinary prayer concentrating on God; second, mental prayer while seeking to know the mystic import of all things; third, the "Dark Night of the Soul" in which self must be renounced; fourth, acceptance of the Will of God; fifth, the state of union wherein the wills of God and Man agree and coincide; sixth, a state of ecstasy in which the soul is transported with joy; seventh and last, a state of ravishment in which the "Mystic Marriage" or perfect Union between God and Man is consummated. These stages are represented as being levels or floors in the Castle and after admission to the lowest, one has to ascend stage by stage up a spiral staircase. It is the Tree of Life or any other system in another form.

These particular Pagans saw their "Interior Castle" as being a sort of psychic meeting place wherein they could be conscious of their Gods and discarnate associates in a common state of inner understanding. A theosophist might call it the "Astral Plane," but they called it simply the "Otherworld." They imagined this Castle as invisible, on top of a high mountain which they had to ascend with great effort and undergo many ordeals in order to be worthy of entrance. They psychodramatized this in their outdoor meetings where the hill they were going to climb represented the "Magic Mountain," and their ordeals consisted mostly of fasting, exhaustive exercise, and other stress techniques likely to produce visionary results. The "Castle," of course, is the psycho-spiritual condition of consciousness they enter after all this sacrificial sweat has been shed.

They described the process thus:

> This is the taper that lights the way
> This is the cloak that covers the stone
> That cuts the cord,
> That binds the Staff
> That's owned by the Maid
> Who tends the Fire

That boils the pot
That scalds the sword
That fashions the Bridge
That crosses the Ditch
That compasses the hand
That knocks the Door
That fetches the Watch
That releases the Man
Who turns the Mill
That grinds the corn
That makes the cake
That feeds the Hound
That guards the Gate
That hides the Maze
That's worth a Light
and into the Castle
That Jack built.

The Castle was visualized as being surrounded by three Rings (see Figure 3). The outer ring represented Life, the middle one Death, while the inmost was called "The River." Each had to be crossed in turn before the Castle could be entered. The outer circle was consecrated with salt to signify human labor and work, the central Death ring with the ashes of willow for mourning, and birch for rebirth, symbolizing the beginning and end of an incarnation, while the inner "River of Time" ring was blessed with a mixture of wine and water, to which might be added vinegar and sugar. Those signified the bittersweet memories of past lives washed out by the promise of joy to come in what Christians might call "Heaven," which these Pagans felt should be their rightful reward after death. The "Queen of the Castle" was a Triple Goddess of Life, Death and Wisdom who roughly equated with Hecate, whose nature was not so frightening as her apperaance. To quote from one Pagan writing his views on Afterlife:

"Our Land of the Dead. Apple Island, Avalon, Caerochen, is a place that to the image-fixed mind appears

Figure 3. Approach to the Castle

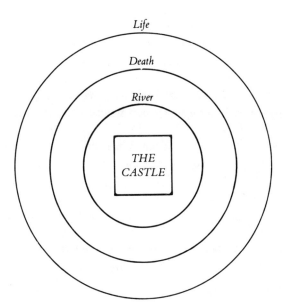

to the eyes as a wooded countryside with a bleak seashore. Across deep pasture lie wooded hills that raise blue skies to the lowering sky. By the sea and across the woods is a small hamlet:

> There you and I, my loves.
> There you and I will lie.
> When the cross of resurrection is broken,
> And our time has come to die.
> For no more is there weeping,
> For no more is there death.
> Only the golden sunset,
> Only the golden rest."

The same writer describes an inner experience of his own which is most revealing. He says:

> "This was the first time I ever saw the Power we call God, or at least a representative of Her. I woke up suddenly to find myself sitting upright in my own body, half in and half out. A dark form was in the room with me, and I felt genuinely frightened. Protesting weakly, I was *hauled* out of myself and taken to a wood where I saw my master for the first time. He was dressed in sixteenth century costume and spoke with a broad accent I had difficulty in understanding. He said; 'Here comes the Lass, let us worship Her.' I looked up from the ground where I was lying and saw coming through the oak trees a White Light and I realized it was a naked woman on horseback but brilliant pure Light also. I have never felt anything like I did before or since, but I was then shot back to myself with a thundering crash and got out of bed shaking and trembling."

This truly remarkable experience is common to many mystics, and each interprets it in terms of his or her own type of imagery. The Truth image is frequently seen as a naked woman, and the White Horse is a very old Celtic symbol of Kingship and sacrifice. The "dark woods" are symbolic of bewilderment and confusion. In other words, the visionary was experiencing an inner enlightenment according to the symbology of his own spiritual system.

This particular Pagan group was not much in favor of drug-induced hallucinations, though they did employ mild herbal concoctions and believed in a salt-free diet for a period of some days before any major rite. They relied much more on strenuous exercise and fasting for inducing a psychically sensitive state. For this, they used two main methods, one called the Mill, and the other the Maze. The Mill consisted of a rapid rotary dance or procession around a small circle until a condition of semi-vertigo occurred. Sometimes they would form this Mill country-dance fashion, by placing a small stone or stick in the ground, gathering around it closely, males and females alternating, link arms around each other's shoulders, bend inwards with gaze fixed upon the ground at the mark (a white stone at night), then start a kicking dance sideways, getting faster and faster until eventually one would stumble or fall, and the whole lot would then finish up on the ground except the musicians.

The Maze was a more complicated performance. A maze-pattern usually of the circular kind had to be traced on the ground. The leader entered it first with a sort of skipping motion and the rest followed in single line chanting a wordless tune mostly in vowel sounds. Steps and directions kept changing with the pattern, and they continued going back and forth through the Maze for a considerable time until they felt, as they described it, "different," and ready to "enter the Castle." This might be only a momentary experince of consciousness with their Inner Selves, or they could be lying or sitting around for quite a while, but they usually "came to" after some minutes and joined the feast round the fire afterwards when they felt inclined.

There were no rigidly fixed words for most of the rituals which these Pagans practiced, though the procedures themselves were fixed. A few customary phrases invoking ancient Deities, and some chant-rhythms were used, but the rest was fairly impromptu. Although they recognized a feminine Diana-Hecate type of Goddess as a worship-figure, they acknowledged a formless and Nameless Deity behind her which must never be mentioned by any name, but was usually referred to as "It" or "That," or "The Old Un." This "Nameless One" was never approached directly by any prayer but always through the intermediate Goddess figure. They did have one rather lovely "Leaf Mask" prayer, in which parts of the face were touched while a formula was recited. The face was imagined as being covered by a seven-pointed leaf. Design and prayer is given at Figure 4.

This "Leaf Mask" idea is connected with the "Green Man" concept, which is visualized as a partly seen human face through a screen of foliage, the lips having a suggestion of a smile. This represents the old "recognition Spirit" we think we catch glimpses of in Nature from time to time. It always seems amused by human behavior which appears peculiar in contrast to its own natural

Figure 4. The Leaf Mask

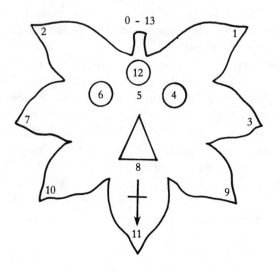

Left = Female    Right = Male

The Blessing is done by touching the face with two fingers of the right hand in the following order, and saying:

(*O, overhead*) O Goddess, Thou who created Heaven (*1, right temple*) and Earth, (*2, left temple*) Order (*2, left temple*) from Chaos (*1, right temple*), Time (*2, left temple*) from Eternity (*1, right temple*), I pray to thee. (*Cross arms and bow.*) Thou that listens (*3, right ear*) to our deepest voices, who shinest forth the pleasing Light (*4, right eye*), who inspires (*5, between eyes*) our inherited wisdom (*12, forehead*) and who protecteth us from the baleful might of the Destroyer (*6, left eye*), I pray thee grant us the inner voices (*7, left ear*) speaking of spiritual things, and let Love (*8, between nose and lips*) be our guiding light. In the Name of the Father (*9, right jaw*), the Mother (*10, left jaw*), and the Spirit that moveth all (*11, chin, then to 12 at forehead, and 13 overhead. Cross arms again*).

inclinations. This symbol is sometimes seen on stone carvings in old churches mainly in Britain. We are really seeing an emblem of ourselves hiding behind the "face of appearances" we present to the

world in general, and the knowing smile of Nature which sees quite
well what we really look like from inside. A reminder that though
we may fool other humans we can't hide from the Spirit which sees
through everything.

One of the most interesting symbols used by these Pagans
was what they termed their "Altar." This was a forked staff or
stang when decorated as shown in Figure 5. They regarded this
totem with considerable reverence, since it summed up their Life-
faith. It was for them what a Crucifix is for a Christian, since their
Sacred Kings were said to have died by being shot to death by
arrows while bound to a tree. Hence the arrangement of a reaping-

---

Figure 5. Staff Altar

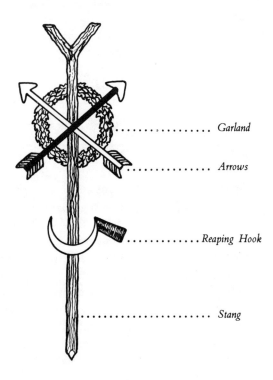

.................. *Garland*

............... *Arrows*

............ *Reaping Hook*

.................. *Stang*

hook for death, the crossed arrows as instruments thereof, and the wreath symbolizing resurrection. Circular wreaths or garlands were originally laid on graves as symbols of hope for a future life. This design also showed the Cosmic Cross. The garland itself varied with the season, and many were the meanings woven into it for those who understood the language of plants, herbs, leaves, and twigs. Sometimes a lit candle or lantern was placed in the fork of the stang to represent the Spirit of Immortality, and the Life-Element of Fire. Water was poured as a libation to Earth-spirits at the base of the stang, and Air was reckoned as the herbal incense burned before the whole symbol. A common formula for the incense was: henbane root, birch-bark, willow-bark, apple and pine gum, roots of deadly nightshade, and white bryony, leaves of sunspurge, cinquefoil, baneberry, foxglove and seeds of bracken. Additives for scent were wormwood, agrimony, rosemary, and vervain. This formula could vary considerably according to the ideas of different groups.

Though they regarded the basis of all magical power as sexual, these Pagans believed that sex was a private matter between those concerned, and it did not enter any of their rites as a spectacle for the remainder. They did have one particular custom as a sex ethic. If a male requested a female to have sex with him, she was quite entitled to refuse and be firm about it. If, however, a female approached a male with a demand for sex services, it would be considered very wrong to refuse unreasonably, because this would be tantamount to "rejecting the Goddess." This could lead to some rather embarassing situations needing all the tact and jurisdiction of the Master or Mistress to smooth over, but problems of that nature were normally "kept within the family."

One curious sex custom was the de-flowering of virgins dedicating themselves to their Deity. This was not always done by human agency, but with the aid of an artificial phallus carved exactly to size at one end of a besom-handle. That end was normally kept concealed in the bound top of the besom itself, so that the whole thing was a secret symbol of the sex act as a household article. Defloration in this way meant that no man could afterwards claim he had taken her maidenhood since she had already "given it to the God" of her own free will. Women were usually seen in triplicity like Hecate, as the Maiden, the Mother, and the Crone or "Old Woman" corresponding with the three phases of the Moon, since these people were Lunar rather than Sun worshippers.

It may come as a surprise to some readers, but the ancient Goddess Hecate had no connection at all with Evil in pre-Christian times. To the contrary, she was the patroness of magic and enchantments who was appealed to for protection against witch-craft. In the Heavens she was Luna, on earth Diana, and below ground Proserpine. She showed three faces, a mare, a bitch, and a sow, all "Goddess" animals of old connected with hunting and sacrifice. She presided over the prosperity of kings and nations, and protected family life and children. Her special place was where three roads met and sacrifices were made to her of dogs, lambs, and honey. She was "Diana of the Cross Roads" and thus the Forked Stang symbolized the triplicity of her nature and mutely proclaimed her presence at feasts held in her honor.

The external appearance of Hecate might seem frightening or startling to some, but human fear is normal when we are confronted with the Unknown. These Pagans always claimed that a sudden feeling of apprehension or unaccountable fear among them was an advance sign of a Divine or supernatural manifestation. In this, they agreed with the ideas behind "Pan-ic," or the strange alarm experienced by people surrounded by woodlands who suddenly "get a feeling of being watched by invisible presences." Ancient Greeks attributed this to the God Pan (or Nature) preparing to reveal himself and frighten those present on his private preserves. It also connects with the biblical phrase, "The fear of the Lord is the beginning of Wisdom."

By no means were all Pagans as cultured as these, but this group is a very good example of what has come down through the centuries with a certain amount of continuity in terms of basic human beliefs. Convinced Christians would certainly condemn them on many counts, the principal one possibly being their denial that Jesus was the *only* Son of God, and also because of their worship of what orthodox Christians might suppose was "the Devil." Those Pagans cretainly accepted that Jesus was an authentic Sacred

King slain on behalf of *his* people like their own "Kings" of past—and present—times. They would deny the existence of a "Devil" altogether. They would claim their "Unknown God" was above Good or Evil, and might work either at its Will, though the author of what most people know as evil was not God at all, but Man. For themselves they were just ordinary folk who wanted only to live in peace like other people, enjoy rural life quietly, and pass to their pleasant "inner pastures" when incarnations were ended.

They naturally kept their religion secret among themselves, and saw nothing peculiar about paying lip-service to a Christian God in village churches on Sundays. In any case, a lot of the Old Testament agreed with what they believed. When the Four Great Feasts of the Year came round at Brigeta (February 2), Beltine (April 30), Lugnasath (August 1), and Samhain (October 31), they kept these in their own way. These older "cross-Quarter days" are connected with hunting and breeding seasons, while the "regular" Quarters, the Solstices and Equinoxes, are purely astronomical and observed by what might be called "orthdox" occultists. Quite often, these Pagans called their Four Feasts by the old Christian titles of Candlemass, Walpurgis, Lammas, and All Hallows and interchanged a number of terms. For instance, they would speak of "Our Lord" and "Our Lady" with a totally different unspoken meaning among themselves. They even had a sort of communion service in which they ate bread with the formula, "Eat this bread in the Unknown Name, with sorrow, care, and fearful dread." They followed this with wine saying, "Drink this wine in Our Lady's name. She will gather you home again." This symbolized birth to a world of toil and unremitting efforts which would be left behind after death for a joyous, pleasant realm of love and laughter.

Our Pagans considered Christianity a twisted and perverted form of their own faith. There were many reminders of this in most old village churches in the shape of carvings and designs or wall-paintings. On the whole, however, they felt Christianity was a sad and joyless belief, condemning perfectly natural human instincts, and having a hard, unfeeling God who understood nothing of Motherhood. What seemed worse was his creation of a Hell for perpetual human suffering. They could not manage to love this cruel Creator image. It horrified them. Their Old Gods would kill, yes, but not torture for fun or revenge. No Hunter tortured a quarry to death. They chased it, killed it, then ate it. End of story.

It is fascinating to trace the elements of the Grail legend into modern times. The Sacred King theme, the Castle, the Hallows, the Quest, the Heros (or knights), all re-combined in each era to tell the tale. We shall find this throughout the whole of Western esotericism. In the end it boils down to the Golden Drop at the bottom of the Magic Cauldron. Keep reducing and concentrating all the different ingredients of esoteric belief and practice to their Ultimate Essence and we get the same "single drop" when we distill consciousness. Everything depends on how we prefer to "boil the pot," and what sort of fuel we want to use for keeping the Fire alight.

That was how these Pagans would have symbolized the process. For them, the Grail was the "Cauldron of Ceredwin" (a Celtic corn Goddess) into which went the whole of their Life— experiences to be steadily boiled down until the "Last Drop before Nothing" remained, and that Drop was *their own Ultimate Reality*. It always pays to read and study the old classic myths and then convert them into terms of modern consciousness. Those traditional tales and legends are not merely quaint accounts of past fantasies. They are factual formulae of our spiritual structure, phrased according to the language of their times, yet they always remain contemporary to those capable of reading their symbolism. That is all part of esoteric practice which calls for learning with patient care and considerable insight.

There is a lot to learn from even this brief account of a Paganistic system in modern Britain with associated extensions into the USA and elsewhere, for though original lines of this particular branch are extinct, offshoots are extant. One of the main points to learn is never to accept things purely on surface value. Always attempt to discover what lies behind the barriers to inner perception. There is a saying that there are only four ways of tackling a wall: over it, under it, through it, or round it. Through it may be too difficult, and round it may be too long, so that leaves climbing or burrowing. Remember, too, that all genuine occult symbology has to contain the keys to its own solution. So it all depends whether you want to use the symbology you have been given as a ladder or a pick-axe and shovel. Either way will get you past it, but ladders are the neatest.

## *Questions*

1. How did early humans typify their Gods?
2. What does the word "Pagan" really signify?
3. Why was a horned God revered by so-called Pagans?
4. What was the pagan attitude to Good-Evil?
5. Describe the "Interior Castle" concept.
6. What were the three circles round the Castle?
7. What were the Mill and the Maze?
8. Discuss the Leaf Mask concept.
9. Choose the nine most important sentences in this chapter.
10. Discuss the symbology of the Stang-altar.

# · 11 ·

# *Cosmic Cycles*

Having covered quite a broad spectrum of the principles underlying the Western Inner Tradition, we now have to continue plodding what may seem to be the same Paths on somewhat higher levels. That is the way Western occultism works, and why it is compared to a "Mystic Mountain" with a spiral track which one ascends. Consciousness is cyclic and advances around its center in a helical manner like other rhythmic energies of our Universe. We may suppose we can think in straight lines, but in fact we do not. We just cannot sense the curvature of consciousness through Time anymore than we feel the curvature through Space of our planet spinning on its axis, or completing its annual cycle round the Sun. Nevertheless, if we do not learn how to live in harmony with the natural laws behind our beings, we can scarcely be very healthy or happy creatures of Cosmos.

In old times, people were taught to recognize the rhythms of Nature through its seasonal changes, and specific Time-Space coordinates were established to celebrate the spiritual significance of earthly events. As we might expect, Lunar cycles were followed before Solar ones, and primitive people counted in moons rather than suns, so their regular gatherings for religious worship and settlement of tribal affairs were normally held at full Moon. Additionally, the moonlight provided illumination for the proceedings and was best for night travel. The ancients were good at combining religion with practicality.

As a result, we have inherited an ancestral "spiritual clock" in our genes which is symbolized by what is known as the Cosmic Circle Cross. It explains a great deal of our apparently irrational behavior which can be traced back to early tribal memories which now exist only as impulses we cannot consciously connect with any rational cause. For example, in early times it was noticed that the behavior pattern of some unstable people altered dramatically at full Moon and these people became known as "Lunatics," It was recognized that this condition could be hereditary. Few may have suspected they were instinctively reproducing primitive, almost primeaval, examples of orgiastic behavior that had been indulged in during the full Moon antics of our most animalistic ancestry. It was a rhythmic reversion to our earliest conditions of evolution in cases where the gene responsible had not been "bred out" or modified during the course of many generations.

Conversely, the same cycles can also bring out the best aspect of human nature. Our ancestors attempted to live in alignment with the forces of Nature which they felt all around them, and this pattern became implanted in the genes they have passed down to us. When, many centuries ago, it was realized by intelligent minds that we were living in cyclic patterns of behavior which seemed related with Cosmic phenomena, the science of astrology was born, beginning with the assumption that human behavior was dependant on planetary positions and therefore our Fate was governed thereby. This could only be so to the extent that humans acted and reacted entirely in accordance with predictable hereditary patterns (which indeed millions do). In cases where individuals exerted the authority of their True Wills and intentionally altered their reaction patterns, the type of Fate they encountered was altered also.

This means that we are far more governed by inherited ancestral genetic influences than by current Cosmic ones, and we can only alter the effects of either by the exercise of "True Will" directly from the higher side of our own identities. This bears out the dictim of many modern astrologers that "The stars may *im*pel, but they cannot *compel.*" Any honest astrologer will freely admit that even the most accurate and detailed horoscope will only outline the *likehoods* of a life, providing a person makes no attempt to change his character or behavior-pattern. It also explains why so many of the Mystery Schools, and also the Christian Church were officially against their members consulting astrologers and fortune tellers. If people really believed their destiny on Earth was unalterable, they would make no attempt to alter it and so would never develop their True Wills as they should during their lifetimes here.

Once it is realized that we are here in this world to *change* ourselves and our consciousness into something better, and this effort is what the spiritual side of our lives is about, there is no reason *not* to consult astrologers or any other kind of oracle which may indicate future trends for purposes of information only. Whether individuals perfer to follow paths of mysticism, magic, religion, or any other means of changing themselves does not make a lot of difference except in method. What matters most is that the souls concerned should select a suitable system for the individual needs of their present personalities and Self-status, then—get on with the job.

A basic problem is that we have this hidden heritage of ancestral rhythms in ourselves which need adapting to the exigencies of existence in our times. Although our lives seem so much faster than formerly, a day now is no longer than a day then. Solar revolutions are the same, there are still thirteen lunations to the year, and the seasons still pass at the same natural rate as in previous millennia. We appear to be living at a much greater pace than our ancestors only because we are packing a lot more meaning into smaller and smaller spaces, and an enormously increased variety and intensity of events into less and less time. So it looks as though we shall have to take the Time-component of Cosmos as a constant, because it relates with definite Solar-Lunar rhythms, and treat the other two components of Space and Events as variables, because they are relative only to human experience.

What we need to do is set up a spiritual sense of rhythms based on the same factors as those which affected our genetics so long ago. Since Time obligingly provides a means of doing this, let us work out a Cosmic Cross symbol which will act as a kind of clock-dial against which we may measure the fundamental frequences of our inbuilt impulses. The advantage of this is that it enables us to make conscious linkages with very ancient energies implanted in us and turn these to present use for forming our future. If we ignore or deny these we risk losing mental peace, apart from spiritual stability. For instance, you may honestly believe you are

Figure 6. Circle Cross of Cosmos

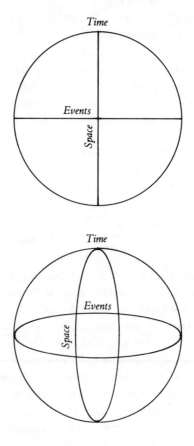

not a religious person, have no interest in Gods or Devils, and care nothing for any sort of supernatural speculations. Suppose, however, you came from a long line of ancestors who *did?* You and your genetics would be in a constant state of subconscious conflict, and that must surely lead to trouble one way or another.

This example could be altered to almost anything. It means only that when we try to live in contradiction to inherited tendencies *without conscious control of such a situation,* many personality problems are bound to arise which are liable to cause trouble for us in contemporary circumstances. So the thing to do is set up something which our ancestral rhythms can recognize and respond to in a harmless and helpful fashion calculated to further our best prospects for the future. This actually happens in a great many ways but what we have in mind here is a sort of cyclic system for constant alignment with the natural forces of our Universe following the pattern of our Western Solar Cross (see Figure 6).

Note that this shows a complete cycle of force-flow from start to finish and back to the beginning again. Although it is actually endless, it can be considered as having four nodal points to which particular Hebrew letters correspond:

*Hebrew Letters*

| | | |
|---|---|---|
| 1. Minimal energy | Yod | Letters |
| 2. Balanced between | Heh | of the |
| minimal and maximal | | NAME |
| 3. Maximal energy | Vau | (Tetra- |
| 4. Balanced between | Heh | grammaton) |
| maximal and minimal | | |

This cycle of Creation continues *constantly* in ourselves and throughout the Cosmos. In our bodies we can sense it in our heartbeats, and it has correspondences everywhere in Nature. We see it working in times, tides, and seasons, and if we are wise we shall learn how to live in harmony with it by reciprocating with its energies. Our ancestors saw it as a daily cycle of dawn, noon, dusk, and night, a monthly one of dark, waxing, full, and waning phases of the Moon, and an annual agricultural round of Spring, Summer,

Autumn and Winter. All these cycles were repetitious of each other on different scales. Basically, the Life-cycle was fundamentally four-fold however one looked at it: 1. birth and growth; 2. active adulthood; 3. decline and death; 4. disembodiment and return to womb. So Life continues indefinitely.

To live in accordance with the Circle Cross cycle was simple enough. You did the equivalents of seasonal activities in sequence, and kept repeating the rhythms according to need. All you had to do was translate the terms of this rhythm into whichever level of Life you intended to exert energy. For instance, if it were physical, you would: (a) summon reserves; (b) exert increasing energy; (c) apply maximum strength to the extent needed or possible; (d) relax back to normal condition. You are using this cycle of events with every physical move you make with your body, and you do this automatically without being consciously aware of the fact. Now you are being asked to direct your conscious attention to it and then see the principle extended into mental and spiritual areas of awareness also.

If the same cycle were *mental* you would; (a) seek or summon an idea from your stock; (b) bring it to focal point in your mind; (c) apply it for whatever purpose it was evoked; (d) replace it in mental storage, possibly modified through usage. Again you do this mechanically without thinking about it and are asked to consider the implications of this. Now look at the cycle from a spiritual viewpoint and you should note that: (a) an experience emerges from somewhere into your circle of consciousness; (b) it develops and intensifies; (c) it reaches and holds maximum impact; (d) it fades back to memory levels again. Such are the cycles of Life that you and every living human are undergoing all the time at different rates for different reasons. You may suppose this is very obvious and commonplace if you stopped to think about it, but how many people do just that? It is *stopping to think about things* which reveals the hidden mysteries behind Life which so many millions miss. So stop sometimes and think often. This is the way to *learn*.

You should recognize also that the quadruple life-beat represented by the Solar Circle Cross is also the sex act in principle from inception to completion. Therefore if you are conscious of the underlying rhythm behind your existence on this Earth, you will "tune in" to the energy-waves of your own genesis. Moreover, you should remember that although the rhythm may be regular, it is an *accented* rhythm with the emphasis on the third beat where the energy builds up to crescendo, as it were, corresponding with the orgasm peak of the cycle. So the beat is, one two, *three,* four. We could lay out some corresponding temporal rhythms like this:

| Daily | Monthly | Yearly | Tidal | Breathing |
|-------|---------|--------|-------|-----------|
| Night | Dark | Winter | Low | Out |
| Morning | Waxing | Spring | Incoming | Inhale |
| NOON | FULL | SUMMER | HIGH | FULL |
| Evening | Waning | Autumn | Outgoing | Exhale |

Do you see that there has to be this variation of energy, this pulse, between maximum and minimum in order to provide *flow* and *motion* to Life? Otherwise everything would be static and frozen as existence without Life, or Eternal Death. While we move we live, be this in body, mind, or soul. Life exhibits a form of energy we know as electricity, a force-flow of power between two extremities of condition called "positive" (plus +) and negative (minus –). The halfway point between these is termed "netural," which is not a zero-state, but a non-active one because it is where one extremity balances the other to cancellation of effect. Electrical energy is symbolized by the Circle Cross with the neutral axis extended so as to make it a Time-coordinate in order to show the number of cycles per second as in Figure 7.

This shows you a symbolic way to look at our Circle Cross as an indicator of electrical potential. It also tells you how to relate a pure cycle of energy as one of a series of regular rhythms affecting Life. You could apply this to mental or spiritual energies as well. It goes on in you one way or another all the time. Whenever your physical brain emits its micro-voltages of electrical impulses, any amount of Circle Crosses are generated. You may as well make them with your active consciousness along other lines linking you with inner dimensions.

Old time spiritual systems tried this by gearing up cycles of Time to rhythmic cycles of Events which they later tied in with

Figure 7. Circle Cross of ordinary household electric current

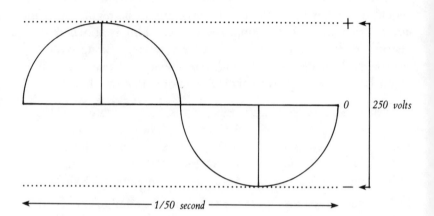

cycles of Space by associating them with stone circles. The Grail cultus much later replaced this by a "Round Table" concept. The Christian Church arranged its calendar to regulated courses of spiritual rhythms based on daily, weekly, monthly, and yearly rotations of specific devotions. Whether or not you are a Christian, the effect of all this is *still in your ancestral genetics,* and you can carry them on quite well in contemporary style to your present spiritual advantage. The guiding principle behind them all is to make yourself intentionally conscious of the Cosmic Life-Spirit in keeping with Its prevailing presentation to humans at the particular period. That is to say you have to attune yourself to however God appears as an Event coinciding with your Time and Place.

This was the whole idea of instituting regular daily rhythms of prayers or ritual devotions at intervals of Night, Morn, Noon, and Eve. These made a revolution of the Circle Cross by themselves and could be arranged in a great variety of ways. The Deity might be addressed as four distinct aspects of Itself, like the Egyptian system of regarding the Solar Boat as constantly sailing round the world and needing different forms of nomenclature at Dawn (RA), Noon (AHATHOOR), Dusk (TUM), and Midnight (KEPHRA). There could be any four changes of the Divine Name invoked, or the same Name in four alterations. Four changes of outlook would do. For example, take Night for dreaming of anything, Morning for developing it, Noon (which might be a period of a couple of hours each side in Summer) for doing it, and Eve for determining it, or reflection over what had been done.

It is perfectly practical to work out ritualized prayers and practices as Moslems and other do which build up repetitive rhythms but there is a danger here that they may become reduced to automatism which summons little or nothing from the heart and soul. It is best to keep all such formulae brief and potent rather than prolong them. Four words with work and Will are far better than four hundred words of wooly waffle. If you intend to practice diurnal rhythmics (apart from your normal course and diary work which constitute that much already), you could do worse than say no more than the Four Magical Maxims, one at each period like this: At Morn, "I Will." At Noon, "I Dare." At Eve, "I Know." and at Night, "I Keep Silence." Provided sufficient power and meaning are put into those words, they will serve the purpose. Try thinking up some likely phrases on your own initiative. Write them down and see what they look like, or record them and consider how they sound. Then pick whichever you like best and try them out for a few weeks.

When it comes to Moon cycles, there are many old ways of harmonizing with them. On the whole, the Dark of the Moon signified ill-fortune and a time to "lie low" or keep activity to a minimum. A new or Waxing Moon was a period to begin anything which was hoped to increase and prosper, such as sowing seeds, investing money, etc. The Full Moon was a celebration time for local or family gatherings, conviviality on a minor scale, worship of the Feminine Principle of Fertility, and also for accomplishing anything of short-term importance. The Waning Moon was no time to begin any new ventures, but only to tend old ones. It meant decrease and loss, so great care had to be exerted in all affairs. This was the period to root out weeds, get rid of rubbish, and dispose of any unwanted surplus.

Now this may seem a lot of superstition, but the principle behind it was rhythmic and regular changes of Life-attitude in conformity with Cosmic happenings. "As in Heaven, so on Earth." The idea was to regulate or control the courses of Earth living so as to match the rhythms of Divine Life as indicated by the perceptible pulses of observable heavenly phenomena. It was a fundamentally good idea which we could well adapt to any age and social situation. It is always better to swim with a tide than against it, as philosophers have remarked often enough without making much impression on human stupidity. If intelligent individuals are indeed to take advantage of favorable Cosmic currents, the simplest way to start is surely to live *consciously* in accordance with those having the broadest effect on our planet like the main Lunar and Solar cycles.

It was a lot easier for our ancestors to arrange their living patterns in keeping with Cosmic phenomena than it is for us. We have to remember that in all rural areas the Sun and Moon were principal sources of light which governed their work programs. It was natural to be more active in Summer than Winter in our North Western part of the world, and this tendency has been bred into our genetics by many generations. For the last few generations, we have been trying to live on a totally different time scale with the result that we are suffering from a sort of genetic "jet lag." Part of our nature is attempting to adapt to the pace of modern living, but the rest of our underlying Self-structures are still tied-in subconsciously with the Time-rhythms of our forebears. That is why it helps now to make at least token gestures of recognition towards these past projections into our present.

Surely it should be possible to plan *some* sort of alignment in your life which would take the Lunar phases into account? It is obviously impossible to lay down any definite schemes for you to follow in modern times, because only you know your circumstances and how best to arrange them. You should certainly take the trouble to find out the phases of the Moon which can be found in any decent diary or calendar or you can obtain one of the many astrological calendars that are available. Then you might try to arrange a few opportunities for quiet relaxation at the Dark period, some efforts at expansion or increasing activities during the Waxing time, major efforts and enjoyments at Full Moon, and emphasis on care and maintenance during the Wane. There must be *something* you could say, think, or do to mark your awareness of Lunar cycles and complete one revolution of a Circle Cross.

If you have the time, means, and ability, you could work out quite elaborate rituals to celebrate at least the Full Moon. This was the time when the noted Thessalian sorceresses of old claimed an ability to "draw down the Moon" and call it out of the sky towards them. Though they did not do this literally, they certainly held group meetings for Diana-Hecate worship and chanted ancient rhythms connected with fertility and fecundity at that time. Additionally, they practiced ceremonial sex with the hope of attracting a "Moonchild" into incarnation. It was then believed that special souls with psychic gifts awaited on the Moon for opportunities of rebirth, and could cross a moonbeam bridge into a human female body exposed to its ending on Earth. Although this may not be believable in our times, here is an interesting modern ritual based on that old practice.

After laying out a circle at their chosen spot, the selected female of a small group stands in its center with a horn of wine in her left hand and a mirror in her right. She catches the rays of the Full Moon with her mirror, and reflects it to the surface of the wine which must also reflect the Moon. She has to coincide the two Lunar images and hold them as steadily as she can. The others hold lit tapers, the men's being bound with red ribbons, and the women's with blue. They pace around the central female nine times deosil. One man enters the circle with a lantern in the left hand and a knife in the right. He says, "Lady, I am between Heaven and Earth for thee." She answers, "Sir, take thy fill, but drink the Cup to its bitter dregs." He plunges his knife into the horn, stirs three times, then splashes the drops to the Four Quarters. After that he kisses the woman, drinks from the horn and passes it around the circle deosil. He is followed by another woman who hands out consecrated cakes or wafers. A charmingly symbolic mime of a sex act.

Orthodox Jews celebrate the New Moon with special prayers, possibly because Pagans made the most of the Full, and maybe on account of the New Moon being specially associated with the principle of increase. It is still considered lucky in some parts to turn money over in pocket or purse at first sight of the New Moon.

The Orthodox Jews have a special prayer which goes, "Blessed art thou, O Lord our God, King of the universe by whose word the heavens were created. They are glad and rejoice to do the will of their Master the truthful Worker whose work is truth, who bade the moon renew itself, a crown of glory to those that have been upborn by him from the womb and who in time to come will themselves be renewed like it to honour their Creator for his glorious kingdom's sake. Blessed art thou, O Lord, who renewest the months."

It is supposed that this is where the superstition arose that it is unlucky to see the New Moon through glass. Since the first sight of a New Moon was said to confer a special blessing on the viewer, an impaired sight of this through the obscurity of early glass might be thought to blight the blessing. It was also considered bad luck to see the New Moon in a mirror, since that reversed the image and made it into a Waning Moon. A Full Moon could not be reversed in outline by a mirror, so it was safe to look then. The appearance of a Waxing Moon is thought to represent a Cup which is steadily filling up from the *right* and therefore fortunate, while the Waning Moon is emptying out from the *left* and therefore unlucky. The Full Moon is the brimming container seen from above (Figure 8). If you take some small bowl-shaped vessel, pivot its edge between thumb and forefinger of your left hand, then rotate it slowly from right to left while watching the outline of its edge change shape, you will see

Figure 8. Phases of the Moon

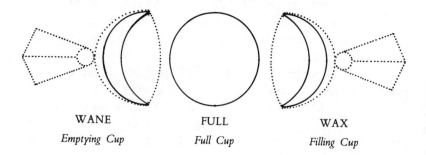

WANE      FULL      WAX

*Emptying Cup*      *Full Cup*      *Filling Cup*

where this came from. Remember it is the right side of the Moon seen first and the left last.

After Lunar cycles, there follows the Solar one of thirteen lunations (plus an odd day). This could be called the major cycle of human life, since it comprises a grain, vegetable, fruit and nut harvest, plus a period of varied animal production, and the average of a single human one. It is the cycle needed to produce one human generation and the wherewithal to keep three generations going. This is ideally a four generation world: one lot born and growing up, another lot adult and doing the hardest work, a third lot having learned from experience passing the benefit of this along to younger ones before they die, and the last lot awaiting opportunities for incarnation again either in the "Otherworld" or back in the womb. It is a great pity that because of over-breeding and unbalance of population things cannot be arranged so neatly on those lines.

The spiritual cycle of the Solar Year turned on the axis of seasonal changes much like enlargements of the Lunar ones. Principal points of the annual Circle Cross are still known as the Four Great Feasts, where everyone able to do so gathered at their local Sacred Spots and socialized in memorable ways. At first these were held in honor of the hunting and breeding seasons at Samhain (October 31), Brigeda (February 2), Beltine, (April 30), and Lugnasad (August 1). The Christian Church later called them Hallowmas, Candlemas, Roodmas, and Lammas. In general, from a human standpoint, they were devoted to honoring in Winter all dead and unborn souls, in Spring the rising youngsters, in Summer the active adults, and in Autumn the seniors and sages. They corresponded also with the main agricultural tasks of clearing and ploughing, planting and sowing, tending and weeding, harvesting and storing. They indicated the Four Points of Life, Excarnation, Birth, Mating, and Death. It is most important to realize that in early times a disembodied spiritual status was considered a part of the Life-cycle of human souls. *A defunct relative or friend was still one of the family.* We could well reconsider our modern outlooks on that topic.

Later, as astronomical knowledge grew more exact, and stone circles were formed as calculators of celestial cycles, the

Great Feasts became shifted to Solstices and Equinoxes, though their older origins are still celebrated to this day, mainly in rural areas. The different systems of esoteric practice have their particular styles of ritual and procedures for observing these important angles of the Cosmic Circle Cross. Most rituals now are quite modern in character, however much they may be based on ancient beliefs and customs. They should never be underestimated on that account, but appreciated as honest attempts to honor our basic ancestral rhythms in present fashion. The Great Feasts are chiefly referred by their initials of WS (Winter Solstice), VE (Vernal Equinox), SS (Summer Solstice), and AE (Autumnal Equinox).

Even if you have no opportunity to attend any such gatherings in person, the least you might do is be conscious of them and keep in mind the spiritual significance of each Solar Season: Spring for planting new "seed ideas" in our "Gardens of the Soul," initiating fresh projects and opening up unexplored areas of our

Figure 9. Circle Crosses of Hour, Day, Month, and Year coinciding

inner worlds; Summer for making maximum efforts at furthering
and fostering our inner interests and aims; Autumn for collecting,
collating, and evaluating them; Winter for quiet meditations,
scrapping useless accumulations of mental and spiritual debris,
overhauling ourselves, and generally getting ready to commence a
fresh cycle next Spring. The important thing is to try to live with
these tides so that they coincide with the Comos and your own life
on Earth.

Living in harmony with the inherited rhythms of your
nature is what the Circle Cross symbol of the Western Inner
Tradition is all about, and why it is of such spiritual significance. It
is really a question of trying to live "wheels within wheels within
wheels," as in Figure 9 imagined *ad infinitum.* We might talk about
the wheel of the Hour, the Day, the Month, the Year, Lifetime and
so forever, yet *all have the same center,* the power-pivot of everything
which we call "God." Only diameters differ according to our
perceptions. Buddhists know this as the "Wheel of Birth and
Death" and believe the best thing to do is get off it altogether into
"Non-Existence." In the West we realize it is impossible to stop the
Wheel of Life while Cosmos exists, but it is possible to expand
awareness of its diameter so that a single incarnation reduces to a
mere momentary flicker and we remain conscious of a continuum
much greater than human life. This all starts with becoming aware
of the Circle Cross concept, and beginning to practice it in your
life.

It has been said that Man's greatest invention was the wheel,
and none of our modern technology would have been possible
without it. There have been civilizations without physical wheels
such as those of the American Indians, but they certainly used the
spiritual principles of the wheel with their calendars and Solar
observances. Modern man has become so familiar with the wheel as
a mechanical device that he is in danger of forgetting its spiritual
meanings, but his genetics have not forgotten, and they keep trying
to remind hurried and harassed humans in our century of the old
rhythms which will always be the basis of our beings. In effect they
are saying, "Steady up there! You can live as fast or slow as you like
providing you do so in a regular fashion. Stop jerking and jinking

around like a hooked fish on the end of a line, and get your life on an even course. Learn how to live like the Universe Itself, in Cosmic Circles, and your life will begin to make real meaning at last."

This is the true significance of a Magic Circle with its Magus in the middle. It is a symbol of how to live properly in a genuine "Magical manner"—something far more important than a medieval madman hoping for spirits stupid or scheming enough to serve all his whims and gratify his greeds. Much more than that indeed. It represents an individual who is centering himself steadily as the spiritual pivot of all his life rhythms which are continually in action around him so that every different frequency coordinates and harmonizes into a single Whole. Try to see the idea of Magic Circles from this point of view. It makes a lot of sense.

Modern living may make it difficult to trace the fundamental rhythms running through it, but this is not impractical or impossible for those able to realize the need of doing so and prepared to take the trouble of working out a program enabling them to partake consciously and, therefore, *intentionally* in the spiritual cycle of Cosmos. Four seconds out of an hour, four minutes out of a day, four hours out of a month, and four days out of a year would do it on a minimum scale providing this was dependably regular. Do you think that would be too much to ask for tuning your life in keeping with that of our Universe?

## Questions

1. What is the curvature of consciousness?
2. Discuss genetic rhythms.
3. Design a diagram of an energy cycle.
4. Co-relate a table of several types of energy cycles.
5. Devise a daily cycle of spiritual rhythms.
6. Why is a new Moon considered lucky except when seen through glass?
7. Devise simple and brief ceremonies for each Lunar phase.
8. Discuss genetic "jet lag."
9. Choose the eight most important sentences in this chapter.
10. How important to you are Cosmic cycles, and why?

# · 12 ·

# *Cycles Continued*

In the last chapter we considered the Cosmic Circle Cross mainly from the Time angle, but there are also the factors of Space and Events to consider and we should learn how they extend into spiritual dimensions. Their cyclic nature is not nearly so obvious as that of Time, nor the perimeters of their circles so clearly definable. Nevertheless they are limits of consciousness, and as such need to be recognized by all who are hoping to extend these limits beyond their present borders.

Let us take physical Space first. The circle of comprehension can be defined to some degree here (Figure 10). In the center is "cell consciousness" extending only to the borders of single biological cells. We are rarely conscious of them unless there is stimulus of pain or extreme pleasure localized in specific cells. Next there is "body consciousness" extending to the limits of our human bodies as a "normal" condition of being. Around this extends the limits of "home" as defined by the closest social circle of immediate relationships with other humans. Enclosing this again is the circle of "locality," meaning the usual limits of spatial life of an average Earth dweller. Outside that again is the "world circle" defining the extent of experience beyond locality anywhere on this Earth. Beyond this is the circle of our Solar System and then that of Cosmos. We can think of these as being "edges of experience."

Figure 10. Limits of Physical Space Consciousness

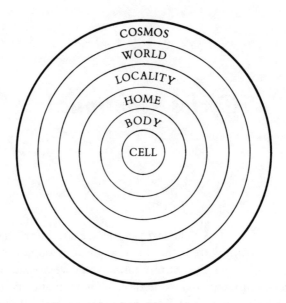

It should be easy to see from this that our evolution as a human species of life advances from the center. The more we evolve, the wider in Space our experience extends, and we are only recently extending it beyond our planet. Although our reference points in Space can only be arbitrary, we relate these to our ordinary bodies and call them up, down, left, front, right, and rear. What we have to note here is that these six physical co-ordinates have their spiritual equivalents as we have learned in an earlier chapter. Some Mystery Schools see this as a Cube of Space because of the six sides, but a cube is also a sphere flattened out six equal ways as you will realize if you think of a spherical balloon being compressed into a containing box.

If you want to build yourself an interesting model of this cubic Space concept, you can do it by first making six small four-sided pyramids as in Figure 11, the height of each being half the square of the base. Paint them blue, yellow, red, deep purple, black

Figure 11. Construction of Cube of Space

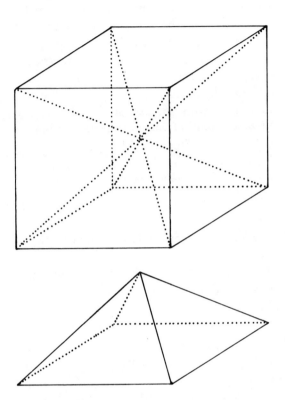

and white. Then assemble them so that they make one large cube with white on top, black at bottom, the sides being purple, red, yellow, and blue in that order. White will represent up and black, down; purple, the rear; then red, the left; yellow, the front; and blue, the right. This lines up with the Life-Elements balanced between highest and lowest forms of Life with the Divine Spark at center. At least this model will give you some ideas of being conscious of Space six ways at once relative to the center of your own being. An ideal way of making a model of this type would be from six differently colored transparent plastics so that their junctions would be discernable.

The purpose of this concept is to help you develop a "spiritual Space-sense." After all, when you entered this physical world, one of the first things you had to recognize as quickly as you could was a sense of which way was "up" and its opposite "down." Otherwise you could never have stood upright. Originally, you had only three ideas of Space: up, down, and "around." The four divisions of "around" came later and helped you to make more accurate movements with your physical body or to estimate the distance and movements of other creatures within your personal range. Now you have to do much the same from a spiritual point of view. Spiritual Space is a set of limitations on your extensions of consciousness in six different directions.

> ABOVE: Awareness of Greater Life on higher than human levels.
> BELOW: Awareness of Lesser Life on lower than human levels.
> RIGHT: Awareness of what is approaching nearer.
> FRONT: Awareness of what is closest.
> LEFT: Awareness of what is getting further away.
> REAR: Awareness of what is distant.

It will be noted that there is an unavoidable element of Time in this Space-sense, and it is not unlike that of a traveller on a road or Path. Maximum attention is concentrated on immediate Space, second degree of attention on the area being approached, third degree on what is being left behind in the distance, and minimum to what is remotely away. Attention to Space above and below is limited to a vague feeling of motion between them. All these Space-sensations have spiritual counterparts on whatever Path of Life we happen to be taking.

How far does the average person attempt to extend consciousness in any of these directions? As a rule, seldom very far except with what is in immediate range, and often not very deeply at that. It is obvious that we must be principally concerned with what is closest to us, but at the same time we need to relate that with the other coordinates in order to evaluate it properly and know the right degree of attention to give it. That is to say, we need to recognize our spiritual priorities and deal with them correctly as they come. Just as in driving we need to know the exact space clearance available in order to manoeuver our vehicle, so there is a need to know what spiritual Space we have to steer our souls around awkward corners and unexpected changes of course.

Estimations of spiritual Space can only be made with experience and practice just as in the case of physical space. Our eyes only help us here because we have binocular vision. A one-eyed person cannot judge distances with any accuracy. Beyond limits of sight, we have to estimate physical distances by maps, hearsay, or imaginative comparisons. It is possible to travel great distances without any real comprehension of them. Only by taking some acceptable standard, such as a foot, yard, or mile, and then relating this with Space can we make any judgment of its connection with ourselves. Why should we not adopt some standard measure of spiritual Space and make our estimation with that? How, otherwise, can we know what is "large" or "small," near or distant in spiritual terms?

It is obviously impossible to adopt any definite standards without general agreement among all concerned, but if we look at the way some of our physical Space standards were obtained, that might supply a few ideas. The Roman mile, for example, was a thousand paces of a legionary, and the word derived from "miles—a soldier." A yard (clothyard) was the length of cloth held in outstretched hand at one end and the tip of the nose turned away to the left at the other. A "hand" for measuring horses was the breadth of a broad palm at about five inches, and the inch was roughly the average length of a male middle finger top joint. All this means that ideas of distance were based on comparisons with human bodily spaces. Could we try a similar system with the soul, and work out some scale connected with spiritual measurements?

Might we suggest that a natural unit of spiritual measurement could be the *Rod*, which would be the spiritual distance to be covered by an average human soul until it has reached the point where it is capable of ruling its inner domains? As a measure of capacity, a *Cup* could be considered as the needed inner content of Love and Compassion required for "Salvation" of that soul. A *Sword* would gauge the amount of applied energy for trimming that soul into the right shape, and a *Shield* might be one pan of a balance to weigh the exact minimum required to pass from one spiritual level to the next. Or the *Shield* could be taken as the weight itself. The *Cord* would therefore become whatever length of Life and experience might be needed for souls to reach their ultimate aim.

Why should we not think of our Magical Symbols in this way? It would help to provide us with *some* standards of Inner Space and "solidity." Even arbitrary standards are better than none at all. Of course, these particular units of measurement are definitely on the high side so far as most humans are concerned. There is nothing wrong with that, but for practical purposes if a decimal application is to be used, many of us would have to think in terms of "milli-Rods," or possibly "micro-Cords." Nevertheless, the four main standards of spiritual Space are attainable by humans who are willing to work on themselves with unremitting devotion.

At any rate, that is a new way for you to think about the Four Symbols. In the language of Inner Space, they are telling you to go far enough, work hard enough, and become sufficiently capacious and solid to achieve the spiritual standards expected of fully fledged members of the Holy Mysteries in the West. As symbols adorning the various Temples dedicated to our Tradition, they are there to inspire anyone who knows what they stand for in actuality. Their magic lies in their meaning and not in the supernatural influence supposed to be attached to them. That should surely be magic enough to please any rational person trying to understand how he fits into the Tradition and what practical use may be made of them.

This is usually a major problem for those enthusiasts who "take up Magic" and insist on "setting up a Temple" for themselves with a lot of expensive equipment. Having gone that far, their question is what to *do* with the stuff in physical Space, so to speak. They feel a burning need to start waving it all around somehow, or handle it solidly so that it might accomplish wonders beyond their own powers of achievement. Their instincts tell them there is something wonderful connected with the symbols, but their intelligence and experience has not then reached a point where they can appreciate just what those symbols really are *as a means of Life* rather than mere ornamental artifacts. It would actually do them more good if they simply picked up any of the symbols and said something like, "All right, now I know what you look like on the Outside. Open the Way for me and show me what you really are on the Inside," then set it up on their altars and sit back to contemplate the thing.

This, however, would be far too tame a practice for most would-be magi who want something more exciting to do with their freshly forged weaponry. There is no reason in this world why they should not invent all sorts of activities involving ceremonial usage of the symbols, *providing they are capable of connecting the appropriate type of consciousness with each as it is being used.* It is not so much *what* is done that matters. It is *how* things are done, and the disposal of awareness during the proceedings. People could dance in patterns around circles exchanging the symbols amongst themselves if this were done with apposite words and music. It is the actual circulation of consciousness that counts, and the "change-overs" from one symbol-style to another. Never forget that the only purpose of a solid Magical Symbol is for evoking its particular sort of consciousness out of you, or for you to project that type of consciousness out of it. Apart from that, symbols are only decorations. Without their meanings they have no Magic whatever.

Once more it would be a good idea to start a notebook or looseleaf collection of ideas and information concerning the Five Symbols. A looseleaf system is probably best because fresh pages can be inserted anywhere. It is amazing that a mass of interesting and sometimes vital information can be acquired in this way. If you start with no more than five pages with a sketch of a Symbol on each, and then note what you have built up in almost six months, you may find yourself having to buy another file cover. To begin your collection, or maybe add to it, here are four "personifications" of the major Magical Weapons as used in one particular ritual of Western practice.

### The Sword

"I am the Sword, dividing right from wrong. I cleave through all confusion, and in action I am Courage, though I rest in

Honor. Mine is government by justice, and I give good discipline. I may bring retribution, yet I am the blade of Healing and I sever sadness from the side of joy. Alternately I am the Arrow, swift and certain to the mark when aimed by clear intentions. On Earth I am the Wind. In Man, Acuteness and in Heaven I present the edge of the Almighty Hand. RESPECT ME."

### The Rod

"I am the Rod that marks whatever lies between extremities, for I commence and close the Circle of Creation. I am the measurement of Majesty and rule with gentle government. Space I span, and Time I regulate. I direct attention to all points of consciousness and indicate intentions everywhere. Alternately I am the Spear-Staff, helping friends or fighting enemies. On Earth I am a Tree, in Man uprightness, and from Heaven I present the pointing finger of the Holy Hand. FOLLOW ME."

### The Cup

"I am the Cup containing every essence of Creation in my compass. All things exist in me, not I in them. Force flows into my Form, and every life is hallowed into One within the chalice of my comprehension. Divine and human Life meet in my depths, mine is the draught of Death or Immortality. Alternately I am the Cauldron of renewal and the Horn of Plenty. On Earth, I am an ocean in its bed, in Man I am capacity, whilst from Heaven I present the hollowed Hand of the Compassionate. TRUST ME."

### The Shield

"I am the Shield that overshadows separated Selves presenting them to one another in the manner of their meaning. Providence is mine, and I maintain both souls and body proving and protecting their integrity. Reflection meets reality within my Magic Mirror, and I am the aegis under which the works of wisdom operate. Alternately I am the Wheel of Life, or Platter bearing the most Blessed Bread. On Earth, I am a field, in Man a personality, and from Heaven I present the proffered Hand of Everlasting Friendship. TAKE ME."

It is always good to have ready-made ritual practices to fall back on, but ideally everyone ought to construct his own versions of at least minor rites designed to serve the Mysteries in the West. The reason for this is because it is the actual effort of consciousness expended in thinking out and putting together the construction and pattern of the rite which is of such importance. This is an act of origination which has been pushed through the Four Worlds and guided into the last level of practical action by human awareness guided by Inner Intelligence. The creation of a ritual is more significant than its repetition, yet fundamentally any ritual is an arrangement of consciousness which can be repeated as a Form, through its Force will naturally vary from one performance to another, depending a great deal on who is directing it.

Have you ever thought that "Magic Words" should have shape and Space as well as Time or Event-duration? If they are to have any reality in inner dimensions, then they should have the equivalent of Space therein, and Space argues some kind of shape or topology. Haven't you ever felt that some words seem sharp and spiky like "peak," "skipping," "crackly" and, of course, "prickly" and other words with S's and K's in them? Then there are "slithery" words like "snake," "squirm," "ooze" and so forth which are mostly self-descriptive; "round" words like "ocean," "oration," "crown," and "rotund" and "aroma;" square ones like "retrospective," "aristocrat," and "penultimate." We already think of "big" words like "totalitarianism" and "little" ones like "it." Words come in all sizes and shapes associated with the concept of Space or area. Then, too, we describe words as being "weighty" or "light" as if they had mass, or "empty" as though they had volume. We also speak of meaning as being "remote" if it is unclear, and "close" if very plain. All these are spatial ideas related to words which show how we connect our sense of Inner Space with the workings of consciousness.

Try out a few exercises in Space-awareness. After you have put yourself in a meditative mood and position, "go inside" your body as deeply as you can get and try to realize the limits of a single blood-cell. For simplicity, imagine yourself a red blood cell. You have no limbs of any kind, no nervous system, so you feel nothing, and yet you do experience alternate states of exhilaration and exhaustion. You are no more than a circular structure about 8½ thousandths of a millimeter, (• that was a millimeter) in size, though that means nothing to you since it is your total expanse. Nor do you know that the reason for your sense of well-being is due to oxygenization reaching you from the lungs of the body you live in, and your exhaustion is due to absorbtion of that oxygen by the tissues you pass through. All you know is that you follow a rhythmic pattern that you don't understand which keeps increasing in intensity as you get more and more exhausted. Then comes a tremendous pressure during which you seem to be turned inside out and you are all nice and fresh again to repeat the process. Such is your entire life.

One blood-cell. Now evolve a bit. Expand to the limits of your whole human body but no further. You are a living, thinking being confined in one body and its brain. Suppose you were totally paralysed and could not move muscles. That is what it would feel like and other humans would have to move your mass around for you as they thought best—or leave you to die. Yet you could still move your mind apart from that body while you had the faculty of imagination, so don't undervalue that precious potential. Treasure and develop it in case of need. It may save your sanity some day. Remember the cause of Cosmos is *controlled creativeness,* and humans can achieve that ability with practice.

Liberate yourself a shade further still. This time to the limits of your own home. Visualize yourself going from room to room, maybe meeting members of your family and enjoying a normal life with them. Include the garden if you have one, and paint your mental pictures from your stores of memory as brightly as you like. After that, widen your range a bit more and take yourself outside your home round and about your locality. Don't go any further than you usually do on short trips visiting nearby friends or something like that. Make it mostly in the vicinity of your town or within easy distance of your own home. Conjure up familiar scenes of your favorite local haunts one after another and keep the idea of distance from your home at the back of your mind occasionally.

When you have exhausted the possibilities of local amusement, free yourself a lot further and go anywhere in this world you may already have been to or would like to visit. Think of yourself catching trains, buses, boats, planes, or just driving to far destinations. Invent one or two adventures for yourself if you feel so inclined. Eventually, try to imagine yourself leaving this world altogether by spacecraft and wandering off around the solar system before you take off entirely on some star-trek looking for Life elsewhere in this Cosmos. Finally, reverse the whole trip sequentially, coming back to your meditating body by stages of Cosmos, Solar System, Earth, Locality, Home, and Self-as-a-Body.

The important thing here is to get a sense of "shift" from one defined zone to another so that you realize the relationship between them. Next you have to repeat the whole exercise in purely spiritual dimensions. Be guided by the "Cube of Space" idea. See yourself as you are, right in the very center of it. You are a brilliant scintillating point of pure Light, shining *where you will* in a disciplined and purposeful pattern. First you "think down" at the blackness below you. All lesser Life is there. Animals, plants, stones, and then just energy. Be conscious of them, then try being conscious *as* them. Realize they are zones of Life just as distinct from each other as those of your world are. Come back from them to your center in proper reverse order. Next push your attention to the upper whiteness above you. Closest to you will be advanced human souls incarnate on this Earth, then discarnate ones, then non-incarnates, then Intelligences existing as Energies. That will be about as high as human imagination is likely to take you though you believe it probable there are higher orders yet between you and the Infinite Energy you call "God" or whatever else. When you have pushed your mind as far as it will go this way, retreat back correctly to your central Self-star.

Looking levelly around you, direct your awareness to the spiritual situation receding from you to your left (remember you are turning on your axis towards the right deosil like our Earth). There, pass into the red sunset all the events and energies which you have coped with and maybe altered so that you became as you are at

184 • WESTERN INNER WORKINGS

present. You cannot recall them, but you will have to deal with them differently next time they come round in changed forms. Make some brief mental notes on how you would like to alter things when you do have another incarnation to live all over again, then leave things alone. There is no more you can do in that direction. Move now to the yellow sunlit patch of the present which shows you your current spiritual position. Here you can really focus attention and examine everything as closely as possible.

This is where you have all the spiritual factors affecting your life within range of your reach so that *you* may be able to affect or influence *them*. Try to think how you could do this, or don't be too proud to ask for inner guidance if you can't. Maybe you only need to write a letter to the right person, take the trouble to visit some particular place, or alter your views on some small point. It is simple things like this which alter your whole spiritual existence and it is only a question of knowing when and how to act with what. Now is your main opportunity for doing this. Do the best you can to get a good grasp on your spiritual affairs as they lie within your reach at closest quarters. They won't be coming round again for a *very* long time, so grab your chance to act on them while it is before you, though you can always repeat this exercise when you have time to spare.

Eventually you will have to move your attention rightwards towards the blue section dawning with your future. (Do note in passing that these are the colors of the center Spheres on the Tree, 5, 6, and 4 in that order.) Here it will be mostly a matter of making resolutions to handle what may be coming somewhat better and more efficiently than you have been doing up till now. Push your mind as far as it will go in this direction (which may not be any great distance, but at least it will help). Try to think of what you should do in various contingencies. Affirm your willingness to do the best you can with whatever is arriving. Have some confidence in your own ability to cope but *never* allow yourself to be contemptuously over-confident. Keep your feelings on the "I can manage—with God's help" level. That will get you by.

Lastly, when you think in the direction of the dim and distant purple past of the night behind you, try to realize the far-off point where past becomes future again. If your death is the future in this life it will be your past in another, and so on, until you reach broader and unimaginable spiritual cycles. Once your Life-limit was that of a single cell. Now you are a Microcosm of cells yet still a single cell of a Macrocomic system, and so maybe *ad infinitum* beyond belief. No need to worry or be apprehensive about what has already become the past and will become the future at some remote period. The best thing to do is go on dealing with what is in front of you and wait till it catches up with you.

If you have performed this exercise properly, you should feel somehow rather strangely "bigger and larger" than when you began it, as if you have gained a new perspective on spiritual Space and brought it into more manageable proportions. What you have actually done, of course, is to alter your own approach-angle to the topic, and that was really all which was needed. In your practice of "Art Magic," you will often find that when you cannot alter some actuality, the practical alternative is to change your own consciousness towards it, and then everything will work out much as you had hoped in the first place.

Now turn your attention to the idea mentioned earlier of giving shape to "Magic Words" so as to increase their significance and spiritual substance. This is where your tape recorder will come in useful to show the difference between "shaped" and "unshaped" words. Try first of all with the vowels, and sound the A as Ah, deeply. Utter each vowel clearly and distinctly as you would in ordinary ritual practice, but with no special thought behind it. Repeat this while visualizing and sensing them as in Figure 12:

*Ah:* as a cube growing larger and larger until it fills the whole room.
*Ee:* as a circle of ripples horizontally away from you.
*I:* as a circle of ripples vertically away from you.
*Oh:* as a globe growing as large as the room and pressing on the walls.
*U:* as a rightward helix growing from floor to ceiling which it presses.

Figure 12. The Five Vowels as Shapes

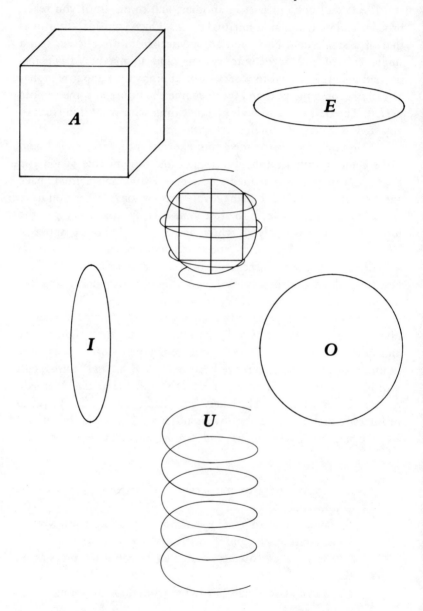

Do that several times, listen to the recordings, and see if you can detect any difference between them. Note that altogether you have formed the Circle Cross of Cosmos enclosing the Cube of Space, and surrounded by the helix of the Truth Cord.

Take any short passage of script you like. Read it first in the ordinary way while recording it, then read it again holding the idea in your mind that every word shapes itself and expands to the edges of the room as you utter it until it is pushed out of the way by the next one. This time don't worry about the actual shapes, but just let them form themselves as they come so long as you feel them filling the place and making it vibrate as they exert pressure within it. As you may know, if a sensitive beam were directed at the windows it could pick up every word you spoke from the ressonate responses of the glass panes. So your words do have solidity in physical Space alone. It is up to you to give them the equivalent in spiritual Space also. Now here comes an odd little thought.

You may have read somewhere that if a planet a couple of hundred Light years away could focus an optical telescope on this world which would reveal close up detail, the inhabitants of that planet would not see us at all, but *our world as it was two hundred years ago.* Humans long dead to us are still active images far enough out in Space. Suppose they also had microphones which would pick up the sounds we make. Once more they would hear words spoken by very long dead people. So whatever you say *remains said somewhere in Space till the end of Time.* Had you ever thought about that? If you hadn't, then begin now and watch what you say afterwards—you never know *when* you might be overheard! Perhaps you may see the possibility of what were once known as "Recording Angels" who faithfully noted whatever was said or done on this Earth. One day, you may have to watch a "playback" of this incarnation from birth to death or, worse still, of many of your lives, when your Time-sense is long enough to make them seem like a few minutes each. Do you think you are likely to enjoy the experience?

There are almost endless meanings to be had from the Cosmic Circle Cross of Time-Space-Events which is the basic symbol of our Western Inner Tradition. Every cycle of Life is represented by it, and it is the sign of Macrocosm and Microcosm combined. Time is cyclic, so is Space, and Events are cyclic, too. The old adage, "History repeats itself" is true enough if we accept it as happenings of human behavior rather than arrangements of artifacts confined to particular periods of Time. Human nature does alter somewhat through the centuries, but so slowly by our time-sense that it is often difficult to discern. It would be nearer the truth to say there is an average level of living souls on this Earth. Anything very much below that average could scarcely be born in human shape (though there are sad exceptions) and those greatly above it need not incarnate in human bodies anymore (though, again, there are glad exceptions). Therefore, the human race as a whole lies within a single range of Life on this planet, and so is relatively constant in nature as a species of Creation. As souls we evolve into and out of it while the Wheel of Life revolves inexorably.

In the fatalistic philosophy of the East it is believed that Fate is unalterable, and what God has decreed cannot be altered by one iota. In the West, we believe that God has an unalterable Plan for Perfection of all Life-species, including ours, but that most of our destiny on this Earth is designed by Man, and that *can* be changed if and when we make the right decisions. Yet we can only change our destiny if we manage to intercept or influence the energies which result in Events on Earth *before* they project into finalized forms on material levels. Once they are actually here among us, virtually superhuman spiritual strength would be needed to change their courses. It would be like trying to alter the flight of a bullet after it left the muzzle of a gun. No amount of magic could do that, and only an idiot would expect such an absurdity.

In our next chapter, we shall spend a little Time and Space on thinking about the Event Circle of our Cosmic Cross. Maybe there is something we might learn to our advantage. More correctly, we should find out what we may do with *ourselves* in order to make good relationships with the events of Life we are bound to experience in our human world. It is no use blaming God for what happens to us here, because most of it, and probably the worst part, comes from Man. At least let us see things in their proper proportions and perspectives. That might make a lot of difference to our views on Magic and the Mysteries.

### Questions

1. Define a "Space-cycle."
2. Describe a concept of "Spiritual Space."
3. Compare physical and spiritual Space-cycles.
4. Make a list of "shape-words."
5. Work out, describe, and practice a "Spiritual Space" exercise.
6. Draft a "personification" of the Magical Weapons according to your own ideas.
7. Associate your own shape-concepts with the vowel letters.
8. Discuss, "Life advances from its center."
9. Choose the seven most important sentences in this chapter.
10. Do you have any ideas of your own which associate shapes with abstract values, and if so, what are they?

# · 13 ·

# *Still Cycles*

Now we come to the much trickier topic of the last component of Cosmos, the circle of Events or Happenings. The unity of any Event is very difficult to describe. It is an energy-effect on and among humans which consumes both Time and Space to varied degrees relative to its own importance or intensity as an experience of human consciousness. For instance, something may happen in a moment of our time which extends an effect lasting for the rest of an incarnation, as when an impact accident results in crippling for life. Conversely, an event may happen very slowly which builds up to the terminal experience of death, as in the case of a slow killing disease. We may die from something as small as a microbe or as big as an atomic explosion, when the results are the same, but the means differ extremely.

First, we have to realize that there would be happenings and events on this Earth if there were no humans here at all. Days and nights would interchange, weather would alter, tides ebb and flow, volcanoes erupt, seasons change, and all other natural events would take place with only Cosmic Consciousness to be aware of them. When human beings themselves became an Event in the Creative cycles, the picture began to alter with the entry of another type of intentional awareness. Originally, the events of natural forces modified our behavior, but eventually our reactions with them aroused awareness which ultimately enabled us to start up our own chain of Events which has been following us through human hereditary and history with accumulating effects all the way.

Most people should be familiar with the old nursery rhyme begining, "For the want of a nail the *shoe* was lost," and ending, "For the want of a Victory the *Kingdom* was lost, and all for the want of a horseshoe nail." The moral was that small happenings could lead to larger and larger ones by chain-reaction until an eventual disaster needed all the increasing energy to cause it, so the power behind that particular series dropped back to flat potential again. The same principle, of course, could be applied with a beneficial result. If we accept this, however, we have to admit the opposite possibility of a maximum happening decelerating in a series of rhythms back to neutral like the boom of a once-struck gong dying steadily to silence after a sequence of reverberations. Additionally, we shall have to see that chains of events can be kept going with repetitious monotony, like the swinging of a clock pendulum moved by a consistent amount of energy supplied regularly.

The cyclic course of events can be broken down into the following four classifications:

1. *Nature:* This may be any kind
2. *Application:* How, and to what or whom it is applied
3. *Intensity:* Its Time and Space components
4. *Effect:* Connected resultant, likely to cause or cancel other Events.

For example, we could classify one natural happening as:

1. Volcanic erruption
2. To cultivated and inhabited area of Earth
3. With considerable force at Pompeii and Herculaneum, Italy, A.D. 79, for several days
4. Both towns wiped out, many dead, thousands homeless and ruined, lives wrecked, cultivation destroyed.

That was only the single turn of one major event wheel in human history. Following that were an uncountable sequence of lesser and lesser events in the lives of those concerned probably for many generations. For instance, our present wheels are spinning still from the effects of both World Wars. Being born after them gives no exemption from their far-reaching influence. Humans inherit Event effects from previous generations as well as their own ancestral genetics. They can scarcely avoid what is already in action when they enter this world. It is bound to affect them to some degree.

We tend to measure our lives by the sequence of events running through them from one end to the other. It would be more correct to measure them by our reactions with those same events, depending on how far or deeply they affect us as living souls. There is considerable variation in the experience-extension factor between one soul and another. Two souls (or more) might share the same Event with as many different effects as there are souls involved. One major problem faced by all mystical or religious systems is how to advise or counsel adherents on dealing with Event effects which they are likely to encounter during a human incarnation. Their findings seem to differ almost as much as Events themselves.

The Christian school of thought is generally to accept anything that happens to you, no matter how dreadful, as being the "inscrutable Will of God" for which you will receive due compensation in the hereafter. You are not to question or dispute this Divine decision, but accept it meekly, partly as a just punishment for your own sins, however trivial, and partly on behalf of other humans whose deserved punishments would be impossible for them to bear, so it has to be shared out among fellow mortals proportionally. It must be remembered that vicarious atonement for sin is a central theme of Christian doctrine, whose single Sacred King, Jesus, was reputed to have agonized for the total sins of all Mankind.

On the other hand, the Christian Church in former times supported a monastic order of life in which both male and female humans removed themselves from the events of mundane society, remaining as unaffected as they could from these, while they set up a series of spiritual events calculated to condition their souls into better states of being. The theory was to withdraw from cycles of events over which they had no control, and substitute other cycles wherein they had considerable control. The monasteries were a kind of spiritual air-raid shelter in which ascetics stayed safely while the laity absorbed most of the nastiness in the world outside. Later generations of Christians came to regard this as a form of moral cowardice and went around belligerantly giving battle to whatever they felt was wrong with our world. In doing this, they caused as much trouble as anyone else.

Few of the Mystery systems regarded unhappy events as being purposely sent by any sort of God. They saw these as being caused mainly by misuse of inner energies by Man, or due to human ignorance and stupidity in refusing to recognize essential Laws of Life. They did admit deliberate and malicious manipulation of energies in order to engineer ill-effects on humans, a great deal of this being set in motion by people for purposes of gain, revenge, profit, or just plain viciousness. A proportion, however, was aimed against us by anti-human forms of intelligence alien to our Life-species which orthodox religions termed "devils." These were offset considerably by oppositional influences from pro-human types of intelligent energies called "Angels." The Great Power most humans thought of as "God" did not normally interfere with these Event-causing energies, but left them to individual creations of Consciousness to work everything out *as They Willed*.

So far, we have been speaking as if Events only happen to us as humans on Earth, but they can also be caused by ourselves as happenings to others. Then again we can increase or decrease chains of events involving us by our reactions therewith. For example, the normal response to infliction of injury by another human being is reprisal in kind, and probably to a greater extent. This usually leads to retaliation which grows in eventfulness until serious damage occurs to both or more parties. That was why the Semitic system allowed reprisal by *no more* than the exact amount of original injury; "An eye for an eye, a tooth for a tooth, and a life for a life," so as not to keep increasing the impetus of a harmful Event-chain. The Christian system went further by asking that "good be returned for evil" in the hope of not only neutralizing it at that point but commencing something beneficial in exchange. This might not have got very far, but at least it was a step in a better direction.

The esoteric teaching on Events of all kinds was that they began and ended in consciousness, manifesting through the "Four Worlds" this way:

1st. The world (or state, level, or whatever) of *Conception,* where the bare idea or notion of an Event is conceived.

2nd. The world of *Creation,* wherein the idea begins to gestate and develop itself.

3rd. The world of *Calculation* wherein the idea takes exact form, shape, and solidifies itself into a practicality for projection in finished form into:

4th. The world of *Concretion,* which is our ordinary condition of consciousness in this human world.

These "Worlds," are the same as those we encounter in connection with the Tree of Life. They were given various names or descriptions, but they are fundamentally the four stages of consciousness whereby Mind materializes its meanings, and Will through Word becomes Work.

The whole point at issue was how members of the Mysteries were to deal best with the impact of Events in this world which hit them from all angles and from every separate level of Life. Many humans became badly unbalanced by some of these Events, and quite a few were dangerously distorted or damaged beyond repair in that incarnation. The consciousness concerned with the Events in life does more soul-shaping for an individual than the awareness dealing with Time and Space. Here we come up against the question of how much control we have over the effects of Events which make contact with our consciousness as human beings, and to what degree we may manipulate this control to cover at least the most probable contingencies.

A good example of this is the control needed by medical specialists who come in frequent contact with horrifying conditions of disease, disfigurement, or human disintegration. There may be little enough which can be done for any such victims, but unless the specialists concerned are able to control the effect of them upon their own psyches, they will become powerless to do even that much because they become liable to break-up on mental levels themselves. Every nurse or doctor in training knows this, and as some say, "You have to harden yourself. You'd go mad if you didn't." True enough, but the problem is how to do this for your own protection and yet prevent yourself from becoming so indifferent to human suffering that you care nothing whatever for your fellow-creatures and are totally unconcerned with what may happen to them.

Quite a reasonable answer to this was given by the dictum, "God hates the sin, yet loves the sinner." That is to say, recognize the distinction between the Events of an individual soul (for each of us *is* an Event in the construction of Cosmos) and whatever Event that soul has set in motion or helped on its way. This is admittedly a fine distinction, but a proper one to make if possible, because it allows estimation of Events to be made on more accurate lines. Thus it would enable a medical worker to be horrified at a disease, yet be deeply sympathetic with the sufferer, so that the two feelings balanced each other, leaving a clear area of consciousness from which to extend intelligent assistance. Opposing Events always tend to cancel each other out, so if they can be "matched" properly, this will usually result in fairly smooth running of the Event-wheel of the Cosmos.

One lesson that has to be learned early in the practice of the Mysteries is the counter-balancing of Events reaching us on one level of Life with their opposites instituted on another. That is to say, use the Law of Compensation in order to keep a kind of constancy and steadiness in the spiritual structure of your own Cosmos. In practice it means that if an Event threatens the stability and running of your individual Cosmic Event-cycle, you have to create an "equal and opposite" Event on inner levels which will help to stabilize your poise and hold you firm on your Path of Progress. What is more, you have to work until this becomes an automatic action operating constantly as a customary act of Life.

First, let it be realized that an ideal condition of existence on this Earth (or elsewhere) would be one of poised power in which our cycles of Time, Space and Events were reasonably regular and consistent with each other so that harmony prevailed throughout their relationships with one another. Theoretically, they would be like a three-plane gyroscope (if there were such a thing), maintaining its stability no matter how everything else related to it. That stability would depend on outside energy reaching it efficiently in order to keep it spinning dynamically. From a mechanical viewpoint, it would need three different types of energy which would neither interfere with each other nor offer enough friction to stop any rotor of the machine. This could be provided by electromagnetic, electrostatic, and vacuum-jet applied forces, none of which need physical contact with the rotors unless you count the air-stream of the latter.

Imagine these three cycles of Cosmos as "wheels," "globes," or even rhythms of Cosmos rotating round yourself simultaneously though at considerable variations of rate. For the sake of making reference points, the Time-Circle is reckoned as horizontal, the Space-Circle as lateral, and our present Event-Circle as vertical as in Figure 13. Now suppose your Event-Circle were an actuality as a

Figure 13. The Three Components of Cosmos Symbolized in Circle Cross Form

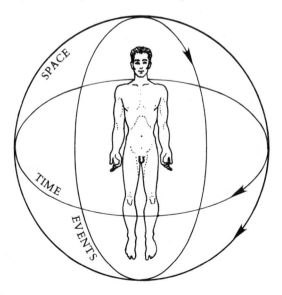

mechanism instead of being symbolically representative of force dispositions connected with your life. The overload from a heavy impact of an Event on your individual circle from external sources could interfere with its smooth working and cause trouble for you unless you might:

A. Avoid or screen yourself from the impact.
B. Absorb and distribute its effects over an adequate area of yourself,
C. Compensate for it by equal and opposite balancing.

To take course A, you would require some presentiment of happenings a little in advance. Course B is what most humans try to do with greatly varying degrees of success. Course C is what genuine Mystics train themselves to manage as well as they can. Note very carefully that this does *not* alter the nature of an Event in any way, but it does alter very considerably the effect of it on your Microcosmos and that is what really matters. Such a "Magical act" may convert tragedy into triumph.

Suppose, for instance, that something nasty has happened to you which was not your own fault, so far as you know. Perhaps a valued possession has been stolen which naturally causes shock when you discover the loss, especially if not covered by insurance. Apart from notifying the police, your immediate need is for psychological first aid. This primarily depends on realizing the vital fact that no amount of your suffering or upset could possibly retrieve your property. You could crucify yourself in your own garden and accomplish *nothing* in the way of compensation. Therefore, any mental anguish on your part would be useless, pointless, and only add to your sorrows without doing the slightest good. Added to that is the unpleasant thought that it would only amuse the thieves if they knew how you felt. So why make them a present of your pain as a bonus?

Using consciousness in that or similar ways, you get the best grip you can on the Event and then originate a counter-current in the opposite direction by thinking and *willing* something like, "I claim compensation for this loss I have sustained. Let this experience in Life bring me some benefit which will be better than the property of which I am deprived. Because I have lost that, then let me gain whatever makes the price look cheap. Which is greater, the generosity of God or the meanness of Man? I await the decision of Divinity with confidence."

The idea is to start up the compensation-current in your consciousness as soon as you can after the Event impacts on you. In that way you prevent the damage that depression or disorientation can cause, at the same time originating cycles of energy which might eventually bring your recompense in material terms. Even though you may never recover your physical property, you may as well convert the loss to spiritual gain which will remain yours long after all your worldly gear has been inherited by others.

A good practical way to commence this system of dealing with Events in a consciously compensatory fashion is by listening to any radio or TV newscast and reacting to every item therein by a counterbalancing comment or thought of your own. Respond to each depressing and discouraging remark with the best "comeback" you can think of. Realize that so many broadcasts are deliberately designed to confuse and upset or distort the minds of listeners and viewers. Refuse to be caught in this trap and turn it to your advantage by converting the impact of ill-events on yourself into something of better spiritual significance.

You could do the same with the printed news media. Instead of sitting supinely in your chair letting all the horrors and stupidities of the day wash over your mind with a despairing film of darkness, react to it as constructively as you can. For instance, you might put up a small prayer for every victim of viciousness you read about. You might send mental messages in the general direction of public figures according to your opinions of them. You could send out ideas for improvements of human or animal conditions in this world. Send any constuctions of consciousness concerned with Event-affairs on Earth, so long as they are intended to be helpful and of some value to the cause of progression towards Perfect Peace Profound. Never lose sight of our ultimate aim. Don't think you will waste time or effort in doing this. No thoughts are ever lost entirely.

We have been speaking of Events in terms of your reactions to them should they be likely to have ill-effects on your psyche, but what about the opposite possibility? Here, again, we need to keep the balance of an Event-cycle steady, but there is no real reason why we should do this by invoking an Event of gloom to counterbalance one of joy. Joy can be compensated out by distribution. In other words, an excessively joyful Event may be considered as an amelioration of a large number of minor Events which, if added up, would total a single Event of an opposite nature to the joyful one. That is to say, a single "Great Gladness" could be taken as a balancing factor against a lot of "small sadnesses" and the overall poise of an Event-cycle preserved. It is always the maintenance of balance which is of greatest importance. The speed and variation of Events may be as great or small as possible, providing their balance is evenly distributed.

Most people of average intelligence in our modern Western world manage to develop instinctively some ability to correct the balance of their Event-cycles but it is still worth while to be conscious of the necessity for balance and to learn if improved methods of achieving balance can be found. Practising ritualists have been applying their art to this for centuries. Ever since the Law of Cosmic Compensation (known in the East as Karma) has been recognized by the human race, schemes have been sought by spiritual specialists for adjusting with it as favorably as possible. For instance, if A murders B in one incarnation, must B murder A in the next and so on? That seemed to be a stupid sort of cycle, yet obviously compensation had to be applied somehow. Again, it seemed inadequate to judge by purely human standards. Cosmos runs by Its own rules that only had to be observed, but which mere human being dared to state with any certainty what those rules were and exactly how they worked?

Quite a few attempted this. The first theory (which still has some adherents here and there) was that humans had angered the "Gods," and so must buy this anger off with bribes or sacrifices. These became ritual Events of their own kind which in varied forms are practiced today. Another idea was that the Gods might be bargained with as in a commercial transaction, and fair trading terms might be established between the human and Divine parties concerned. One way or another, a great number of ceremonies and procedures evolved from the central idea of altering Events involving humans by changes of consciousness connected with them on different levels of Life. The most modern survival of this idea seems to be the conviction that it is not so much the "Mind of God" we need to try and influence, but the mind of Man. Events "sent by God" we can cope with all right, but when it comes to Events caused by Man there is far more likelihood of peril to the peoples of this planet. Therefore, practitioners of the Mysteries in our days are chiefly concerned with types of ritual aimed at alterations of human attitudes by setting up currents of consciousness which it is hoped will infiltrate and influence the instinctive intelligence of Mankind in general into better courses of behavior and consequently an improvement in the average Event-pattern.

Individual adjustments of Event-cycles have to be made by those concerned for themselves. Nobody else is likely to alter them for you from outside, as it were. You have to take hold of them from Inside and balance them out from there as best you can. No one in his right mind would suppose this an easy task, but it has to be tackled sooner or later by all attempting to make spiritual progress in their lives. Some Mystery Schools advise one method, and some another. These all depend on your ability to prevent the impact of Events from damaging the spiritual structure of your psyche and you must be equally able to initiate inner chains of Events calculated to cause correspondingly compensative effects. Christian Mystics would say this could only be accomplished by the "Grace of God" acting through you because you prayed for it. Other mystical systems might say that you should develop the faculty by your own efforts in conjunction with superior spiritual helpers anxious to advance your progress along the Path to Perfection. Though every system might disagree with the other in favor of its particular methodology, all would be unanimous in admitting that the achievement and maintenance of spiritual balance and poise amid every disturbing and confusing Event of Earth-life is of primal importance as a prerequisite of successful spiritual living.

Here it is proposed that you should try the practical symbology of the Cosmic Cross for gaining this essential state of stability. In one sense, it is like riding a bicycle. Nothing keeps you upright and in motion except your impetus and balance which is an acquired art. So is Cosmic cycling. First you have to experience the idea of being in the center of the Three Cosmic Circles of Power. They are rotating around you on their axes at different rates. Now you must realize this would not be physically possible, so you visualize them not as mechanical wheels, but as globes of three different energies capable of occupying the same Space-shape relationships, but interacting therein independently. Our previous suggestion of atmospheric pressure, electromagnetic, and electro-static energies would serve as symbols for this, but you could choose others if you make them feasible in your mind. Let suppose you build up a picture around yourself which feels like this:

Around you horizontally from left to right rotates the globe of Time as an alternating mass of electrostatic energy. It pulses like an electronic clock, and you sense it ticking inexorably as it measures your incarnation from birth to death. Around you laterally, over your head and beneath your feet from left to right is the atmospheric pressure–driven sphere of Space which expands or contracts as it revolves. Around you rotating from head to foot, front and rear, is the electromagneticaly propelled sphere of Events. Alternately, you might imagine this as a treadmill which you work yourself with every step you take upon the Path. Whichever analogy you employ, get the images absolutely clear in your mind with the fundamental ideology of Time, Space and Events revolving round you in three directions. Like riding a bicycle, so long as they keep going steadily and regularly you will be all right, but if not, you are liable to get hurt. See the scheme as simply as that.

As you should realize, the most difficult part to balance is the Event cycle. If you can, you have to steer your way past Events that might obstruct your Path, get safely through those which are difficult, or over the minor bumps and potholes while you absorb the shocks with nothing worse than small discomforts. In that sense, driving your "Cosmic vehicle" is very similar to riding a bicycle along a problematical country pathway. You have to be constantly on the alert for oncoming emergencies, yet at the same time relaxed enough to enjoy the ride. Remember this is a spiritual structure *of your own construction,* so it is carrying you along Inner Paths of progress which are *relative* to Events encountered on Earthlife. Nevertheless if you can develop expertise on the spiritual Inner Paths of Life, this will considerably influence your travels along the Outer ways.

Once you are accustomed to imagining your Cosmos around you, try to sense yoruself controlling its course through Creation. Make imaginative journeys through different Events which would normally upset you, but take yourself through these calmly and steadily because you are compensating for them all the time. Do the same with imaginary Events which might make you euphoric with delight, but again keep a firmly compensatory throught-control over your event-cycle in front of you, and distribute the delight over a wider area of yourself so that the total effect evens out and holds you in balance. One useful point about this exercise is that you can do it while engaged with any routine type of occupation (except of course while actually driving a physical vehicle along a terrestrial road). You can do it while walking along, or during almost anything which leaves the imaginative part of your mind free to operate, and best of all, you can and should *enjoy* it.

The really valuable effect of this exercise is that it helps associate control of your relationship with Events together with a simple symbolism in your consciousness, and that is a great spiritual advantage: to realize that you are not just something an inscrutable Fate knocks indiscriminately, from one Event to another in this life, but a living individual soul with an ability to hit back if you have to and bounce to a better position. Surround yourself with the Cosmic Circle Cross and be your own Time, Space and Events in spiritual dimensions. It is the symbol of Divine Dynamism which you need to invoke as a spiritual stabilizer whenever you feel your sense of inner balance threatened or shaken.

If you felt yourself slipping or falling physically, you would instinctively grab at anything at all to save your body from possible injury. Everyone should have an inner equivalent to clutch in case spiritual poise should be upset. Pious Christians might call a Jesus image to mind, or a very superstitious person might stroke a lucky charm and mutter a spell. Both would be calling consciously on a symbol which they associated with salvation from whatever was endangering their peace of mind and soul. As a result, a summons would forthwith be sent to the subconscious reserves of energy from whence supplies might be drawn to deal with the problem confronting them. You might call this a sort of "Save me!" or S.O.S. symbol, if you like. So why not make the Cosmic Circle Cross of spiritual stability *your* S.O.S. symbol as an emergency emblem whenever you feel yourself slipping? Why let Life on this planet push you around hither and thither? *Get inside your own Cosmos and compensate* so that you hold your course steady alone Inward lines whatever happens on the Outside.

These are only *some* of the significant meanings behind the Circle Cross Symbol. More and more should come through to you as you medittae on it and *live* with it. Perhaps by now you realize why it is such a vital and fundamental design woven into the Western Mysteries. Again and again you have to be told that the symbols of the Holy Mysteries are not there only as reminders of our past or to make anything seem more impressive in the present. They are there for your *practical use,* and to serve the minds and souls of those who use them. So the next time you start thinking about the Sacred Symbols of our Inner Tradition, ask yourself, "What is that *for,* what does it *do,* and how can I *use* it?" If you reach any conclusions, try working out a few exercises which you feel would improve your handling of that Symbol. It is the only way to develop your abilities represented by those Symbols.

From the Circle Cross came the Round Table of Arthur, in the center of which the Sangreal was said to appear in fulfilment of the promise, "Where two or three are gathered in my name, there will I be within the midst of them." Later, the Grail was symbolized as a red rose when the Rosicrucian Movement took over many of the old Mystery procedures with more up-to-date methods in Renaissance times. Other meanings apart, the symbol of the Rose displayed above a gathering of people meant that all said or done beneath it must be kept closely secret by all present. Hence the phrase *sub rosa*—under the rose. To this day, we call any central ceiling decoration or moulding a "rose," and it is almost the last relic of the old mysteries in modern homes. You cannot escape the

Circle Cross in one form or another wherever you go in the West. So keep it circulating in yourself always.

For the time being, though, we shall leave this almost inexhaustible theme and consider some points of ceremonial procedure in Western esoteric practice which, being part and parcel of our Inner Tradition, deserve their place in this overall study course.

## Questions

1. What, to you, is the cycle of an event?
2. Give several examples of: a. Major events arising from accumulation of small ones; b. Lessening effects from the fading of a major happening.
3. Trace an event from inception to manifestation through the Four Worlds.
4. Discuss: "God hates the sin, yet loves the sinner."
5. Do you have any systematic procedures for dealing with events, and if so, show this schematically.
6. How do you set up counter-currents to events?
7. Give three examples of event-compensation.
8. Do you have any personal "Save me!" formula, and if so, what is it?
9. Choose the nine most important sentences in this chapter.
10. How is stabilization by the Cosmic Cross system like riding a bicycle?

# · 14 ·

# *Sacred Ceremonialism*

**S**ome details of ceremonial practice should be studied before any would-be member of the Western Mysteries attends formal ritual gatherings. This is one point on which Western occultism as a whole is extremely weak. Secrecy of procedure is so deeply ingrained among practitioners that they are apt to lose touch with the original reasons for this, its purpose and application. Somehow they expect candidates for initiation into their particular group to have no prior experience of Mystery practice, and to accept what happens as amazing revelations of supreme spiritual importance. This is just about as unreasonable as expecting a modern person to approach the nuptial couch with no knowledge of the sex act. That *could* happen, but it would be regarded as exceptional in our times. Candidates do indeed present themselves for initiation without previous knowledge of ritual procedures, but why *should* they? What is so wonderful about ignorance?

Most of the now unnecessary secrecy and "hush-hush" policies about ritualism in the Western Mysteries is a hangover from previous periods when ritualism was not only totally mis-understood by outsiders, but could land everyone concerned in deep trouble with civil or Church authorities involving loss of liberty, property, or maybe life. There were excellent reasons for "occult secrecy" then. In early Christian times, rumors abounded that Christians were secret cannibals who ate their God and drank his blood, thus practising ritual murder. Later, Christians were to believe that Jews sometimes killed Christian children for the sake of their blood to mix with their Passover bread. The only likelihood of safety lay in silence, so this was strictly enjoined and enforced on members of all Mystery Schools, even to the point of death for betrayal. Some groups even today (though very few now) still administer oaths to candidates invoking terrible penalties for revealing ceremonial secrets to outsiders. A classic penalty was having the throat cut from ear to ear, and the body buried between high and low tides. Another was to be shot to death with five black arrows. At least candidates knew what to expect.

Now the knowledge of the Holy Mysteries in the West is not confined to secret societies consisting of human beings with their lives to safeguard. The Mysteries are essentially the beliefs and spiritual standards we hold within us as being too sacred to brandish around and speak of openly before those who might treat them with indifference, contempt, or hostile ridicule. No one devoid of such a sense of respect for sacred topics can possibly understand the significance of the Mysteries. Without respect and reverence, the Mysteries have nothing to offer humanity, and the symbol for reverential respect has always been—silence. Or at least very subdued speech. When silence is employed as a symbol for the sacredness of the Mysteries, as in the case of the Rose Cross for instance, it is beyond value. If used to confuse others or enhance self-importance for no good purpose, it is only foolish. Knowledge of when and where to speak or keep silence is vital in the Mysteries. The golden rule is not to talk until the necessity for speaking becomes crystal clear, then say what needs to be said and no more.

Ceremonial is an artistic skill which needs to be learned like any other skill such as dancing, speaking, acting, or combining body, mind and soul for purposes of spiritual import. There are good ritualists (relatively few), passable ones (not enough), and then really incompetent ones (plenty). All might improve with enough practice and attention. Not everyone has that particular flair for ritualism which marks an expert at any art, but at least a competent and capable performance might be expected of average attenders at Western Mystery gatherings if they are prepared to work on themselves.

It is often wrongly supposed that only those conducting a ceremony are ritualists, and the rest are mere spectators, like an audience in a theatre. This should *never* be so. *All* partakers in esoteric ceremonies are to be regarded as active ritualists, and they are equally part of the rite with the principals or Officers who activate it on Earthly levels. No occult ritual should ever be considered as a show of some kind put on for the entertainment of those attending. It is essentially a physically symbolized presentation of spiritually synthesized power put into action for some specific purpose. Everyone present is (or ought to be) part and parcel of the action as a practising ritualist whether or not they are physically active in it. The moving and speaking Officers can be compared to conductors of orchestras. They are coordinators, but it is the instrumentalists who make the music which is the object of the whole gathering. Without that music there would be nothing but aimless gesticulations and antics. A conductor's baton does not play a note by itself. Silence is conducting sound.

Using the orchestra analogy again, unless every musician is an accomplished performer on his instrument, there could be no harmony worth hearing. Imagine the horrible outcome of attempts by professionals to render a concerto played by untaught children free to hoot, scrape, bang or twang anything they wanted, plus a conductor with no knowledge of music who only wanted to wave his hands around because he thought he heard a tune somewhere. Even imagining the racket is painful, but scarcely more so than an incompetent collection of ritualists "tone deaf" to inner dissonances caused by their untrained and unskilful combinations of consciousness. Magic is not unlike music in many ways, and musicians have to practice for many hours by themselves before they are normally considered ready to begin practice with others. So it should be with ritual practitioners in the Holy Mysteries.

It might well be asked why, if the objectives of esoteric rituals are spiritual, we need any form of physical symbolism at all, and if the action could not be accomplished without the formalities of ceremonial. The answer is that since we are living in this world as human creatures of flesh and blood, we cannot very well ignore the Life-energies applying to this condition of consciousness. If we were purely spiritual beings existing without incarnate bodies, we could indeed do without the material means of signs, ceremonies, or any form of energy-adaption through symbolism. But we are *not* such wonderful sorts of beings, only plain, common, ordinary humans trying to improve ourselves in the best way we can. We cannot deny the facts of our bodies, but only interpret them as being related with spiritual actualities in one way or another. So our bodies are symbols of our souls rather than the reverse. While we are burdened with bodies, we need some kind of physical symbolism to translate the natural Life-energies of this level to more subtle states of activity. We also need physical symbols with spiritual significance for bringing inner energies to bear on mundane matters. Hence the reason for ceremonial activity to symbolize spiritual equivalents.

Another good reason for ritualism is for the sheer sake of expressing ourselves thereby as active agents of Life. People dance, sing, play, or perform activities for no other reason than that this satisfies a need for expressing energy in "extra" existence. The old dictum of Descartes, "I think, therefore I am," is interpreted as, "I act, therefore I am." Why should not ritualism, religious or otherwise, be considered an art form second to none in human estimation of behavior? If a practitioner were asked why he or she fulfilled themselves with ritualistic activities the reply might be, "Because I enjoy it and achieve myself therein," and who would consider such an honest answer inadequate or unjustified? Certainly no one with the slightest understanding of real spiritual values.

The actual meaning of the word "ritual" is only "in the manner or style of," signifying the way things are or ought to be done. Strictly speaking it would be incorrect to say anything like, "I would like to practice ritualism," or "I am going to attend a ritual tonight." There should really be a specification of the type of ritualism referred to, such as, "a mystical ritual," "a military ritual," or whatever else. Ritualizing any procedure in the proper sense, means establishing suitable forms and methods for doing it, and generally working to that standard every time it is repeated.

This does not mean that any such forms must never alter or improve, only that they do exist as current or customary usage. Nothing more or less.

So whether you work according to ritual systems others have invented, or invent your own, you will still be practising ritualism whenever you repeat a formalized process. To practice an occult or mystical ritual means that you must use an established method for dealing with whatever occult or mystical principles may be involved. It is the *customary usage* which makes it a ritual, otherwise it might only be an experiment or a "one off" happening. Nothing wrong with that. Just a matter of definition. It is always best to be as clear and focussed as possible about meanings attached to symbols, and words are possibly some of the most potent symbols we have in Western esoteric practice. The clearer, more conscious a definition we can make of any word, the more magical that word will become. Vague ambiguous words are only sonics without sense, and the only value to any word lies in the consciousness it can contain.

Most Western esoteric ritualism is concerned with coordinating consciousness between body, mind and soul so that contact is made with spiritual energies for specific purposes. This means that there is something for the body to do which should involve the mind in thinking and the soul in feeling so that both principles invoke the attention of spiritual awareness. One might almost call it a chain reaction. For example, dancing or circumambulating awaken the bodily functions, singing or chanting move the soul, the meaning of the words stir the mind, and the coordination of all these energies directed to an inner target arouse the spirit. That is the A, B, C of Western (or any other) mystical or magical ritualism. The rest is a matter of whats, whys, hows, and whens, depending mostly on the whos. The only difference between the ordinary religious rituals which anyone can attend, and the eclectic private rites of secret and occult congregations is one of method and meaning. Most of the fundamental principles are common to both so far as "psycho-mechanics" are concerned.

Intelligent members of the ritualistic churches often wonder why so little of the procedure is ever explained to them carefully, or why it is so inadequately accounted for if they do ask. The same might apply to a lot of Lodge or Temple practice. Much of it should be self-explanatory to any rational mind, but a great deal of the symbolism is not meant to be explained anymore than a Zen "koan" is, and for the same reason. Some symbols are deliberately designed so as to arouse "Cosmic curiosity" in the minds and souls of beholders and receptors. *It is the effort to try to solve the meaning of the thing* which stirs the minds and souls to rise above their average levels, and in so doing they encounter a lot of other spiritual experiences which teach them the "occult truths" they sought to know. That was mostly why the Celtic Mystery practices were so fond of riddles, string and knot puzzles and other challenges to insight and intelligence. They were "awakeners" demanding the engagement of interest, imagination, and real effort on the part of those seeking the solutions, and giving considerable pleasure if a satisfactory one was found. Achievement all round by setters and solvers alike.

This is also why so many of the old time rituals had strings of questions, challenges, and unexpected events in them which could be quite disconcerting. They were not only character and intelligence tests for participants, but also arousers of hidden abilities and potentials. It is said that we never know what we can do until instant demands are made on us in emergencies, and this is quite true. The designers of those rituals knew this quite well, and contrived situations calculated to have exactly that effect. This worked well enough so long as the element of surprise remained intact, but as the secrets leaked out (which they nearly always do in the end), candidates prepared themselves in advance with textbooks answers, and eventually proceedings degenerated into semi-farcical affairs of parading round the place in costume with sponsors who whispered standard replies into candidates' ears as they encountered each fresh challenge. This was not much more than modern radio show personnel holding up large cards marked "LAUGHTER" or "APPLAUSE" to obtain artificial audience response.

The physical part of modern occult rituals depends on which particular system or group is working. By no means are all these methods acceptable in common among every assembly. Each selects a combination of whichever practices seem to suit its purpose of association. For instance some will accept nudity, flagellation, and sex practices as ritual procedures, while the majority of others would certainly not. Some rituals are charged with emotional content like revivalists meetings, with lots of singing, dancing, ecstatic cries of excitement, and everything short of group sex. Others are stiff, silent, gloomy, enigmatic and chilling in nature. There are as many varieties of ritual as there are types of people to work them, and the only criterion to decide whether they are occult or not, is whether they are performed in public or private. Even there, some gatherings which are practised in public may be occult in effect because the inner content is not perceptible to an average awareness.

If any ritual can be classed as behaviorism, the components of mystical ritualism should be categorized as behavior of body, mind, and soul, geared to spirit by a linkage of symbolism and motivated by a single common intention. Unless such a coordination takes place in actuality, no form of ritual involving spiritual energies can possibly be effective. Handling the physical symbolism of ritual procedures by itself produces no more than mime and movement. If you cannot coordinate body, mind and soul with a spiritual intention, you will never make a mystical ritualist. This may not be such an easy thing to do as you might suppose, and nothing but practice and discipline will develop such an ability. Why not try it out in principle now and find the "feel" of it, then the rest should be simply a matter of application and arrangement.

First, the physical symbolism. Pick up a common pen or pencil in the ordinary way and by pure intention alone convert it to a magic Rod. It has to represent the projection of your Will from the focus of its point. Aim the point at some flat surface a short distance away and start drawing steady rhythmical circles in the air. Next comes the mental involvement. Choose some simple yet most meaningful phrase such as "Thy Will be Done" and keep repeating this is your mind. Now bring in the attention of your soul by feeling and trying to appreciate the significance of that saying. Wonder whose Will or what Will if you like, so long as you can hold the feeling of a Divine Intention fulfilling itself. Lastly, strive to recognize a sense of existence beyond body, mind, or soul altogether, the Spirit which *You are* apart from any incarnation. Realize that It alone knows your "True Will," and is really competent to rule your life on any level. When you have managed this, stop circling your "Rod" with its point in the center, turn it round and slowly bring the point towards you till it touches your body approximately over the heart, and conclude with the mental invitation "In Me." Finally lay down the pen or pencil where you got it from, or put it back in your pocket.

*If* you performed this little ceremony properly, you should now understand something of what mystical ritualism means, because the fundamentals are the same as those behind the most elaborate esoteric rite. Everything else is only a question of degree and intensity. It is the coordination of consciousness through the inner levels of Life directed at a single aim which is important. That is what is meant by the injunction to "BE OF ONE MIND IN ONE PLACE AT ONE TIME." Being unified in body, mind, soul, and spirit with one Will.

Do you see from this that you could work "occult rituals" anywhere, with an absolute minimum of equipment, any time you please providing you fulfill the "unity" clause? Conversely, you might attend a meeting in the most expensive Lodge or Temple imaginable, and take part in nothing more than a charade. You might ask what was the point of holding such a meeting, but the fairly obvious reply would be for the purpose of increasing effect by multiplication of casual consciousness. Nevertheless it makes no difference how many people are present unless they all know what they are doing and are able to focus their forces effectively as a whole. The difficulties and problems with this can be appreciated only by those who have tried to be coordinators of massed human consciousness. A lot of the blame must rest with whoever is responsible for training group members. If members have never had ritual principles properly explained to them, and sufficient practice sesssions to experience how inner attitudes and dispositions of energy should be arranged, they can hardly be critized for ineffectual operations.

All this, however, is the purely human end of the ritual range. The other end is beyond reach of human hands and is held by spiritual specialists on higher levels of Life altogether. That is to say so far as the best types of inner contact are concerned. It is perfectly posssible to seek lower and far worse sorts of cooperators along inner lines, and people frequently do for the sake of greed-gratifications or similarly sinister reasons. This is not a place for commenting with any detail on this topic. It is only mentioned to show a need for linking up with inner intelligences (once called Angels or Devils) who are concerned with human affairs for their own purposes, and therefore are likely to help or hinder our progress along parallel Inner Pathways.

What our occult or religious rituals do if they are properly carried out is attract the attention of spiritual beings because the convolutions of our consciousness shaped by ritual practice make specific patterns in the structure of their particular Life-spheres. We could compare this to sending out a transmission which can be received by specially constructed sets in tune with certain frequencies. It is actually the coordination of body-mind-soul energies that sets up signals recognizable by inner intelligences. This is relatively rare among humans accustomed to concentrating mainly on Earthlife conditions. Most of our inner energies dissipate and become absorbed by ordinary surroundings and circumstances. It is only when we are pressured by extremes of pleasure, pain, or some similar cause that our energy levels coincide sufficiently to emit signals intense enough to reach other ranges of recognition. Alternately we can do this ourselves by regularly ritualized practice in a disciplined way.

This is roughly the method by which ordinary prayer is assumed to work. A symbolic posture is taken up by the body, meaning is made by the mind, and feeling is expressed by the soul. Once the three attitudes coincide consciously, contact becomes established with spiritual spheres of existence which hopefully will allow attention from thence to connect with the earthly caller. There is no infallible guarantee that this will happen, but the likelihood is extremely probable. Communication does depend very greatly on alignment between the Life-levels—the importance of this point can scarcely be overemphasized.

It is principally to engage the body in symbolic movement that orthodox Jews adopt the practice known as "dovening" during their prayer sessions. This is very effective if done properly. It amounts to making a slight back and forth movement from the waist in rhythm with the verbalized orison, and it may be done seated or standing. The result produces a very mild auto-hypnosis favoring liberation of mind and soul from lower levels. This is not entirely essential to prayer practice and does not suit everyone, so individuals have to decide whether or not to use it during specific types of prayer. The nearest Christian custom (apart from revivalist meetings) seems to be a quiet clicking of rosary beads reminiscent of a whirring Buddhist prayer-wheel. These are all ritualizations for the same practical purpose, to keep the body and mind circulating in set rhythms so that the soul and spirit can communicate with higher orders of Life.

One of the problems encountered with occult ritualism is the misunderstanding prevalent among those eager to practice it but with no experience of it. They usually start off with all kinds of absurd expectations and demands which have little or no hope of gratification, then when they finally realize that these are not going to be fulfilled, they drop the whole thing with disappointed annoyance. Unhappily, ceremonial procedures attract these erratic and unstable souls, because they seem convinced they can find the answers to all their problems handed to them on a magic platter by an obliging Archangel sent specially to serve them—or perhaps by a cringing Demon humbly awaiting their command. Nothing less than total failure will eventually prove to them that this is a fallacy.

The ritualism of the Western Mysteries is *not* designed to produce "psychic phenomena" such as materializations or anything of a spiritualistic, seance nature. If this happened, it would probably be *incidental* rather than consequential, and would mean that someone (or more than one) who happened to be present was endowed with what were once called "mediumistic tendencies." The aim of most modern Mystery practices is to produce *mediators* rather than mediums. There is a very fine distinction here which needs careful explaining so that there will not be misunderstandings, disappointments, and unnecessary ill-feeling. Anyone determined to be satisfied with nothing less than objective and tangible psychic phenomena should seek elsewhere than among practitioners of the Western Mysteries. Groups dedicated to that particular style of approach to inner life do exist and are not particularly difficult to locate. Application should be made to them rather than to any Temple, Lodge, or other Earth-based association of esoteric Western Mystery practice.

The main distinction between mediumship and *mediatorship* is that in the former case unreserved control of mind or body is placed at the disposal of the alien entity which then assumes responsibility for what may be said or done. In the latter case it is *not* so, the mediator being in full control of his or her faculties, but prepared to mediate, or act as an agent between other humans and the spiritual source of influence or intelligence with which he or she has established contact. The main reason for this is that Western Mystery Inner teachings generally hold it wrong or inadvisable in principle to allow an individual consciousness to be "taken over" by any other than the appointed owner. Despite all safeguards, a body or mind which can be controlled by another entity offers too great a risk of undesirable usage by "anti-human" intelligences. It is impossible to put up one hundred per cent protection against this, and even a low proportion of instances would be unacceptable in very close working circles of the Mysteries.

Now this does *not* mean there would be terrible risks of "Black Magic" and fearsome happenings from any person so misappropriated. *On the surface* there would be no evidence anywhere of harm happening. Miles and miles of "spirit messages" could pour forth with one platitude after another. Using those messages as a "carrier wave," however, a great deal of extremely subtle and spiritually injurious "Inner propaganda" can be put over on unsuspecting human hearers. This is not unlike certain authorities on Earth who cleverly employ perfectly sound and even noble ideology to impart concealed political influences especially to entrap young and inexperienced people eager to embrace almost any worthwhile-sounding cause. It would be absurd to suppose this does not happen, because that is plain fact undisputed by anyone with commonsense. Just the same thing goes on along inner lines, and has been happening from many ages past.

It is no more than dangerous stupidity to suppose that "all is sweetness and Light in the Spirit world," and that nothing harmful can happen to humans who believe in the beautiful. Try telling that to some human terrorist aiming a gun at you at close quarters. You would soon face the facts of the Spirit World before you expected to. No Archangel would be likely to materialize and save you. Well, would you *really* expect that? There are deadlier projectiles than bullets which only kill or injure physical bodies. Inner influences affecting minds and souls have done more damage to the human race than all the bullets we have ever fired at each other, and most of these influences have reached us through the mediumship of humanity. Not specifically "spiritualistic" mediumship at all, but simply *any* human being who allows himself to be used as a means of dissemination for those influences on earthly levels of Life. It is the *principle* of mediumship which the Western Mystery teaching regards as being potentially dangerous, rather than specific instances of it which may indeed be perfectly innocuous.

*Mediatorship* is something quite different. There, a cautious control is kept on whatever approaches the receptive areas of inner awareness. "Filter systems" are set up to check contamination as far as possible. All sensible precautions are taken against invasion or subversion by "sinister" or "Left Hand Path" operators, whether human or otherwise. Only when the mediator is as certain as he can possibly be that an inner intention or intelligence is harmless or beneficial, does he consent to act as its agent and "pass it along" towards fellow humans or anywhere else. A genuine mediator is a *trustee* of an "Inner Estate," the administration of which he will some day expect to be called before an accounting authority. Therefore mediators will realize the responsibility and onus of such a position.

Real mediation is *not* a question of "getting spirit messages" and secondhanding the information (or misinformation) to other humans. It means actually becoming a link in the Life-chain conjoining consciousness between one order of being and another. For example, you might mediate the power of Love between Divinity and an animal or a plant as well as another human. Reversing this, you might mediate their love of you back to Divinity if they could not do this well enough for themselves. This is about the highest function possible of genuine priesthood for a human soul to achieve. By no means is everyone capable of collecting and arranging consciousness so that it makes certain of direct contact with Divinity. Those best able to do this for themselves may extend their ability on behalf of others if they are prepared to mediate or act as contact-links. Perhaps the best explanation of this was once out as a "Priest's Prayer" of unknown authorship:

### The Priest's Prayer

Thou brother Priest, who countest less
The measure of our sinfulness
Than the broad reach of our desire,
Touch thou my life with Fire!

Visit my heart with any pain
So be it to my peoples gain.
Brother, thou knowest all my need
To be their priest indeed.

Let them not suffer any loss
For sin of mine; For every cross
Thou layest on them, let them bear
Only the lighter share.

If they have sinned, yet lay their hand
On me who at thine altar stand.
Ah! Thou who tendest this poor vine,
Tread out the grapes, and all the Wine,
Be theirs—and Thine!

That would be mediation in the highest sense of the word, and beyond the ability of most human ministers in religion. No reasonable person would expect that much of an average priest, but it is certainly a standard to uphold and think about. There is an old proverb which says, "The lot of the mediator is to have his garments torn," and there is not only homely truth in that. Mediators often do pay for their well-meant attempts at intervention, and they have to learn the proper occasions of mediation. In any case, no one can possibly mediate more or other than the inner energies they are able to contact by their own efforts. All the ritualism in the Western Mysteries is geared to developing and increasing the capability of mediatorship or priesthood in the original meaning of that term among practising members. It is not a priesthood that parades itself and preaches at people publicly, but one which very quietly and effectively mediates the hidden energies of the eternal here on Earth for mortals to benefit by.

There is no such thing as an esoteric ritual which will work wonders by its automatic performance alone. If that were possible, a tape recording of it played to an empty room would be equally effective. Everything depends on the dispositions of consciousness fed into the inner structure of rituals both by humans from the Outside and their spiritual co-adjutants from Within. Mediation must be mutual if it is to operate at all. In old times, some of the Mystery mediators "assumed the God" by dressing and acting in that character before those wishing to communicate with that particular Deity. They felt that petitions presented to Its living simulacrum on Earth must reach an intended destination in Heaven. They knew quite well it was another human being dressed up, but they were not speaking to that human as himself. They were invoking the power he represented.

About the last relic of this today is the human priest in the confessional. The penitent is not supposed to speak to him, but to the God whom the priest mediates through his office. Devotional images of the Savior and saints take the place of costumed "God-Men." Methods of mediatorship have altered very greatly down the ages, even if the fundamentals remain the same. It is necessary to realize that the rites of Western Mystery practice are carried out for very definite and cogent reasons, and not for aimless amusement or amateur dramatic entertainment. They are always *worked* and never played at.

## Questions

1. Comment on "occult secrecy" with reference to ceremonial practices.
2. What is the symbol for reverential respect, and why?
3. Define ceremonial per se.
4. What is the literal meaning of "ritual"?
5. What makes any ritual esoteric in a spiritual sense?
6. What is the cultural value of ritual practice?
7. Discuss the procedure of prayer.
8. What is the distinction between mediumship and mediatorship?
9. Choose the ten most important sentences in this chapter.
10. Assess the value of ritual procedures in modern times.

# · 15 ·

# *Mediation and Meaning*

We were speaking of mediatorship and its primal importance in the Western version of the Holy Mysteries. A mediator of any kind is essentially a "middleman" or a "combiner of consciousness;" the third line of a triangle; the Middle Pillar of the Tree; any Path linking two Spheres; whatever links Power to performance. Electricity is a Power, and a motor will perform, but neither would be of any practical value unless the mediation of conducting wires connected them together. So a human mediator is really someone who enables interaction to take place between two different classes of consciousness. Unless this were possible we should never have got very far as a Life-species on this Earth. Some humans had to push the limits of their intelligence a little further into the unknown, make contact there with something that enlightened it, work the whole thing out as seemed best, then mediate the results to other humans one way or another.

Genetic lines of descent are really a form of mediation from our ancestors. They provide the wherewithal that links us with our human Life-origins, and every generation modifies it a bit for the next one. We all mediate something somehow for somebody. Here, however, we are thinking specifically of mediating purely spiritual energies along particular Paths of action. In order to appreciate what these energies are it is only necessary to visualize a world entirely without them: a world without Love (in the true sense); a world with no beliefs in anything better than optimum supplies to meet maximum material demands; a world without hope beyond physical limits; a world controlled by computers owned by an anonymous consortium which exists nowhere on their tapes or silicon chips; a mechanical, robotic, passionless, painless, and utterly pointless world, almost beyond the imagination of extremist "Doomsday" writers.

One of the worst symptoms of psychosis is total (or almost total) lack of feeling, an inability to emphathize with anything or anyone. If a human were to suffer appalling agonies in front of people afflicted with this complaint, they *could not* experience the slightest feeling about it or make the slightest move to help their fellow-human. Their *ability to mediate has left them.* Nevertheless in many cases some desperate stirrings of departing normalcy insists on trying to re-establish communication by almost *any* means. This results in the patient attempting to injure himself physically in some painful yet seldom fatal way, such as burning a hand, hitting himself with something sharp and heavy, or any other kind of local damage. Physical pain is not only acceptable, but welcome and reassuring. In extreme cases even severe bodily injury is scarcely felt as painful and the patient becomes more alienated than ever. This terrible Selfstate is a well-known clinical condition. A world deprived of spiritual energies would be something like that for most of us.

Looking at the other side of the picture, we have to conceive of a world in which a majority of inhabitants have marked degrees of mediating the right kind of Inner energies: a kindly world and a *caring* world; one in which the poise and harmony of all conscious life therein was of paramount importance and everyone was concerned in maintaining it; thus by implication, a happy and healthful world because its peoples were sharing the same Spirit inspiring their perfection. There might be a million different religions and as many opinions as there were human minds, but in the mediation of a common conciousness derived from an identical source, the Spirit of Life Itself, every living being would experience its relationship with all the rest.

How does anyone mediate anything? The same way that any form of energy is mediated, by becoming a conductor for it from supply to demand. If you were an electrical mediator, you would be a metal strip of some kind, if a gas or liquid, you would have to become a pipe, or as a mechanical mediator a rod, belt, or wheel. That is to say, you would have to be suitable for the job within definite specifications. This is equally true in spiritual dimensions of living. Though most people have some mediatory abilities, it does call for rather special attainments of character and nature in order to mediate the finer spiritual forces which charge our consciousness with existence-altering energies and have the effect of advancing human souls along their pathways to Perfection.

Jesus is usually considered by orthodox Christians to be the only mediator between themselves and the Godhead. As part of that Godhead, he voluntarily became Man, and therefore partook of two natures, human and Divine, thenceforth mediating both through himself, and will do so for any human sincerely believing this possible. Mystics of other faiths would grant that, apart from his uniqueness and exclusiveness. They would see the quality of mediatorship as being one for every soul to achieve for itself before it can hope to advance beyond ordinary human levels. The gift, power, ability, or faculty of passing on to other souls something of the spiritual energies and experience gained by contacts with higher than human consciousness—that is the type of mediatorship sought for in the Western Mysteries. Put in absolutely nursery language (which is quite often the most effective), "leaving the world a bit better than you found it." Though we may realize quite well the discouraging enormity of such an injunction, that is not an adequate excuse for never atempting it.

The ritual example of mediation which might convey some meaning in this instance is how far a Christian priest can mediate the meaning of Christ to communicants when he offers the consecrated bread and wine to them saying, "The Body and the Blood. etc." How many ordained priests even try to mediate that Spirit towards each soul they serve? If they do not so attempt, then they are failing lamentably in their office. Centuries ago there were many theological arguments about whether wicked or unworthy priests could say a valid Mass. The official findings were that the personal character of the priest had no effect on the validity of the Mass because the rite was sacred in its own nature, and the ordination of the man was automatically sufficient to make the rite effective by itself.

Regularly communicating Christians with any spiritual sensitivity might have accepted this as the edict of an authority but they could not feel this was true in practice. Their own instincts alone told them a different story. How could a gabblement of Latin by a man obviously racing through a routine with little attention to meaning, followed by a casual or disinterested pushing into their mouths of a bread wafer at highest speed, communicate anything to them of the Spirit prepared to sacrifice Itself by becoming human in order to help them become Divine? A technical communion was not necessarily a *true* communion, and those who could feel and experience this difference for themselves preferred to seek the services of priests who had the ability or gift of what we now like to call "charisma" derived from the Greek and meaning "grace, or favored gift" in the sense of being given some special faculty by God.

Now "charisma" may be a "gift of God" (as other abilities are) but it is one which can be developed and brought out, or allowed to lie dormant and idle. Remember the parable of the hidden talents. Contrast the unsatisfactory type of communion service just mentioned with one administered by a priest whose mediatory faculties had been cultivated and increased. He would be able to present the Spirit of Christ to people through his own person. The love, feeling, power, presence, and other attributes associated with Christ of the figure of Jesus would all be *there* in every move that priest made, and it could be felt and experienced beyond any shadow of doubt. There could be no mistaking it. That is *real* mediation.

It is also possible to experience *partial* mediation as in instances where perhaps a single aspect is specially mediated. For instance, you might find a priest able to mediate the indignation or anger of Jesus, yet none of his love or compassion. Another priest who could mediate the Love-aspect might be incapable of mediating the wit or wisdom displayed by Jesus, and so on. Nevertheless all these would still be genuine mediations well worth encountering. In old times this was understood, and resulted in "specialist priests" who were noted for their types of mediation. It was seldom expected that any single mortal could mediate more than *part* of any Divinity, and maybe to very limited degrees, but even a slight contact was reckoned as a great deal better than none at all.

You might think that this means no more than straight-forward acting in the character of a God, like a stage actor would. Yes, it means just that—*plus*. Very much *plus*. Remember that the drama was a *sacred art* in olden times, and this was why. It was consciousness from higher levels of Life contacting humanity and *inspiring* humans to evolve above Earth-animal standards which have steadily raised us to our present levels, and *still does so*. In earlier days this was a lot more noticeable than it is at present. Anyone speaking or behaving oddly or differently than usual among small tribes was supposed to be "moved by the Gods." *Sometimes* there could be an element of truth in this, especially if what was said or done proved helpful or uplifting to those around. Unhappily, not *all* inner influences came from higher sources, and not *all* peculiar behavior was motivated by other than natural causes, so earlier generations of humans were just as mixed up as modern ones. Added to this, a lot of what passed for mediation in Temples of old (and closer to our own) times was no more than what might have been called "priestly persiflage" or deliberate dishonesty for the sake of power and money. Mediatorship is a gift that can be easily misused either intentionally or unconsciously, but this applies to all human faculties and is part of our evoultionary process. We simply have to take it as it comes, and develop our gifts as carefully and conscientiously as we can. The important thing is to recognize a hidden faculty and determine to deal with it in a disciplined and responsible manner.

This is where ritual practice comes into the picture, because any ritual can be a controlled and organized procedure bounded by reason and proved reliable by usage over prolonged periods. Nothing whatever in human experience can be guaranteed as one hundred per cent infallible or foolproof, but procedures with a high percentage of reliability are always preferable to those of lower standards unless an element of risk is being intentionally allowed for. Ritual practices for mediating spiritual influences toward human beings have existed in all cultures and ages into our present times, and show no signs of disappearing altogether. These could scarcely have continued if humans had found no purpose or value in them, and their extent and variety seem as wide as human minds and souls can make them. Their impact and involvement in human history is incalculable. They cannot be denied, dismissed, or ignored by anyone trying to account for human behavior and genetics. They have made their mark indelibly on mankind.

No ritual practice *causes* meditation because it is an inherent faculty, but ritualism does regulate and control it within pre-determined limits. By setting up and formulating the framework of a ritual, the type and even the degree of mediation possible to human operatives can be standardized and relied upon providing those operatives are capable and properly poised people. In extreme cases where they may be incompetent or worse, they can scarcely work any serious harm to others with ritual procedures properly designed for opposite effects, but they may indeed unstabilize themselves by trying to mediate inner energies which they could not conduct through their own natures. This does happen when over-ambitious or unwisely enthusiastic individuals try to mediate energies far beyond their current abilities. Had they listened to reason and commenced practice with lesser matters, building up abilities from that point, it would have made far more sense. *Never try to mediate anything that commonsense warns you is more than you can carry with confidence.*

In the Western Mysteries, ritualists usually start mediation exercises through the symbology of the four major instruments of Rod, Sword, Cup and Shield. Here these are taken to represent the chief characteristics of an average human being in the act of Life, that is, as a living and intelligent creature dealing with others of its kind. For practical purposes, the symbols can be considered as four attitudes to adopt which may be mediated quite normally towards any fellow humans we are likely to encounter in the usual course of living. These are:

1. **The Rod.** *Courtesy.* A kind of general affability and conventional behavior in relation to others of your own level, so that rules of reasonable harmony and balance are observed.

2. **The Sword:** *Caution.* An alert and observant watchfulness to make sure that any anti-social activities are noted and if possible checked, or other possible dangers averted.

3. **The Cup:** *Concord.* Amity and affection with love and joy. The best possible relationships with others.

4. **The Shield:** *Concern.* Attention to and interest in people and their doings, feelings of protective care, and willingness to help with their problems.

These are four distinct and comprehensive lines of contact between you and others. Each is a distinct category of consciousness in itself which can be combined with the others and yet retain its own characteristics. If you intend to make the Magical Instruments (or Weapons) into control symbols for these, all you need do is invent or follow out associative ritualistic exercises. The idea is to connect them so closely in your consciousness that invoking the concept of a symbol or symbols in your mind will forthwith enable you to adopt and mediate the attitude attached to it towards whoever or whatever you direct it at.

You could begin by picking up your physical Rod Symbol and making measured gestures with it while saying or thinking something like, "It is good to have some standard measure of behavior to one another in this world. This makes things easier for all of us alike. We have to have some reasonable rules of conduct to adopt in the business of running an organized society and common culture. Let this Rod signify my mediation of such an attitude towards everyone else." Then point the Rod wherever you will, imagining various people you know in very ordinary ways of living, and attempt to mediate this flow of feeling to them as if it were radiating along the Rod from you in their direction. Experience it as an actual energy if you can, which is active when you point the Rod away from you, and passive or dormant when you rest the Rod horizontally from left to right across your body.

Next, with the Sword, make your gestures as if facing a potential danger with warning rather than threatening movements, and say something like, "I will defend my peace of mind and soul with all my might and skill as any living being is entitled to. I am not asking for any trouble, nor mean to make any, but if it is forced on me against my will, then I shall uphold my honor by justified action. I would prefer not to fight, but if there is no other way out of danger, then I will sell my life as dearly as I can. I am watching every move made against me, and at the first sign of attack will defend myself as best I may. Yet all I ask is Peace. Leave me alone." Point the Sword around, imagining likely enemies or sources of hostility. Move very cautiously or warily with as much alertness as you can manage, then mediate this attitude along the Sword-blade while you hold it as powerfully as possible in your mind. Neutralize everything as you lower the Sword point to the ground or rest its blade on your shoulder, resuming the alert attitude quickly as you suddenly point the Sword again at imaginary antagonists which fade away before your concentrated caution.

When you have the Cup in your hands, relax, smile, soften your voice, think of those you love or want to love, or just wish to be happy and content with. Then tell them what they mean to you and how much you need to make yourself wanted by them. Perhaps you could put it, "Wouldn't it be wonderful if all of us in this world could only be happy and harmonious together without any worries and with nothing but Love in our lives? Maybe one day some super-scientist or mighty magician will discover the most marvellous elixir of all time, a draught which makes mankind love and trust each other unreservedly. That would truly be the Golden Drop in the bottom of the magic cauldron, or the contents of the Sangreal which would make us of the Holy Blood. I drink to the dawning of that Delivering Day." You could have a real drink in the Cup and drain it while you mediate this wonderful wish as hard as you can at everyone you imagine. Think of it outpouring towards them and bringing all the happiness you would wish them. See that as a magical memory when you set the Cup down with reverence.

As you take up the Shield, see yourself as being closely concerned with what happens to other humans in this world whether or not you know them personally, and whatever their condition in life. It *does* matter to you how they are treated because their welfare and yours are tied up together. You cannot help caring somewhat more for those nearest and dearest to you, but at least you can extend that care to cover a few fellow beings. Gesture with your Shield and say or think, "I *do* care what happens to you. I may not be able to do much to help, but at least I can send shielding thoughts and prayers. It does matter to me what you think and feel because we are all in the same world and part of one another whether we like it or not. We have been told to bear one another's burdens, and this Shield is also a Platter on which I offer you the Bread of Brotherhood in the Blood. Receive my recognition and regard thereby in common consciousness." Bear your Shield flat like a paten, and offer your caring communion to those you think of, mediating it as sincerely as you may the while. Then lay the idea down with the Shield wherever you put it.

Do you see the scheme behind this ritualism? It gears your inner awareness to the radiation of spiritual realities throughout the world. Through these exercises you have actually been sending out mental and spiritual energies into the ambience of consicousness connecting you with other souls. This may not be to any great amount or intensity, but the fact that a sincere effort has been made to mediate spiritually significant energies of existence along ordinary earthly lines, is a lot more important than you might suppose. It is a question of "every little bit helps" which is a truism we may not think highly of, but cannot very well deny as a reality.

When you have practiced this particular type of mediation for a while and are used to doing it without physical symbols, you may discover that you are better at one of the attitudes than the others. This is normally the case, and you will have to judge results for yourself. The point here is that if you are going to work with others in any sort of group, you will need those who mediate your weakest symbols better than you do. In other words, if you are a natural Sword, you will most likely find the Cup difficult to mediate, and so you will need the company of those whose best and natural mediations are the Cup, Shield, and Rod. A really well balanced circle will consist of people able to mediate the Cup, Rod,

Shield, Sword, and Cord, each one mediating their own symbol somewhat predominantly to the others so that all together a maximum contribution of consciousness is made, and the circle becomes truly dynamic.

You could vary this exercise in many ways. Simply cut a Tarot pack, and mediate the attitude of which ever suit comes up for a few moments then change to whatever appears next. If a Trump, you would naturally have to cut again till one suit shows itself for you to mediate. In older times, you would have had to mediate these attitudes by adopting the stance or appearance of conventional Gods. These postures can still be seen in Oriental folk dramas, but they have not survived too well in our culture, their last relics being the medieval Mystery plays, and the "Mummeries" which are occasionally still produced in European rural districts. In traditional "Mumming Plays," the character of the Old Man, or "Father Christmas" displays the Rod or Staff as a broomstick; the "Turkish Knight," the Sword: "St George," the Shield (and counter-Sword); the "Doctor," the Cup (as a bottle for the "Magic Drop"); and usually "Idle Jack" or the Fool as the Cord with the rope or string which he brandishes about.

Mediating the Cord is not so easy. It is especially a connecting or continuity symbol of the Truth-tie linking all Life together. You probably realize that all matter is only a collection of separate atoms related by—yes, by *what?* Nobody really knows, but whatever that force may be, it is the Cord of Cosmos. The "Cord" of any circle is the one who not only ties the others together, but also links them with other circles. A cord can loosen as well as tighten, so what is needed is a concept of the Cord as something which holds everything together at exactly the right tension everywhere, firm where it has to be firm, and elastic where stretching is needed. Adaptability in all directions. You could try a few exercises by circling round with an actual cord or long piece of string, looping or connecting it from one piece of furniture to another while saying something to the effect of, "Life is this joined to that forever and forever, a series of events strung together by our conscious observation and memory of them. Our bodies are cell linked to cell, our minds thought linked to thought, and our souls feeling joined to feeling as long as they last. Time, tied to Space, tied to Events makes Cosmos conscious and the one thread tying everything together for a single purpose is—*Truth*. Separate, we stand for ourselves, together, bound to each other by the bond of Blessed Blood, we belong to the Supreme Self we seek to serve, and through that Self we have Eternal Life of which this is the token."

For that particular mediation, the Cord should be colored red to symbolize the linkage of the Holy Blood within the Sangreal of which each of us should hope to become a single cell eventually, if we are not already one. You have to think of your "fellow-cells," untold millions of them all making up the "Blood of God" yet each single one of unique importance. Everyone joined into the most significant "Blood Brotherhood" in existence. Such is the symbolism of the Cord in this context which you should sense when mediating its meaning.

You do not need physical proximity for mediating spiritual energies though, of course, this may enhance reciprocal responses. On spiritual levels you are automatically part of Life extending throughout the Cosmos, and what you mediate into that Life-stream will eventually reach its objective in principle. In a way, this is not unlike banking a small sum of money. The cash in notes you hand to the teller is only a symbol representing a value determined by a fiscal authority—printed paper, no more. That symbol does not go into a mysterious box with your name on it, nor does the bank wrap it up and send it to somebody in your name with a charge for the service. It does no more than record your deposit on its computers which then enlarge your credit by that amount. The paper symbols are then re-circulated through carefully controlled channels.

In a relative fashion what you mediate along spiritual lines is monitored through the "Recording Angel" system we mentioned earlier, and becomes available as "supply" to other humans if they request it in the right way. They will not receive the *identical* energy you put in, but they will be entitled to whatever your effort has pushed in their direction by impetus delivered at the other end of the line, so to speak. No energy is ever lost, but only transformed and re-distributed. So you can mediate as much as you like. Somebody will get some benefit somewhere, and your "Inner credit" will be enlarged, becoming part of the "treasure you lay up in Heaven."

By commencing the conscious control of mediation in this simple way with the Four (or Five) Symbols of the Western Inner Tradition, you will be practising the principles of mediation needed for much more complicated conditions and arrangements of consciousness. The Spheres of the Trees, for example. You mediate those by passing them through yourself in a predetermined direction for some specific purpose. This was really what their "Magical Images" were meant to be: character concepts for mediators to "assume" in order to manage the particular type of energy associated with any particular Sphere. Put another way, if the forces typified by any Sphere formed themselves into human shape, that would be what they ought to look like. So reverse the process. Make yourself in the semblance of a Magical Image, and in theory this should make it easier for you to mediate that type of energy.

Though this sort of thinking was not exactly accurate (for instance, dressing up as a nurse will not bestow the least medical competence), there was some degree of reason in the idea. Assuming the appearance of some thing does incline people to think or speculate about it, and that by itself opens up their minds and souls to the ideology and meaning behind whatever it is. If your conscious attention can push on with enough determination from that point you might get somewhere into Inner Dimensions sooner or later. In old time Mysteries it was believed that if you dressed and acted as a God, the reality of that God in a higher state of Life could use you to project its consciousness through on Earth-levels. Nowadays we realize there is no need to dress the part if we can formulate our consciousness in appropriate fashion by ourselves. That is what the "God" works with, but it is still nice to have some ideas of appearance on which to base our beliefs.

There is no absolute obligation to choose the conventional "Magical Image" figures of the Spheres on the Tree in order to mediate their meanings. You could perfectly well invent ten attitudes or appearances of your ordinary self in human form as symbols of such mediation. For instance, what do you think is the best way for you to appear as regards facial expression and body-attitude if you were trying to mediate Sphere 2, *Wisdom,* and Sphere 3, *Understanding?* Do you think anyone could tell which you were trying to express by looking at you? Never mind about exposing your dramatic talents to anyone else, try them on yourself first.

Go and look at your self in a full length mirror if possible. Sit or stand before it as you please and watch your image critically as if it were that of someone else. Now start mediating *Wisdom* by concentrating on that Sphere alone, and feel it passing through you towards others. If you feel impelled to make any special gestures and position your body and limbs some way, do this and study the effect in the glass. See if anything appears "right" or "wrong" to you. If there is anything you can fix quickly, do so, and if not, then make a note to guide future experiments. Don't be put off because you look nothing like your own concepts of a Wisdom-image, just keep concentrating on that one Sphere and see if your bodily appearance is altering in any way to match your mind. Don't worry too much if it doesn't seem satisfactory, at least you have made an attempt. Should you be happy with the result, remember it carefully, for that is the attitude to adopt in future if you want to mediate Wisdom. Don't decide too quickly, though. Have several runs-through before you finally adopt any definite image for regular use.

If you want to be conscientious, go through all the ten Tree concepts one after the other, trying to find suitable attitudes and expressions for mediating their meanings. You may use simple "props" if you like which should be quite "ordinary life" things such as pens, rulers, drinking glasses and so forth, things you would pick up normally and use as a matter of course. You could wear different kinds of clothing so long as they were customary for you. Whatever you do, never exaggerate your stances or expressions to points of absurdity. Keep everything within the bounds of reason in respect to their effect on others. If you think you are trying to convey an impression of Wisdom and this only invokes amusement in someone else, then you are obviously failing to mediate properly. Mediation isn't as easy as you thought, is it?

Should you ever manage to mediate the ten Spheres effectively to even a slight extent, you might perhaps get photos of yourself in each pose and study them as Magical Images of your own Tree of Life. You could do this easily enough with a delay-action camera set up against the mirror if you do not have a trustworthy friend to take them. It is by no means necessary to make such pictures, but they would be interesting reminders for you to look back on some years later. So would tape recordings of your voice mediating the meanings of the Four Symbols. Don't forget to date them. Maybe you can see now where all this mediating should be leading to: hopefully, a state of existence where humans are capable of mediating God for and at each other, or rather a condition of consciousness wherein God is mediating Itself for Itself through us. In other words, God will be living consciously in and *as* us. Does this mean anything to you? It certainly means something to the God in you. Think that one out.

However, if you want to be an active worker of our Western Inner Way, you should be concerned with mediating the Sangreal Spirit through whatever branch of our Tradition you may be following, because it applies to all, and is in itself the fundamental factor underlying every distinct division of esotericism within the West. Call yourself what you like, you still cannot avoid your ancestry or deny your birthblood, and that is how the Sangreal works through you in this world. The most you can do against its action is refuse to recognize it consciously and objectively, which would be just as pointless as refusing to admit you have a heart inside your body or red blood within your veins.

You are perfectly entitled to reject every idea about the Sangreal which you encounter, but that will only alter your objective relationship with it, which affects yourself alone. Why not approach the Sangreal concept on a broader basis and consider what others have done with it and how it affects the lives of all Westerners having the slightest claims to any sort of spiritual status? In any case, knowledge should always precede action, so please feel very welcome to participate in the next series of Sangreal studies before you decide to do anything at all on your own initiative.

Come along then, Companion.

## Questions

1. Define the responsiblity of a mediator.
2. Do you think a fundamentally bad person could mediate good influences?
3. Why was drama once a sacred art?
4. What, if any, are your special abilities at mediation?
5. What are the mediative characteristics of the Four Magical Symbols?
6. How would you mediate the Cord-symbol?
7. Are there degrees of mediation, and how would you define them?
8. Depict someone with little or no abilities of mediation.
9. Choose the ten most important sentences in this chapter.
10. Have you watched yourself in a mirror while attempting mediation, and could you observe or sense changes between one type of mediation and another?

# Valedictory

What we have presented so far is a rapid and comprehensive review of the main theme of Western Inner Tradition teachings which could be described as individualistic integration with Infinite Intelligence, summed up long ago as KNOW THY SELF. That is what our Tradition is all about from one end to the other.

There are bound to be criticisms concerning the exclusion of specific topics, especially those closest to a reader's interest. It may be asked, for instance, why there was no mention of Astrology, Alchemy, Ceremonial Magic, Crystal-gazing, Druidism and so forth right down to Witchcraft, Water-divining and Zoism. Such was never the intention behind this work. It is neither an A-B-C of anything nor an encyclopedia of occultism. There are plenty of those around for the benefit of interested investigators. If you want to study specialized subjects, then buy or borrow the appropriate literature.

From first to last, this work is meant to awaken, channel, and cultivate your interest in seeking for and, most of all, *belonging with* a spiritual *wholeness* of a uniquely Western character. This is not a matter of specific sectarianism, but of inborn inheritance. None of the Occidental esoteric associations such as Rosicrusianism, Transcendentalism, and the like, have any exclusive claims whatsoever to our Inner Tradition. The fact that they uphold it from their particular angles does not automatically entitle them to sole ownership. The most they can claim is honorable participation. Membership is by birthright and subsequent socio-spiritual activities are purely an affair of choice and conviction.

Our Western Inner Way is neither inferior nor superior to the Eastern one, and any arguments or speculations on this issue would be a total waste of time and misunderstanding of principles involved. Inherent natures are such in themselves, and to try to force them into unsuitable frameworks would be intrinsically wrong. By all means let us comprehend and complement other cultures in this world, but surely each thrives best in its natural environment. The fostering of our own culture begins with respect for its equivalents elsewhere.

We speak of "Eastern" and "Western" spiritual Traditions, and realize there has been a "Northern" one as well, surviving not only as Shamanism extending across to North America, but also as the more sophisticated yet ruthless "Norse" system incorporating Odin, Thor, and the dramtaic God-Figures favored by Wagner and Hitler alike. What few people realize is that the time of a Southern Inner Tradition *has yet to come.* The strong likelihood is that it will issue of our Western Way, transplanted to the Southern hemisphere mostly by our descendents born and naturalized there. Arising from their inherited genetics, there will eventually spring up a spiritual Inner Way having an identity of its own with a vital part to play in our esoteric evolution. There are already signs of such beginnings evident for those able to read them.

All that we who are yet with our "old" Tradition can do is care for what we have and help those who are trying to make more of it by renewal and re-interpretation. They deserve every encouragement and support we can give them, for they will not be competitors but co-adjutants in a world which sorely needs every single spiritual effort that anyone can make. Quite a new and suprising type of consciousness has to be developed by forthcoming incarnates so that they can cope with problems menacing the fate of mankind regardless of traditional loyalties. The more effectively we can concentrate the esoteric energies of our specific Traditions towards such an objective, the better it is likely to be for all of us.

The general understanding with most esoteric systems is that apart from a curriculum of studies and a standard of instructional competence, there should exist some means of concerting consciousness at material levels of Life for spiritual purposes. Orthodox religions have their congregations with customs and rituals. So do much smaller sects and societies. There is a common need among humanity for companionship and mutual support when dealing with affairs involving the principle of Divinity. The old feeling of "safety in numbers" is particularly prominent with those who recognize the reality of Inner Existence. Though they are competent to treat with It individually, they usually prefer to combine their consciousness together when approaching It for reasons affecting them collectively. Hence, the various Lodges, Temples, and other groups of assembly.

Now there is nothing whatsoever in this world to prevent people following the Sangreal Ideal from doing the same things if they want to. Lodges and Temples are only buildings or rooms in buildings. Symbolic equipment consists of nothing more than artifacts. Rituals and liturgical procedures are arrangements of behavior linked with skilled script-writing. All these mechanics of mysticism are readily available to whoever is willing to devote time, money, and organizing energy towards coordinating them on physical levels of Life. If any sort of a Sangreal Sodality seriously intends to manifest itself as a materialized happening among mankind, a few short years should be sufficient to establish it on this earth as a fully functioning affair. Whether or not that will ever come to pass depends absolutely and entirely on *you* and others whose interest and enthusiasm may have been aroused beyond the limits of lethargy. Put as briefly as possible, if you want to enjoy association with others of the Western Way according to Sangreal ideology, then don't wait for anyone else to build up a higly organized structure worthy of your entrance, but start making it yourself. Building begins first in your heart, then in your home, and only after that as a communal construction.

The companion volumes of this Sangreal Series are designed to help you with your individual Quest. One of them deals with the numerate side of our Tradition which is generally terms "Qabalah" and concerns an approach to Ultimate Entity via a sequential and relatable set of values leading out of each other toward that End. Otherwise, "looking for God by numbers." The remaining book is undoubtedly the most important from a purely spiritual point of view. It supplies the full details and analysis of the Sangreal Sacrament that is celebrated in the form of a Mass with a unique meaning which brings the Grail within reach of all participants. It gives other information which may stimulate your search for the Sangreal Sodality as a concentration of Western esoteric culture in this world.

Even if you feel no especial affiliation in that direction and possibly prefer allegiance to oriental inspired esotericism, it can scarcely injure you to know the inner workings of another human spiritual system which aims at the same Ultimate by an alternative route. There should be no antagonism or rivalry between fellow travellers to an identical destination along differing lines of enlightenment. At least if you should not be inclined to help your own inner kindred attempting the Quest, please do not try to hinder them on whichever Way they are taking. Nobody is likely to be helped by standing in somebody else's Light.

So if you have stayed the course as long as this, you might as well see it out to the present point of ending, which could be another beginning for you and for many. Who knows what the eventual outcome may be? The one certainty is that only good of some kind is mostly likely to eventuate. Questions of how much good, who will benefit by it, and is it going to be in sufficient time to annihilate evil cannot possibly be answered except by subsequent history.

The last pertinent question in this section is: *What are you going to do about it all?*